Thomas M. Leitch teaches English and
directs the Film Studies Program at the
University of Delaware.

D1605615

What Stories Are

Narrative Theory and Interpretation

WHAT STORIES ARE

Narrative Theory and Interpretation

Thomas M. Leitch

THE PENNSYLVANIA STATE UNIVERSITY PRESS
University Park and London

Library of Congress Cataloging-in-Publication Data

Leitch, Thomas M.
What stories are.

Includes index.
1. Narration (Rhetoric)
2. Discourse analysis, Narrative.   I. Title.
PN212.L45 1986   808.3'00141   85-43559
ISBN 0-271-00431-2

To Richard B. Sewall

Contents

Preface

I began work on this book five years ago with three expectations. Since I had been spending some time on the theory of poetry and had become increasingly impatient with what I took to be the excessive emphasis most theorists placed on evaluation in defining poetry (so that to call a discourse poetry was automatically to call it good), I welcomed the opportunity to work with a collection of materials whose ontology would not depend on value judgments. I looked forward, too, to the task of mapping out the work of previous theorists of narrative, to put their theories into a coherent relation with each other by developing a terminology which would allow me to bring them into some sort of accord, or at least to indicate illuminating discords. Finally, I was excited by the prospect of dealing with the most fundamental aspects of narrative, the prediscursive qualities that made stories stories. Despite the pioneering work of Vladimir Propp in the Soviet Union and the more recent studies of A.-J. Greimas in France and Gerald Prince in America, I felt that most studies of narrative discourse emphasized discourse over narrative: Seymour Chatman's influential *Story and Discourse* seemed much more interested in discourse than story; Scholes and Kellogg's earlier study *The Nature of Narrative* hardly dealt with ontological problems at all; and more recent theorists like Gérard Genette and Franz Stanzel left ontological problems behind, I thought, as soon as they decently could. I anticipated with pleasure writing about stories as stories, not as events treated a certain way in narrative discourse.

All three of these expectations, of course, were disappointed. I found almost immediately that I could not hope to define stories except in terms of some presumed norm of adequacy, however minimal. And it took little research to persuade me that to survey and impose order on recent work in narrative theory would be the work of a lifetime—perhaps, since the surveyor would inevitably fall further behind the more he read and wrote, the lifetime of Tristram Shandy. But it was not for some time that I realized that there was no way I could define *story* in terms of a structure of actions or events without reference to a specific discourse—that narrative was inescapably a kind of talking or writing or acting rather than an order of events. What I ended up writing, therefore, was not the book-to-end-all-books on narrative, a book that, summarizing and placing all previous work on the subject, would be swayed by no parochial value judgments or detours into mere narrative discourse, but rather a much more tendentious study of narrative in rhetorical or transactional terms (as opposed to the structural approaches of Greimas and Chatman and the more purely phenomenological approach of Horst Ruthrof's *The Reader's Construction of Narrative*), a study of the conditions under which a given discourse might be displayed as a story and of the relations stories established with their audiences that permitted them to operate as stories.

For help in this regrettably modest task (my original project would no doubt have justified many more impositions), I have many people to thank. Mark Amsler, Leo Braudy, Ernest Callenbach, Elliott Gilbert, J. Hillis Miller, Arden Reed, William T. Stafford, and several anonymous readers read or listened to parts of the manuscript in progress (a few hardy souls consuming the whole thing) and gave me the benefit of their encouragement and criticism. A section of Chapter 3 appeared in a slightly different version as "Closure and Teleology in Dickens" in *Studies in the Novel* 18 (Summer 1986), a section of Chapter 4 in an earlier version as "Donald Barthelme and the End of the End" in *Modern Fiction Studies* 28 (Fall 1982), and an earlier version of Chapter 9 as "To What Is Fiction Committed?" in *Prose Studies* 6 (Autumn 1983); I am grateful to the editors for permission to reprint. Yale University awarded me a Morse Fellowship for 1981–82 to begin work on this book, and the University of Delaware provided a Humanities Faculty Grant for the purchase of a microcomputer which was instrumental in completing it. I wish I could thank Lisa Elliott for her cooperation as well, but her sacrifices over a period of five years so that I could write a book on the difference between stories and other things would only reflect the use of the word by mothers of small children who are trying to secure their cooperation in dressing themselves or in not rolling on the supermarket floor. Cooperation of this sort is strictly a one-way street. She and all those who have given me their cooperation without any hope of repayment deserve my profound gratitude.

Part One
Narrative Ontology

1
What Stories Aren't

Everyone knows what stories are—fortunately; for it is excessively difficult to say just what they are. Despite the recent efflorescence of work in narrative theory, the problem of formulating a rule which shall distinguish things that are stories from things that are not, a rule which would establish what makes a story a story, has remained unresolved. Numerous critics have addressed this problem, but no one has yet defined narrative with the authority of Aristotle on tragedy: "Tragedy . . . is the imitation of an action that is serious and . . . complete in itself" (*Poetics* 6.1449b).[1] Critics since Aristotle, adopting his distinction between the representational modes of *mimesis* (showing) and *diegesis* (telling), have customarily defined narrative as the essentially diegetic representational mode. This distinction provides all the precision most audiences require: Dramas, although they may intermittently have recourse to a second-hand account of events (Jocasta's story of the prophecy about her son, Gertrude's account of Ophelia's death), are preeminently mimetic enactments of experience; narratives, although they sometimes employ the mimetic strategies of drama (as in directly reported dialogue), are essentially diegetic representations in which experiences are assumed to be recounted by a storyteller. Drama tends toward mimesis, narrative toward diegesis. As Robert Scholes and Robert Kellogg have written, narrative works "are distinguished by two characteristics: the presence of a story and a storyteller."[2] Specifying the storyteller as an indication of narrative's diegetic character allows us to distinguish between narrative and drama but leaves another question: What is a story? This question remains the most fundamental in narrative theory, and the most difficult to resolve.

Narrative as Drama

Story is a difficult concept to define because it elides so easily and insidiously into other concepts that it is almost impossible to establish a definition which includes all stories but excludes everything else. Scholes and Kellogg, defining plot as "the dynamic, sequential element in narrative," agree with Aristotle that "in a temporal art form the dynamic and sequential element is the primary one" (4, 207–8). Of course, all literary works, including Emerson's essays and Petrarch's sonnets, have a plot in the sense that an audience perceives them sequentially like music, not simultaneously like photography and sculpture.[3] Surely, however, it would be a mistake to define all diegesis as narrative. Most narrative theorists agree that what distinguishes narratives like "The Gift of the Magi" from nonnarratives like "Self-Reliance" is the representation in narrative of a diegetic world within which the audience perceives events sequentially. These theorists have taken as axiomatic the distinction between what Seymour Chatman has called "the content or chain of events" within the diegetic world of the narrative and "the means by which the content is communicated."[4] Chatman, following structuralist practice, calls these aspects of narrative *histoire* and *discours*, or story and discourse, but he compares these categories to the Aristotelian *logos* and *mythos* and the Russian formalist *sjužet* and *fabula*. Chatman's use of the word "story" to describe the diegetic content of narrative is therefore well established in narrative theory, but neither Chatman nor most other theorists undertake to explain the difference between stories and nonstories.[5]

It is not surprising that narrative theory has traditionally avoided the question of narrative ontology, of what makes stories stories, for past theorists who undertook to define narrative met with indifferent success. The first of these theorists whose work has survived, Aristotle himself, was philosophically disposed to favor drama over narrative, and throughout the *Poetics* he refers to narrative as if it were an inferior subspecies of drama, its rules and conventions essentially those of drama, and its success proportionate to its dramatic qualities. He does, it is true, distinguish carefully between the manners in which epic and dramatic poetry are presented: The poet "may either (1) speak at one moment in narrative and at another in an assumed character, as Homer does; or (2) one may remain the same throughout, without any such change; or (3) the imitators may represent the whole story dramatically, as though they were actually doing the things described" (3.1448a). His other distinctions—the greater length and variety of epic poetry, its dependence on the stately heroic meter, which most readily accommodates the rare words and metaphors in which narrative abounds, and its greater affinity for marvelous and irrational events which need not be dramatically enacted—all follow from the difference in the manner of presentation. But Aristotle is willing to abandon this distinction in order to defend the superiority of tragedy to epic. The accusation that tragedy is often badly acted, he argues, "does not touch the art of the dramatic poet, but only that of his interpreter," because "Tragedy may produce its effect even without movement or action in just the same way as Epic poetry; for from the mere reading of the play its quality may be seen" (26.1462a).

More important than the question of Aristotle's success in making a distinction between dramatic and narrative works is his tendency to define narrative in dramatic terms. The kinds of epic poetry are for him the same as those of tragedy; its parts, except for the omission of song and spectacle, are the same; it contains no elements which tragedy does not share. Moreover, a narrative plot "should clearly be [constructed] like that in a drama" (23.1459a). Except for noting the consequences of its mode of presentation for narrative, Aristotle does not entertain the possibility that a narrative plot, or narratives generally, might be constructed on principles independent of the model of tragedy, principles inherent in narrative as such.

The description of narrative works in terms borrowed from the criticism of drama, which amounts to treating narrative as a kind of drama, persists in our time most clearly in the neo-Aristotelian criticism of the Chicago school. This persistence takes several forms: Elder Olson's unwillingness, in his *Theory of Comedy*, to consider any nondramatic works; Ronald S. Crane's analysis of *Tom Jones*, *Persuasion*, "The Killers," and "The Short Happy Life of Francis Macomber" in terms of a single dramatic action each is presumed to imitate; and Wayne C. Booth's discomfort with *A Portrait of the Artist as a Young Man*, whose ambiguities make it impossible to determine just what its action means or is. The Chicago critics, writing with constant reference to Aristotle, have repeatedly sought to make his concepts and distinctions responsive to the range and variety of modern literature.

The neo-Aristotelians, however, are not the only modern theorists of narrative indebted to Aristotle. The major school in Anglo-American criticism of fiction, a school whose principles have been adumbrated by Henry James, codified by Percy Lubbock, and inherited by most critics writing in English before the advent of structuralism, owes a subtler but equally pervasive debt to Aristotle. When Lubbock wrote in 1921 that "the whole intricate question of method, in the craft of fiction," is "governed by the question of the point of view—the question of the relation in which the narrator stands to the story,"[6] he defined the criticism of fiction in essentially rhetorical terms, terms which were still current when Booth published *The Rhetoric of Fiction* in 1961. Indeed, Booth's attack on Lubbock's dogmatic preference for objective or "dramatic" narration reaffirmed Lubbock's major premise—that any theory of narrative must be organized around the problem of the author's point of view.

Success in fiction depends for Lubbock on providing some authority for a novel's narrative assertions within the novel itself, so as to mask its status as imitation or fiction. Speaking of *Madame Bovary*, Lubbock observes that "the art of fiction does not begin until the novelist thinks of the story as a matter to be *shown*, to be so exhibited that it will tell itself" (62). A given scene (the term is Lubbock's) may be presented pictorially, as it appears to someone's consciousness, or dramatically, in terms of external description. When the consciousness so represented is different from the author's, like that of Strether in *The Ambassadors*, both methods are dramatic, for "nobody is reporting his impressions to the reader. The impression is enacting itself in the endless series of images that play over the outspread expanse of the man's mind and memory" (170). Lubbock's preference for mimesis to diegesis, and his choice of James as the exemplary craftsman of fiction, define novelistic success in dramatic terms: the more successful the novel, the less narration it contains, and the more pictures or dramatized scenes.

Lubbock's account is based on James's theory and practice as expounded in the Preface to the New York Edition of *The Awkward Age*, where James congratulates himself on having created "really constructive dialogue, dialogue organic and dramatic, speaking for itself, representing and embodying substance and form," and contends that "my first care *had* to be the covering of my tracks—lest I truly should be caught in the act of arranging, of organising dialogue to 'speak for itself.'"[7] James's determination to organize his novel along the lines of the well-made play echoes Aristotle's dictum: "The poet should say very little *in propria persona*, as he is no imitator when doing that" (24.1460a). Like Aristotle, James borrows the language of dramatic criticism for his narrative theory and so makes narrative in effect a special and inferior species of drama.

But James and Lubbock are not Aristotelians in the sense that the Chicago critics are. The peculiar quality of Aristotle's influence on the critical tradition they inaugurated is indicated by James's inability to write a successful play. It is true that *Guy Domville*, the climactic work of James's dramatic career, failed in part because James's touch was too delicate for an audience which preferred *Arms and the Man* and *The Importance of Being Earnest*. But James's own gifts were for narrative, though narrative of a particular sort. When he wrote in his notebook the year following the failure of *Guy Domville* that "the scenic scheme is the only method that *I* can trust, with my tendencies, to stick to the march of an action,"[8] he overlooked or took for granted his conception of action as a relation between a pictured consciousness and a dramatized world. The phrase "drama of consciousness," which aptly describes the action of James's major fiction, encapsulates the paradox on which that fiction is based: Consciousness can be dramatized only in terms of overt action, but it is an imaginative value only as it transcends reduction to a series of actions. James's characteristic theme, the unsuccessful attempt to translate consciousness and the external world into each other's terms, requires either a theater like Shakespeare's, whose conventions allow direct access to the characters' thoughts, or the form of narrative fiction.

James was slow to appreciate the essentially narrative character of his imagination because his conception of action remained executive rather than philosophical: He is interested in dramatic action as a rhetorical figure for consciousness, not as a basis for defining human behavior. James prepares for a criticism and a pedagogy in which the forms of drama are institutionalized as rhetorical strategies because he adopts Aristotle's preference for drama to narrative without accepting the philosophical presuppositions on which that preference is based.

What Aren't Stories

The earliest theorists of narrative defined it in dramatic terms because drama and the theory of drama possessed a cultural centrality and a respectability that narrative forms like the romance, and later the novel, lacked. In his seminal essay "The Art of Fiction" James attempts to confer the comparatively exalted status of the drama on his own work by borrowing its terms and concepts. More recent analysts, however, have placed narrative within the context of other modes of discourse.

In their textbook *Film Art*, for example, David Bordwell and Kristin Thompson offer a representative account of the relation of narrative to non-narrative films when they distinguish among four possible formal systems. In categorical films, "the filmmaker presents a subject by cataloguing a set of conceptual types." In rhetorical films, "the filmmaker presents a logical or persuasive argument" in a film which "goes beyond the categorical type in that it tries to convince the viewer of some quality about the subject; it does not simply provide information about it." In abstract films, "the separate elements of the film organize according to 'pure' formal principles. . . . The basic quality of abstract films is that they rely on the viewer's attention to similarities and differences in material qualities of the film medium: color, graphic compositions, movement, editing, sounds." Narrative films, by contrast, present "*a chain of events in cause-effect relationship occurring in time.* . . . A narrative begins with one situation; a series of changes occurs according to a pattern of causes and effects; finally, a new situation arises which brings about the end of the narrative." Causality is an important criterion for narrative because "a random set of events cannot be a story." The sequence

> (1) "A man tosses and turns, unable to sleep. A mirror breaks. A telephone rings"

is not narrative because it establishes no causal or temporal relationships among its events. On the other hand,

> (2) "A man has a fight with his boss; he tosses and turns that night, unable to sleep. In the morning, he is still so angry that he smashes the mirror while shaving. Then his telephone rings; his boss has called to apologize"

is a narrative sequence because causal and temporal sequences are made clear; "the narrative develops from an initial situation of no conflict between employee and boss, through a series of events caused by the conflict, to the resolution of the conflict."[9]

Bordwell and Thompson's book stands alone among introductory textbooks on any mode of narrative in its attempt to place narrative in a rigorously defined context of alternative forms. Such rigorous distinctions, however, cannot always be maintained in the analysis of actual films. In Marv Newland's cartoon *Bambi Meets Godzilla*, for example, most of the film's running time is devoted to a frame showing Bambi peacefully browsing in the grass as the credits roll: "Directed by Marv Newland. . . . Written by Marv Newland. . . . Screenplay by Marv Newland. . . . Bambi's wardrobe by Marv Newland." Two seconds after the last credit, a gigantic foot comes down from the top of the screen, crushing Bambi, and the film is over except for two closing credits and a tiny motion showing Godzilla's toes curling. This film is surely a narrative in Bordwell and Thompson's terms, since it has all the requisites of a story; yet it also makes significant use of categorical form (the credits, which become in retrospect an important part of the film's joke) and abstract form (since its effect depends, like that of all animated cartoons, on "the viewer's attention to similarities and differences in material qualities of the film medium"). *Bambi Meets Godzilla* is in fact a hybrid, not an example of any one form; an audience who perceived only its narrative qualities and accepted it as a complete sequence of events would miss the point of the joke (that is, the buildup of the title and the opening credits seemed to portend a much more extended encounter between the principals—although the nature of their actual encounter, as we realize in retrospect, is far more probable).

Of course, *Bambi Meets Godzilla* is an unusual film whose effect relies on the mixing of narrative and non-narrative elements, but almost every narrative film imaginable is in fact another hybrid. *Casablanca* relies for its effect on arousing the audience's sympathy for the Free French and enmity against the Third Reich; *Gone with the Wind* gives a great deal of information about life in the antebellum South; John Ford's westerns have a pictorial beauty based on purely graphic elements. Such elements do not, of course, make these films simply rhetorical or categorical or abstract, but they do indicate the intimacy between narrative and non-narrative forms.

Bordwell and Thompson's definition of narrative in terms of events linked in causal or temporal relationships, and especially the distinctions they draw between examples (1) and (2), recall a simpler time when narrative theory was not the subject of debate because audiences knew what stories were and what to expect of them. Narratives presented a situation characterized by instability, developed a conflict out of that instability, and concluded with a resolution.[10] But the advent of modernist fiction, especially in the short stories of Chekhov, Joyce, Stephen Crane, and other authors in whom nothing often happened, or in whom events seemed impressively meaningless, made it not only more urgent but more difficult to distinguish between stories and nonstories. In most of the stories in *Dubliners*, there is little or no conflict between characters, though considerable conflict within the principal characters. If these stories are narrative, does it follow that any representation of psychological conflict is narrative? Is Hemingway's "Hills Like White Elephants," which establishes a conflict that is never resolved in the story, a narrative? Bordwell and Thompson's original definition of narrative ("a chain of events in cause-effect relationship occurring in time") does not make conflict essential to narrative. Does it follow that any series of events whose causal or temporal relationships are clear is a story? It has become a cliché among the readership of *The New Yorker* that stories published there, although easy to follow, are frequently obscure because they don't have any endings. Ever since modernist writers made irresolution and closing indeterminacy fashionable in narratives like "Heart of Darkness," *The Castle*, and *A Passage to India*, storytellers have continually demanded that their audiences accept more elliptical promises of resolution. The result has been to expand the frontiers of narrative to a point unimaginable a hundred years ago and to make the boundaries that separate stories from nonstories the subject of constant dispute. If stories recount states of affairs which are causally or temporally ordered, then what isn't a story? Most theorists would agree:

(3)   Once upon a time they lived happily ever after

is not a story, even though it uses (in fact, consists entirely of) two phrases
we associate exclusively with narrative. As the "story" Charlie Brown
pretends to read to Lucy in the comic strip *Peanuts*, it is a nonstory in
narrative clothing, a pointed refusal to engage in the act of storytelling.[11]
Gerald Prince, who has done more than anyone else writing in English to
clarify the difference between stories and nonstories, has ruled that "narrative is the representation of *at least two* real or fictive events or situations in
a time sequence, neither of which presupposes or entails the other"[12]—a
definition that disqualifies (3) as narrative because it represents only one
event.

Prince's definition, however, does not treat all attempts to weasel out of
storytelling equally, for when Lucy pretends to read her brother Linus a
story consisting of the sentence,

(4)   A man was born . . . he lived and he died,[13]

her utterance is according to Prince a narrative, however minimal; indeed,
most of Prince's discussion in *Narratology* is devoted to such minimal
narratives. Counting such examples as narrative maintains the logical
consistency of Prince's definition but strains its correspondence to what
most audiences would consider narrative (though Linus in this case is
suitably impressed). Defining stories, as Prince does, in terms of the
diegetic events they represent allows the term *narrative* to cover such
examples as

(5)   When General Sherman's troops marched through Georgia,
      Scarlett O'Hara and her family lost their old way of life. Some
      years later, Sam Spade, a private detective in San Francisco,
      tried without success to secure a costly jewelled statue of a bird,

but surely no one would accept this example as a narrative; although it
conforms to Prince's rules, it contains too much information for one
story—how are the problems of Scarlett O'Hara and Sam Spade related?—but not enough for two. A sufficiently ingenious audience could
postulate links between the two events, but these links would in all
likelihood be thematic (e.g., "Life goes from bad to worse") rather than
causal.[14]

Causality itself has often been taken as an indication of narrativity. In
E. M. Forster's famous distinction,

(6)   The king died, and then the queen died

is a story, whereas

(7)   The king died, and then the queen died of grief

is a plot, which places primary emphasis on causality rather than temporal
sequence. Now either of these examples could well serve as the basis for a
successful story, but neither of them seems adequate in its present form. If
I said, "I just heard a deeply moving story," and went on to recount either
(6) or (7), my audience would undoubtedly feel cheated. Forster's third
example,

(8)   The queen died, no one knew why, until it was discovered that it
      was through grief at the death of the king,

although he contends that "it moves as far away from the story as its
limitations will allow,"[15] is in fact the most successful story of the three
because it is the only one which gives the audience the opportunity to
wonder in what way the expectations it arouses will be fulfilled; the crucial
phrase "no one knew why" makes it the only one of Forster's examples
with a middle.[16]

Causality is not, however, a necessary and sufficient condition for narrativity because even examples whose causality is clear are not always
perceived as satisfactory stories. The problem with

(9)   A man learned of a plot against England from a woman who was
      killed in his flat later that night. Eluding the police and the
      killers, he set out to warn the authorities, but then changed his
      mind and went abroad to live

is that although the causal links between the events are clear, the rationale
of the entire series is not. Even if it is more probable that a man would
behave as the man here does than as Richard Hannay actually does in *The
39 Steps*, the opening event of (9) establishes a conflict whose resolution is
implicitly promised; at the very least, the ending of (9) is too vaguely
described to fulfill the promise of its much more specific complication
("killed in his flat later that night"). On the other hand, an example like
A. E. Housman's poem

(10)   Reader, behold! this monster wild
       Has gobbled up the infant child.
       The infant child is not aware
       It has been eaten by the bear,[17]

which recounts only one event (the infant child's unawareness is not really
an event, and even if it were, it would be entailed, in Prince's terms, by the
first event here), is at least arguably a story whose closing event mocks, by

its tautological vacuity, the premise which its opening establishes and so decisively reorders the audience's expectations.

Since causality cannot alone distinguish between stories and nonstories, there is a temptation to consider other features as possible touchstones of narrativity. Intelligible sequence is obviously an inadequate criterion, since many non-narrative discourses are better described by one of Bordwell and Thompson's non-narrative categories. To narrow the requisite of narrative to *temporal* sequence, however, produces immediate difficulties, since many novels like *Tristram Shandy* and *The Good Soldier* present events in a sequence remote from the order in which they are said to have taken place. Nor does it help to define narratives as those discourses from which a causal or temporal sequence of events can be recovered, for, as Nelson Goodman has argued, a temporal sequence of events can be recovered from any discourse, whether or not it is narrative: "A picture of a forest tells implicitly of trees growing from seedlings and shedding leaves; and a picture of a house implies that trees were cut for it and that its roof will soon leak."[18]

If the presence of sequential implications makes "The Love Song of J. Alfred Prufrock" and "Dover Beach" and "Religio Laici" narrative, then the term can be applied to virtually any discourse and so becomes meaningless. If we intend to save *story* as a critical term—to distinguish, that is, between stories and nonstories—we need a more precise formulation of a story than the sequence of events implied by a given discourse, and a formulation more closely aligned with our habitual experience of stories.

Saving the Story

It is of course possible that the term *story* cannot be defended as a critical category, a property of all and only narrative works. René Wellek has suggested in "Genre Theory, the Lyric, and *Erlebnis*" that *lyric* is a term whose bewildering variety of applications makes it too elusive to serve as a useful critical category; the same may be true of *story*. Theorists have found it virtually impossible to define story (as against discourse) as a constitutive feature of narrative without either arguing in a circle, by defining narratives as works which imply stories, or becoming impractically vague, by defining all diegesis as narrative. The extent of their difficulties is evident in the work of Frank Kermode, whose impressive and influential work on narrative continually reveals the power of stories without ever distinguishing them from nonstories. In *The Sense of an Ending* Kermode discusses the shape of fiction in terms of its ends, which image the ultimate and eschatological end of humankind. "Men die," observes Kermode, after the physician Alkmeon, "because they cannot join the beginning and the end";[19] the purpose of their fictions is to establish a notion of human identity by defining the present moment, "the middest," in terms of a mysterious but imaginable end. Clocks, notes Kermode, say *tick-tick*, but people humanize this sound by calling it *tick-tock*, providing it with a beginning and an end, a miniature plot defining "a special kind of middle" (45).

Nowhere in *The Sense of an Ending* does Kermode propose a distinction between narrative plots or narrative fictions and other sorts of plots or fictions; his focus is on the implications of teleological thinking for fiction and history generally, not on generic typology. But his illustrations persistently raise questions about the relation between, for example, narrative endings and the more general subject of poetic (or aesthetic or discursive) closure. He acutely observes that although Sartre denies the Aristotelian belief that "without potentiality there is no change," Sartre's own novels perforce contradict his beliefs. "Change without potentiality in a novel is impossible," Kermode concludes, because "a novel which really implemented this policy would properly be a chaos. . . . All novels imitate a world of potentiality, even if this implies a philosophy disclaimed by their authors" (138). Kermode's other example of a "Megaric" or anti-Aristotelian novel, *Paterson*, a text which has struck most commentators as neither novel nor narrative, raises the question of whether the "fixation on the eidetic imagery of beginning, middle, and end, potency and cause" is characteristic of novels, of narratives, or of all fiction. More generally, what is the place of narrative within the fictive realm?

Such questions are tangential to Kermode's argument in *The Sense of an Ending*, but in *The Genesis of Secrecy* (subtitled *On the Interpretation of Narrative*) they become more pressing. Kermode extends his argument in the later book by defining narrative as an interpretation of a world inherently "unfollowable." Narratives commonly image problematic relations and situations in terms of dramatic events and characters, so that the need to account for the Crucifixion, for example, leads Mark and the other evangelists to adopt the plot function of Betrayal, which, incarnated in the figure of Judas, ultimately becomes a character with a life and interest of its own. Narrative sequence is at once "the great mnemonic" and the silencer of "awkward questions";[20] hence historians characteristically prefer narrative as more authoritative than explanation. Although narrative begins as demystification, however, an interest in their own requirements of coherence, fullness, and verisimilitude leads all but the most schematic narratives to say "more than is strictly necessary to make [their] point" (34). Since gratuitous details tend to encourage a multitude of interpretive

justifications, it follows that " 'narrative' always entails a measure of opaci-
ty" (25)—the more completely a narrative separates itself from the point it
was created to gloss, the more fully it opens itself to the imputation of
multivalence and mystery. Kermode summarizes this process in his contribution to the 1979 Chicago symposium on narrative by considering narrative as "the product of two intertwined processes, the presentation of a
fable and its progressive interpretation (which of course alters it). The first
tends toward clarity and propriety, the second toward secrecy, toward
distortions which cover secrets."[21]

Kermode's line of inquiry is so useful and provocative that it is surprising to find that he never makes his definition of narrative explicit. Because
Kermode discusses no alternative modes of organization to the narrative
mode, narrative comes to appear as the only way of ordering the unfollowable world. In his analysis in *The Genesis of Secrecy* of the evolution of
Judas from plot function to character, for example, Kermode conjectures
that "he entered the story for the first time at the moment of the Arrest,
and was expanded backwards," and remarks, "It takes very little to make a
character; a few indications of idiosyncrasy, of deviation from type, are
enough, for our practiced eyes will make up the larger patterns of which
such indications can be read as parts" (94, 98). But are such elaborations
and hermeneutics specifically narrative? Or are they equally characteristic
of any works which focus a fictive consciousness—of Browning's dramatic
monologues, or Landor's *Imaginary Conversations*, or "Hugh Selwyn
Mauberley"? One can agree with Kermode that situations or beliefs and
characters tend to generate each other as agents enact their potentialities in
a narrative which requires in turn instrumental agents with requirements
of their own without concluding that this generation is invariably narrative.

Again, when Kermode concludes in "Secrets and Narrative Sequence"
that "secrets . . . are at odds with sequence, which is considered as an
aspect of propriety" (88), it is not clear why "sequence" should mean
narrative sequence (as, in the instance, it does) and not logical or expository or thematic or associative sequence—the sort of sequence exhibited in
In Memoriam or Browne's *Urn Burial*. Kermode offers Keats's Grecian urn
as an object which lacks "intelligible sequence" and captures our attention
by promising temporal developments which never actually take place, so
that "this lack or absence must be the most important thing about it" (84).
But Kermode, presenting the thwarted promise of narrative as the poem's
structural principle, overlooks the equally important organizing principle,
not of the urn, but of Keats's poem: the logical sequence of argumentation.
If secrets are those aspects of a text most at odds with sequence, most
consigned to obscurity when sequence is foregrounded, then sequence

must be defined more broadly, in terms which include not only narrative sequence but expository, rhetorical, and psychological sequence as ways of ordering the world. Kermode obliquely acknowledges this necessity in the Preface to *The Genesis of Secrecy* when he describes his interest in "problems of interpretation . . . especially as they presented themselves in narrative, but also, because narrative seems so central, in many other areas" (vii). But he stops short of establishing the relation between narrative and those other areas—between narrative and midrash (81–84), for example, as alternative modes of interpretation.

In Kermode's account of the development of narrative, the logic of the story, its events and agents, generates discursive features which in turn generate new plot functions and agents, but the two logics of story and discourse, tending respectively toward revelation and secrecy, are fundamentally contrary. The conflict between the imperatives of story-logic and discourse-logic is the basis for Jonathan Culler's important essay, "Story and Discourse in the Analysis of Narrative." After considering narratives whose events generally determine their discursive form but which are at crucial points themselves determined by the discourse (so that, for example, Sigmund Freud, recounting the analysis of the patient who has come to be known as the wolf-man, hypothesizes the patient's witnessing a primal scene at the age of a year and a half as a requirement of his present neurosis and the discourse of his dreams and conversation), Culler remarks: "Since the distinction between story and discourse can function only if there is determination of one by the other, the analyst must always choose which will be treated as the given and which as the product. Yet either choice leads to a narratology that misses some of the curious complexity of narratives and fails to account for much of their impact." Thinking of discourse as simply generated by the events of a story fails to explain the frequent determination of story events by the discourse. But thinking of story events as themselves a function of discourse, "a series of predicates attached to agents in the text," ignores the fact that "even the most radical fictions depend for their effect on the assumption that their puzzling sequences of sentences are presentations of events." Culler concludes: "Neither perspective, then, is likely to offer a satisfactory narratology, nor can the two together fit together in a harmonious synthesis; they stand in irreconcilable opposition, a conflict between two logics which puts in question the possibility of a coherent, non-contradictory 'science' of narrative. . . . One must be willing to shift from one perspective to the other, from story to discourse and back again."[22]

Culler is constrained to deny the possibility of a systematic narratology because of his determination to pursue the conflict between the claims of story-logic and discourse-logic to its conclusion; his entire analysis follows from his distinction between story and discourse. Yet perhaps he makes this distinction too easily; perhaps indeed it is neither necessary nor defensible after all. Culler approvingly quotes Mieke Bal's unusually explicit definition of story (*histoire*): "The story consists of the set of events in their chronological order, their spatial location, and their relations with the actors who cause or undergo them."[23] This definition is presented as if it referred to a natural or actual order of events in the diegetic world, the order in which they "really" happened; and in some closely similar form, it has been accepted by theorists from Aristotle to Seymour Chatman. But defining stories in this way, as we have seen, makes it impossible to distinguish stories from nonstories, since nothing in Bal's definition, or in any definition that begins by separating story from discourse, explains why some chronological sequences of events are stories and others are not, or why rearranging chronological sequences of events sometimes produces narratives like *Tristram Shandy* and sometimes produces non-narratives like Freud's *Interpretation of Dreams*. If we decide that only the nature of the discourse itself determines whether or not a given sequence of events is a story, then story itself becomes a discursive product, not a presumed anterior or prediscursive set of events. The conclusion is inescapable: Since there is no way of distinguishing between stories and nonstories without reference to the discourses which present them, story is indeed a discursive category. Although narrative discourses do present agents, events, and relations, those agents and events and relations are not a story, merely the material for a potential story—and for many alternatives, such as Bordwell and Thompson's categorical, rhetorical, and abstract forms of discourse.

Placing narrative modes alongside other kinds of discourse, as Bordwell and Thompson do, allows us to see, for example, that narrative is the only one of their four formal systems which relies on the audience's ignorance about what is to come. Audiences may well be ignorant about impending developments as they watch categorical, rhetorical, and abstract films, but their ignorance, at least regarding certain details (why will Norma Desmond kill Joe Gillis in *Sunset Boulevard?* what was the foolproof method Walter Neff used to murder Dietrichson in *Double Indemnity*, and why didn't he get away with it?), is absolutely essential to the success of narrative. As soon as the audience knows everything that is to happen, narrative becomes ritual. To broaden Kermode's formulation, stories imitate a world of potential, of coming-to-be, not of having-been. This insight is fundamental to an ontology of narrative discourse—to narratology, as it has recently been called by Prince and others.

It remains true, of course, that narratives require their readers to attempt to recover the "natural" or "correct" chronological order of their events, but that "natural" order, once established, is not what makes a series of events a story. "Narrative," as Tzvetan Todorov remarks in "Primitive Narrative," "is a discourse, not a series of events";[24] there is no such thing as a prediscursive or unarticulated story. Since what makes a given series of events into a story (more accurately, what makes different states of affairs into a series of events) is the manner in which the discourse presents them, it will be necessary to use the terms *story, plot,* and *narrative* rather differently in this book from the way they are usually used.[25] Plot, the constitutive trope of drama, is the trope by which narrative images human action, an action involving either the relations among different agents the narrative presents or relations between the storyteller and the audience. A story is not what a narrative presents, it *is* a narrative, since no story exists outside or independent of a narrative discourse. As for narrative itself, it is a mode of discourse which it will be the project of this book, and in particular the following chapter, to define.

2
Narrative as a Display Mode

If narratives cannot be defined as discourses which represent stories, how can they be defined? Critics seeking a *sine qua non* which all and only narratives possess have suggested such features as sequence, change, action, closure, turning or peripeteia, and events as such as peculiar to narrative discourse, but these features are shared by non-narrative works (action and peripeteia by drama; events by drama and medical and legal studies; sequence, change, and closure by a much wider range of works). In the absence of a convincing narrative differentia, other critics have defined narrative categorically, as a distinctive member of a larger class. This is the ostensible method of Aristotle, who divides poetic imitation according to its medium, its objects, and its manner, distinguishing on this last point between dramatic and narrative works. Aristotle's example demonstrates how important the broader class is in characterizing the particular species: His definition of poetry in terms of its end (imitation) rather than its medium (verse) is constitutive of all that follows.

The problem with defining narrative in contradistinction to the other members of a larger class of works is the variety of classes in which narrative might plausibly be placed. Aristotle's analysis places narrative within a particularly literary context: Epic is set against drama on the basis of their modes of presentation. Using modern literary modes, we might distinguish between stories and essays or lyric poetry, although here the mode of presentation (writing) fails to distinguish each species from the other. If the class is a mode of discourse—narrative as something told— stories (for example, anecdotes) could be set against gnomic opinions, directions, gossip or chitchat, and so on, on the basis of their grammatical tense. If the class is that of works designed to be assimilated in only one sequence, narratives could be set against chronicle histories on the basis of their imputation of causality.[1] If the class is spectacle—narrative as something worth paying attention to—novels could be set against mail order catalogues, feature films against documentaries or travelogues, painting sequences like Hogarth's against the sequence of paintings in an art gallery (an arrangement usually chronological rather than narrative), on the basis of their continuity (of action, of character, of theme) and coherence (unlike catalogues and art galleries, narratives are designed to be experienced as wholes). Given, however, that narratives have comprised works in prose, in verse, in painting, dance, and film, besides oral recitations, none of these classifications does justice to the variety of narrative forms, purposes, and situations.

Consider the most aggressively commonsensical attempt to define literary genres by differentiating between their technical features, Northrop Frye's definition of each genre in terms of its "radical of presentation," an Aristotelian concept of manner: "Words may be acted in front of a listener; they may be sung or chanted; or they may be written for a reader."[2] From these distinctions Frye derives the genres of, respectively, drama, epic, lyric, and fiction. Frye contends that "the purpose of criticism by genres is not so much to classify as to clarify such traditions and affinities, thereby bringing out a large number of literary relationships that would not be noticed as long as there was no context established for them" (247–48), and his account is most illuminating for works whose conventions presuppose multiple radicals of presentation, such as *Paradise Lost, Faust,* and *The Ring and the Book.* Useful as Frye's definitions are in practical criticism, they do not aim to provide a satisfactory ontology of narrative, which, having no distinctive radical of presentation, is parceled out between epic and fiction. Nor does Frye's classification make any provision for nonverbal narratives like silent film.[3]

A more comprehensive schema of literary genres, based on a combination of intention and manner of presentation, is that of Paul Hernadi. Since "one *could* say that verbal art evokes imaginative worlds in four fundamentally different ways: thematic works present, poems enact vision; plays represent, narratives make us envision action,"[4] Hernadi uses a four-part typology in which narrative modes are set against lyric modes, which they least resemble, and distinguished from thematic and dramatic modes, which they tend to elide into. Like Frye, Hernadi considers the borderlines of his categories at great length. The principal advantages of his typology are that it makes room for silent films (which could be placed among dramatic modes, since these have wordless pantomime as their logical extreme) and that the thematic category acknowledges not only the existence of such literary genres as the essay and the fable but the variously pervasive tendency in lyric and narrative works toward general statement.

Aristotle would no doubt take exception to Hernadi's opposition of dramatic to thematic modes, for he considers tragedy as the central poetic mode because of its emphasis on a thematic teleology. His thematic account of tragedy, together with Frye's and Hernadi's postulation of such mixed modes as lyric drama, suggests a third approach to the problem of defining narrative: Instead of positing a narrative *sine qua non* or differentia, we might define narrative in terms of a characteristic program or rationale, a way of seeing or shaping the world. All modes of discourse, in this account, would have the status of images or incarnations of a given set of philosophical beliefs about human behavior and the nonhuman world. Such an approach to narrative ontology could take as its model Aristotle's rationale of tragedy; for although Aristotle defines mimetic modes in terms of their presentational differentia, his distinctions are based ultimately on a philosophical rationale of human experience.

The reason Aristotle takes tragedy as a privileged model for all poetic modes is implicit in his discussion of plot (*mythos*), which he asserts to be a more important element in tragedy than character, for "Tragedy is essentially an imitation not of persons but of action (*praxis*) and life, of happiness and misery. All human happiness and misery takes the form of action; the end for which we live is a certain kind of activity, not a quality" (*Poetics* 6.1450a). This sounds magisterial and unexceptionable, but, as E. M. Forster has pointed out, few modern critics would agree with Aristotle: "We believe that happiness and misery exist in the secret life, which each of us leads privately and to which (in his characters) the novelist has access."[5] Aristotle gives the dramatic plot precedence over character for the same reason he prefers drama to narrative: Lacking a modernist notion of consciousness—nowhere in Aristotle are the faculties of remembering, speculating, feeling pain or desire, or intending linked as modes of mental awareness—he defines human experience in terms of public action rather than Forster's "secret life."

Indeed, it is not going too far to say that Aristotle uses tragedy (particularly Sophocles' *Oedipus the King*) as his model of poetic representation because Sophocles' tragedy defines man in terms of his own freely chosen, morally consequent action. Aristotelian tragedy images human experience in terms of actions rather than qualities because it defines human identity in terms of radically free moral decisions. What makes human beings powerful, in this view, is their capacity to act freely and rationally, to make intelligent decisions about themselves and others; what makes them tragically limited is their inability to foresee in sufficient detail the consequences of these decisions. A successful tragedy presents an agent in a situation which dramatizes simultaneously and to the greatest extent his powers and his limitations, but it is the action and not the agent which is the proper focus of tragedy.

Although this analysis obviously does not apply in detail to most tragedy since Aristotle, it is surprising to see how, in its broad sense, it continues to apply. Playwrights as different as Shakespeare and Ibsen continue to treat tragedy as the imitation of an action; they simply conceive action itself in different terms. The plot of *Hamlet* involves not three actions but one—the avenging of a royal father by a son—but this action is so equivocal that Shakespeare presents it through three analogous and intertwined versions, so that together the vengeance of Hamlet, Laertes, and Fortinbras dramatizes the action more comprehensively than any single version could do. (Compare the continuing quest for vengeance in the *Oresteia*, which dramatizes different aspects of the problem sequentially rather than contrapuntally.) Most of Ibsen's prose plays similarly present a single action, though Ibsen places more emphasis on the social and psychological springs of action (in *Ghosts* and *The Wild Duck*) and the possibility of conversion as a dramatic action (in *A Doll's House* and *Little Eyolf*). Even more radical departures from Aristotle—*The Cherry Orchard*, *Waiting for Godot*, *The Lesson*—most often pose as more or less overt critiques of Aristotle's assumption that human experience is defined by purposive action and thus continue to develop the philosophical debate which makes them intelligible.

That Aristotle himself defines the human subject in these terms is clear from his other works. In the *Nicomachean Ethics* he defines individual character in terms of action rather than consciousness: "By choosing what is good or bad we are men of a certain character, which we are not by holding certain opinions. . . . It is activities exercised on particular objects that make the corresponding character" (III:2.1112a; III:5.1114a). Anticipating the objection that character is a cause rather than a result of action, he contends that character can be formed only by the deliberate imitation of moral actions: "It is not the man who does these [just and temperate actions] that is just and temperate, but the man who does them *as* just and temperate men do them" (II:4.1105b).

Elsewhere Aristotle goes still further in postulating the capacity for free and morally consequent action as the defining quality, not only of a given person, but of the human animal generally. In the *Physics* he distinguishes responsible men from children and lower animals, who are "incapable of deliberate intention" or of "moral action" (II:6.197b). Finally, in "On the Soul" he defines the soul as the cause of the body in the efficient, formal, and final senses (II:4.415b) and characterizes the soul in terms of "the powers of self-nutrition, sensation, thinking, and motivity" (III:2.413b).

Insofar as a creature partakes of these powers—that is, insofar as it is capable of behavior directed toward a desired end—it has a soul which animates and motivates it. Hence plants, which feed themselves, are more alive than rocks; the lower animals, which are capable of movement and sensation, are still more alive; and man, who alone is capable of rational action, is most alive. The ability to proceed deliberately toward a freely chosen end is for Aristotle the defining quality of the human soul.

Tragedy in the Aristotelian tradition defines human experience as determined to a great extent by social position or psychology, fortune or circumstance; but it is the free action, however rare—Oedipus's decision to seek out the murderer of Laius, Phaedra's confession of her love to Hippolytus, Hedda's rejection of her role as Tesman's wife in favor of her role as General Gabler's daughter—which provides the pivot for each play, because it is only through such actions that people demonstrate at once their aspirations and their limitations. To trace a single action from its problematical beginning to its catastrophe is the project of tragedy, which emphasizes the teleology of rational action in order to present what might be called a dramatic view of human experience. The analysis of human experience in terms of actions and their consequent ends has been largely superseded in the modern mind by the Cartesian analysis (to which Forster alludes) of human experience in terms of consciousness—we are what we think, not necessarily what we do—but the generic prescriptions Aristotle based on his analysis of human nature have seldom been challenged in any systematic way. The most considerable attempt by a modern critic to construct a generic typology on a philosophical basis—a philosophy of experience rather than simply of representation[6]—is that of Georg Lukács in *The Theory of the Novel*. In order to prepare for his historical analysis of the novel as a fictional mode, Lukács distinguishes between the world-views of drama and epic: "Great epic writing gives form to the extensive totality of life, drama to the intensive totality of essence." This distinction is more than procedural, for Lukács's conception of epic and drama, like Aristotle's account of tragedy, presents the modes in question as images of a philosophical system or ways of imagining a world: "For the epic, the world at any given moment is an ultimate principle; it is empirical at its deepest, most decisive, all-determining transcendental base."[7] This radically historical empiricism Lukács proposes as the hallmark of narrative literature, as against the "formal *a priori* nature" of the drama, which works by abstracting the essential meaning from a world in which philosophical meaning is felt as inherent. Drama seeks to incarnate and enact this transcendental meaning, narrative to propose contingent meanings, intimations of transcendence, in the world as it empirically is.

In his 1962 Preface to *The Theory of the Novel*, Lukács pronounces his earlier methodology too positivistic and abstract and characterizes his project as an attempt "to form general synthetic concepts on the basis of only a few characteristics—in most cases only intuitively grasped—of a school, a period, etc., then to proceed by deduction from these generalisations to the analysis of individual phenomena, and in that way to arrive at . . . a comprehensive overall view" (13). The later development of Lukács's career indicates that he found generic typology an unpromising application for the Marxist aesthetics which so decisively influenced him shortly after *The Theory of the Novel* appeared: His commitment to dialectical materialism, which made him even less sympathetic to the drama as a genre, rendered all categorical generic distinctions suspect. For critics who do not share Lukács's later principles, however, his early project is *mutatis mutandis* still valid. What philosophical views of the world and of human experience are implicit in the forms of narrative? If the rationale of Aristotelian tragedy is a conception of people as creatures capable of rational action, what is the underlying rationale of narrative? In order to answer these questions, it will be necessary to examine at some length the needs and desires stories fulfill for their audiences.

What Makes Stories Worth Telling?

One problem traditional narrative theory has failed to resolve is why story events sometimes produce narrative discourse and sometimes other kinds of discourse, such as those Nelson Goodman calls studies and symphonies.[8] A related problem, which Goodman does not consider, is why different audiences often perceive a given discourse in different terms. Doting parents accept their children's recitals of events, hopeful legatees their senile uncle's reminiscences, and cowed employees their boss's pointless anecdotes as stories, even though disinterested parties would analyze them quite differently. Most of the examples I dismissed in Chapter 1 as non-narrative could be recovered as stories by an audience so inclined. For example,

(1) The king died, and then the queen died of grief

would be a perfectly adequate story if introduced with a non-narrative line like, "I know something even more heart-rending than that."

(2) The king died, and then the queen died

would be accepted as an adequate story by someone trying to establish the order of deaths in order to ascertain the proper disposition of the kingdom.

Indeed,

  (3)   The king died

is a narrative—a news "story"—which, fleshed out merely with a time and
proper name, would probably hold the interest of the late king's subjects
for days on end. A discourse like

  (4)   A man learned of a plot against England from a woman who was
        stabbed in his flat later that night. Eluding the police and the
        killers, he set out to warn the authorities, but then changed his
        mind and went abroad to live,

even though it does not fulfill the ostensible promise of its complication,
might well be considered a successful story by an audience which preferred plausibly motivated actions to unity of plot; in outline, (4) bears
some similarity to John le Carré's novel, *The Spy Who Came in from the
Cold.* More extended examples could be multiplied, as witness the debate
over whether Alain Robbe-Grillet's novels and Donald Barthelme's short
stories are really narrative.

It is possible, of course, to conclude that the rules for stories, although
tolerably clear, are ambiguous at the frontiers, or that different audiences
will relax the rules for stories on special occasions. Given the necessity of
defining narrative in terms of particular discursive sequences, however, it
seems more logical to conclude that the definition of narrative is always
context-dependent, that whether a given discourse counts as a story depends on the circumstances under which it is told—the historical moment
of its composition, the relation between storyteller and audience, the needs
or demands which the story has been introduced to fulfill. Lucy's brother
Linus accepts

  (5)   A man was born . . . he lived and he died

as a story, but to most readers it is a parody of storytelling, or (to be more
fair to Lucy's intentions) a plot summary.

Narratologists have been reticent on the subject of plot summaries
because it is difficult in ontological terms to distinguish between a story
and its summary.[9] Summaries are by definition shorter than the stories
they summarize, but brevity alone is neither a necessary nor a sufficient
criterion: Henry James's "Project" for *The Ambassadors* is longer than
most short stories, but it is still recognizably a summary, whereas "a man
lived" is not even recognizably a summary. Prince's account of narrative in
terms of two or more events which do not necessarily entail each other
provides a useful way of distinguishing stories-plus-summaries from other
kinds of discourse but does not differentiate between them.

We might say that summaries were simply poorer or more schematic or less satisfactory stories, and that, more generally, different discursive representations of the same events do not mark a difference between stories and nonstories but simply between better stories and worse. It may seem extreme to characterize (5) as non-narrative when we can take the more reasonable position that it is an unsuccessful narrative; after all, everyone makes a distinction between bad poems like "Trees" and nonpoems like the Manhattan Yellow Pages. This apparently reasonable position, however, overlooks the fact that audiences cannot understand any utterance or discourse except by perceiving it as an example of a certain kind of discourse, that audiences are strongly disposed to assume that a given utterance is an adequate example of *some* kind of discourse, and that narratives usually contain (for example) lyric or thematic elements. As Goodman has demonstrated, stories under the pressure of sufficient abstraction or discursive transformation are therefore perceived, not as less interesting or satisfying stories, but simply as adequate examples of some other kind of discourse. F. W. Murnau's silent film *The Last Laugh* might be summarized by the formulation

(6)   He who laughs last laughs best,

but this formulation is not another story, however unsatisfactory; most audiences will accept it as a perfectly satisfactory apothegm unless they are given some specific contextual cue to interpret it in narrative terms. Regardless of the ensuing complications, we must use the term *story* to mean "minimally adequate story"; otherwise, there is no discourse which a sufficiently ingenious audience cannot recover as a story, and since the boundaries of what constitutes an acceptable story are constantly being pushed back, the term will apply to any discourse and so will become meaningless.

Evidently, then, the whole concept of story depends on a context which involves not only a particular discursive mode and selection of states of affairs but also the particular circumstances governing the storytelling transaction. It might seem impossible, if narratology is radically context-dependent, to give an account of narrative ontology which is not simply a catalogue of circumstances under which particular audiences have accepted particular discourses as stories. Although it is not possible to define stories apart from their audiences, however, it should be possible to say something about the conditions under which a given audience will accept a given discourse as narrative. This is simply to say that narratology must begin by recognizing the fundamentally transactional nature of stories and proceed by defining them in terms of their transactional status. Consider another discourse, this one quoted by Mary Louise Pratt from the field-work of the sociolinguist William Labov:

(7)   Well, this person had a little too much to drink and he attacked
me and the friend came in and she stopped it.[10]

This is what Labov calls a "danger of death" narrative, a story told in
response to the question, "Were you ever in a situation where you were in
serious danger of being killed?" (Pratt, 70). Although the response takes
the form of a series of clauses presenting a sequence of temporally ordered
actions, it is not a story but rather, like Charlie Brown's discourse to Lucy,
a pointed refusal to tell a story, because it is not *tellable*, to use the term
Pratt has borrowed from Labov to describe stories that are worth telling.

Pratt defines tellability as "display-producing relevance." Some utterances, she contends, are designed primarily to communicate information
(answers to questions, for example), whereas others are tellable without
such close reference to their immediate context because they "represent
states of affairs that are held to be unusual, contrary to expectations, or
otherwise problematic." The speaker of a tellable utterance "is not only
reporting but verbally *displaying* a state of affairs, inviting his addressee(s)
to join him in contemplating it, evaluating it, and responding to it. His
point is to produce in his hearers not only belief but also an imaginative
and affective involvement in the state of affairs he is representing and an
evaluative stance toward it. . . . Ultimately, it would seem, what he is after
is an *interpretation* of the problematic event, an assignment of meaning and
value supported by the consensus of himself and his hearers" (136). The
difference between most stories and their plot summaries, we might say, is
that the stories display states of affairs which the summaries merely report.

Tellability is clearly context-dependent, for most stories are no more
universally tellable than most home movies are universally watchable.
Whether or not a given version of the same states of affairs is accepted as a
story depends on its context and the inclinations of its audience. In
general, the less dependent a story is on the interests of a particular
audience, the more tellable it will be. Ross Chambers goes so far as to
argue that a distinctive feature of narrative fiction is its "power to control
its own impact through the act of situational self-definition."[11] Certainly
there is an intimate relationship between tellability and contextual de-
tachability. Thus,

(8)   I knew a woman once who killed her husband. Stabbed him in
the bathtub one night,

although an adequate contribution to a men's discussion of unpleasant
women and a dazzling contribution to a children's discussion of notable
acquaintances, seems to invite a reply like, "What was she like?" or "What
made her do it?" that would supply more of the details which would
establish its tellability, whereas

(9)   A man returning victorious from war was killed by his wife
      shortly after his arrival home

could plausibly be introduced apart from a particular conversational context—for instance, in a news report which would add nothing but particular names and places. The emphasis in

(10) A general, having spent seven years away from home in an
      effort to help his brother-in-law bring back his wife's sister
      from an elopement with her lover, was killed on his return by
      his wife and her own lover

on motivic and thematic parallels makes it even more independent of an
immediate context and so more readily tellable: The victim is no longer the
husband of some woman I once knew, or an anonymous soldier, but a man
destroyed by the kind of family loyalties to which he has committed
himself, and the kind of sexual betrayal he is committed to avenging. A
man presented in such terms is a likely subject for identifications among a
relatively wide range of audiences. These identifications are focused more
sharply by the ironic details of

(11) An Argive chieftain, descended from a family whose history
      was marked by power struggles, murders, and a blood curse,
      pledged to his brother-in-law to help recover his wife's sister,
      who had eloped with her lover. When the allies' fleet was
      unable to sail, the chieftain sacrificed his daughter in order to
      propitiate the gods. After seven years' absence, he returned
      home victorious with his concubine, but they were both killed
      by his wife and her own lover,

which present the chieftain in a number of contradictory roles—descen-
dant, ruler, husband, brother-in-law, political and military ally, father,
lover, cuckold—whose collisions, it seems, must inevitably destroy him.

(12) [The complete text of *Agamemnon*],

which adds a great many further details, often seems unnecessarily digressive to students encountering it for the first time, but its long choral
speeches are only apparently digressive: Like the details increasingly
prominent in each successive discourse, they show why the murder of
Agamemnon is a complete and significant action, not just an isolated
incident. In Pratt's terms, such details, by providing a more self-contained
rationale for the story, make it less context-dependent and more universally tellable. Even (12) is not normally studied as if its significance were
wholly independent of its context. The murder of Agamemnon has problematical consequences of a sort that require two more plays to work out,

and the trilogy ends by connecting the final resolution of the action to the founding of the city for whose citizens the play was first performed—a return, in a more sophisticated form, to the sort of importance claimed for (8). Although modern readers of Aeschylus commonly take account of these connections, however, his story about Agamemnon would probably be considered more widely tellable, more convincingly a story, than any of the shorter discourses (8) through (11).

Aeschylus's version of this story is tellable because the details he presents elaborate more fully its teleology, the rationale which will retrospectively establish the thematic significance of the entire sequence. But a story's tellability need not depend on novelty or teleological complexity: An accomplished storyteller, Pratt points out, "can pile detail upon detail, and can even be blatantly repetitive, because he is understood to be enabling his audience to imagine and comprehend the state of affairs more fully and to savor it for a longer period of time" (146). The way the storyteller displays this state of affairs in order to enable the audience to savor it more fully does not necessarily give them any new information, because narrative material is displayed according to a principle of enjoyment, not a principle of communication. Discourses become tellable stories precisely through the ways they display the states of affairs they present.

It does not follow from this that every story that glosses the summary, "Boy meets girl, boy loses girl, boy recovers girl," arouses the same response or displays its incidents in the same way. Our appetite for what we usually consider different versions of the same story is based on the expectation that each version will display not simply a given situation or plot or state of affairs but different aspects or implications of that situation: the contrast between the unexpected delight of a new love, the pain of separation, and the joy of reunion, for instance, or the ingenuity with which the principals overcome the obstacles to their love, or the wittiness or tenderness or frank eroticism of their behavior toward each other. A rhetorical view of storytelling will help to focus and extend Pratt's conception of "display-producing relevance." A given story is told to secure a particular complex of responses (emotional, analytical, aesthetic) in its audience; within the story, certain elements are displayed in order to evoke those responses; other elements are employed in order to focus the leading elements more sharply. Henry James divided the materials of fiction into the matter and the treatment; we might use the older distinction between relative ends and means within a given work, those elements intended to be displayed as such and those intended to display other elements. The simplest example would be hard-core pornography, whose author invents (and whose audience tolerates) a plot and characters barely compelling enough to support or enliven a series of sexual episodes which it is the story's point to display. An avowedly pornographic book or film which did not titillate its audience would fail as pornography no matter how penetratingly it displayed the psychology of its principals, for the point of pornography is to display something further down.

The example of pornography indicates that stories often display something other than the dynamics of their plots; indeed, E. M. Forster judged it a weakness of *The Ambassadors* that it displayed nothing else. The plot of a narrative can indeed be an excrescence, as it is in pornography. Even Boccaccio, whose *Decameron* offers an unexcelled field for studying the range of narrative display, occasionally commits himself to a story which displays something strangely at odds with its plot. The story of Titus and Gisippus (Day 10, Tale 8) has a complicated plot: Gisippus, having given his friend Titus his affianced bride Sophronia without her prior knowledge, loses his wealth; finding himself alone and impoverished in Titus's homeland, and believing that Titus has snubbed him, he falsely confesses to a murder; Titus, now recognizing his old friend, confesses to the murder himself, as does the real murderer, wonderstruck by the friendship of the others. But Boccaccio spends very little time unfolding these incidents. Most of his story is devoted to three set pieces: Titus's debate over whether or not to abandon himself to love, his argument with Gisippus over which of them should marry Sophronia, and his justification of his behavior to an audience of Sophronia's and Gisippus's relatives. The rest of the tale, despite its intricacy, stands as a rather perfunctory postlude to this last speech, and it is easy to see why. In a tale ostensibly told to celebrate friendship, the means by which the friendship between Titus and Gisippus is established—Gisippus's willingness to trick Sophronia into marrying Titus instead—have implications so disturbing and antisocial that Boccaccio must spend more time justifying his complicating action than resolving its consequences. Teleological development is here merely a pendant to the rhetorical development the story actually displays.

Works defined within a formulaic genre like pornography or science fiction tend to display the limited features prescribed by the rules of the genre: pornography the titillating possibilities of sexual intercourse, science fiction the problems implicit in future technological development, and so on. Even here, however, we can discern different emphases and elaborations within a given structure which indicate that different implications of a given situation, and not simply the situation itself, are being displayed. In *Adventure, Mystery, and Romance,* John G. Cawelti has traced the way Westerns since *The Deerslayer* have redefined their formula by displaying different aspects of the American West. The historical evolution of the detective story could be described in similar terms. For early writers like Poe, Gaboriau, and Conan Doyle, the figure of the detective, whether as an exemplar of analytical intelligence or an avatar of melodramatic romance, is at the center of each tale: It is enough for the story to follow the detective through his investigations, because what is displayed is the process by which the detective gathers evidence and solves mysteries. Later writers like G. K. Chesterton and E. C. Bentley, by prolonging the interval between the detective's discovery and his public interpretation of evidence, displayed the formula's potential as an intellectual puzzle, a potential most fully realized in Ellery Queen's "Challenge to the Reader": Now that you have seen everything the detective has seen, can you solve the mystery before he does? Hard-boiled writers like Dashiell Hammett and Raymond Chandler, reacting against the artificiality of such puzzles, retained the plot of mystery and detection but emphasized its subterranean affinities with violence, corruption, and habitual criminals in order to display the social implications of violent death. More recently Ross Macdonald, by substituting the convention of universal guilt for that of the criminal scapegoat, has extended the metaphorical implications of the hard-boiled writers, and the police procedurals of Ed McBain and J. J. Marric have returned, *mutatis mutandis,* to Poe's emphasis on the process of detection itself.

It might seem that such variations within a given generic formula are difficult for readers to perceive, but every work has many ways of indicating which aspects of the formula are being displayed—chapter endings, for example. The chapter endings of Agatha Christie's detective novels tend to display puzzling clues or unexpected revelations, with a view toward tantalizing the reader's curiosity and challenging his powers of interpretation. Chandler's novels, by contrast, display the sardonic wit of his detective, Philip Marlowe, by featuring his wisecracks or aphorisms at the ending of many chapters. Chandler's chapters, though shorter than Christie's, carry a correspondingly greater sense of discreteness and closure. The resistance of less reflective mystery and adventure stories to intermediate closure or division into discrete episodes inspires in its simplest form the cliffhanging chapter endings of the Nancy Drew and Hardy Boys children's stories, which present sudden, perfunctorily motivated calamities most often resolved in an equally perfunctory way in the first few sentences of the following chapter.

The multiple implications a given sequence of actions has available for display are especially obvious in different versions or transformations of the same specific material. The process of adaptation from one medium of presentation to another, particularly the transformation of novels and short stories into films, has been extensively studied. In *Authorship and Narrative in the Cinema,* for example, William Luhr provides a detailed discussion of six films based on "The Strange Case of Dr. Jekyll and Mr. Hyde," each of them displaying different implications of Stevenson's story. Just as an actor, in his specific choices about how to play Hamlet, necessarily adapts the words of Shakespeare's text to what is essentially the different medium of stage production, so that whole process of adaptation to a new medium entails numberless particular decisions about which implications of a given character or situation to display. The different possibilities a given situation premises are nowhere more striking than in adaptations to the musical stage, where successful productions like *Man of La Mancha* (or unsuccessful ones like *Ambassador,* starring Howard Keel as Strether and Danielle Darrieux as Madame de Vionnet) often display possibilities for theatrical spectacle and production numbers undreamed of by Cervantes and Henry James.

Tellability and Narratology

Observing that great films have been adapted from mediocre literary sources and abysmal films from great sources, Luhr concludes by rejecting the "assumption . . . that narrative quality is transferable."[12] The broader implications of Luhr's argument, as we have seen, are fundamental to the problem of narrative ontology. For example, the tellability of a given narrative may depend so intimately on the resources, constraints, and challenges of a given medium that the narrative may not be tellable in any other medium. During the 1930s the graphic artist Lynd Ward published a series of "novels in woodcuts," which told stories through a series of wordless images. In outline or verbal summary, however detailed, Ward's stories (e.g., "a failed painter contracting for a brush which brings him success finally realizes he has pledged his soul in exchange") sound far too banal to interest adults, especially since his chosen medium allows little in the way of incidental elaboration or circumstantial complexity. But Ward's stories are successful examples of their kind because the medium of the woodcut makes us accept the bold composition and visual stylization each picture displays and the mordant wit with which Ward often connects his images in place of other kinds of complexity.

In discussing the process by which an audience assimilates comic strips, Seymour Chatman has occasion to translate an essentially nonverbal comic strip into a series of "abstract narrative statements." In Chatman's terms, his version of the comic strip "is not at all the story per se; it is but one more (and poorer) manifestational representation of it. Story, in my technical sense of the word, exists only at an abstract level; any manifestation already entails the selection and arrangement performed by the discourse as actualized by the medium. There is no privileged manifestation."[13] Our account of stories as *by definition* tellable allows us to go still further: Chatman's verbal rendering of the comic strip is so much "poorer" than the version it glosses that it is not a story at all, not because it is only a single manifestation of a given series of events, but because the comic strip uses these events as the basis of a tellable story in a way Chatman's version does not. Barbara Herrnstein Smith makes a similar point when she attacks Chatman's "two-leveled model of narrative structure" on the grounds that Chatman's "story" is only another *version* of a given narrative rather than its underlying *structure,* that since "no narrative version can be independent of a particular teller and occasion of telling and . . . every narrative version [including what Chatman calls the story] has been constructed in accord with some set of purposes or interests,"[14] there is no such thing as a story apart from a series of particular narrative versions and situations.

Chatman, in a reply to Smith's critique, has defended the notion of prediscursive or extradiscursive narrative structure as a "construct" (as against "a Platonic idea"), a theoretical reconstruction or extrapolation of the portion of a given story "which is *purely* narrative in structure, independent of . . . medium, that portion having its own structure—in natural language, in the language of dance, in the language of comic-strip drawing, or whatever."[15] Distinguishing between Smith's "narrative pragmatics," with its emphasis on "conditions for the production of narratives," and his own "narratology," or study of narrative ontology, Chatman defines the analysis of narrative structure as valid apart from the conditions which create different versions of a given story: "Of course the differing ways we each pronounce a phoneme is a function of our differing life-histories; but what has that to do with phonemic theory? . . . Just as linguistics argues for a logical model, not a behavioral account of actual speech performance, narratology offers a theory which assumes the task of defining its subject (all and only narratives in the universe of texts) on a logical model, with no reference to the contingent life histories of those who make or partake of stories" (804–7).

The point at issue here is not whether a distinction can be made between narrative discourse and the events it presents—obviously such a distinction is always available to the analyst—but whether that distinction can be made the basis of a narrative ontology, whether the stories thus postulated can be defined as "all and only narratives," or whether narrative is by definition radically situational—whether the adequacy of a given narrative, its status as a tellable story, can be determined only by a given audience considering a particular manifestation in a particular presentational medium, presented in a particular historical and cultural situation. Chatman succeeds in maintaining the distinction between story and discourse, but not its relevance to narrative ontology. There is, as Smith might say, no such thing as the Cinderella story; there is only a Cinderella subject, which can serve as the basis for numerous stories, and can serve other purposes as well.

Tellability and Narrativity

Clearly, stories can be tellable for as many different reasons as there are storytellers, audiences, and storytelling situations. Although a tellable story will typically feature a certain degree of coherence, psychological development, and teleological motivation, any of these requirements may be suspended under the appropriate circumstances. In fact, an audience determined to be encouraging, polite, or obsequious can absolve a storyteller from any rules whatsoever, as parents accept an infant's babbling as a satisfactory language for the nonce. Stories told in answer to questions are, as philosophers of language have pointed out, not bound to be intrinsically interesting as long as they answer the questions adequately. More generally, the requirements for tellability are appreciably relaxed for any story presented as true; or, to put it another way, a truth claim often serves as the primary basis for a story's tellability. Stories beginning, "You're not going to believe this, but . . ." or "I knew a man once who . . ." are often accepted as tellable because they display the very unlikeliness of the events or the privileged position of the storyteller as a repository of vicarious experience and worldly wisdom: Indeed, Walter Benjamin has suggested that such privilege was once accorded tellers of fictitious stories when stories were regarded as a mode of wisdom. As Benjamin distinguishes between "the art of storytelling" and "the dissemination of information,"[16] however, most audiences would probably distinguish between the newsworthy and the tellable—between stories which conveyed verifiable information relevant to the audience's interests and those whose tellability did not rely on such claims. Although I will return to this distinction in Chapters 9 and 10, I have introduced it now in order to justify my emphasis on fictional narratives as a paradigm for all narratives. If the fundamental requirement of all stories is that they be tellable, the rules for tellability will be strictest for fictional stories.

Considering fictional narrative as a model for all narrative allows us to focus on the essential question of narrative ontology—the question of what makes stories tellable as stories (apart from what makes them tellable as information, as personal revelation, and so on). The pragmatics of narrative discourse might suggest that there is ultimately no distinguishing feature which makes stories tellable as such, that their adequacy derives entirely from thematic material they share with other discursive modes or from their relevance to their immediate contexts. But Robert Scholes's definition of a narrative as "a text which requires and rewards narrativity" indicates an activity practiced by every audience for stories in whatever medium; they translate a sequence of words or images into a temporal and causal sequence of actions which is coherent and meaningful: "A fiction is presented to us in the form of a narration . . . that guides us as our own active narrativity seeks to complete the process that will achieve a story."[17]

Scholes's argument, which defines narrative and narrativity—the process whereby an audience constructs a coherent story from the fictional data (images, gestures, sentences) presented in a given discourse—in terms of each other, might be illuminated by an example. Imagine taking a child to the movies—for example, to a Marx Brothers film like *Duck Soup.* Even if she understood all the dialogue (or were content to ignore what she could not understand), a child without an adult's expertise in the conventions of film narrative would constantly be asking pointless questions. When the film cuts from Groucho inside the palace to Groucho getting into a motorcycle sidecar outside, she might ask, "How did they get outside?" After the scene has ended with Harpo's driving away alone, she might ask, "What happened to the sidecar?" when she sees Groucho without it in the following scene. After the scene is played for the third time—this time Groucho gets onto the motorcycle, but Harpo drives off alone in the sidecar—she might ask at intervals through the rest of the film, "Why can't we see the motorcycle again?" All of these questions show an ability to comprehend events as such without the ability to follow a story whose effectiveness is based on selecting events, establishing significant relations among them, and ordering them so as to make certain points. The ability to supply connections between successive shots—the hero and heroine embracing by moonlight, followed by the heroine cooking bacon in a sunlit kitchen—and the ability to see when a comic routine has reached its topper or punch line and exhausted its potential are part of the audience's narrativity, a narrativity most of us learn as children.

At its simplest level, narrativity entails three skills: the ability to defer one's desire for gratification (so that even if the opening five minutes of a film do not make obvious sense or provide pleasure, we still assume that the film will ultimately justify our attention); the ability to supply connections among the material a story presents; and the ability to perceive discursive events as significantly related to the point of a given story or sequence. The application of an audience's narrativity varies with the medium of presentation (and indeed with the genre and storyteller, as one brings different skills to bear on Antonioni than on D. W. Griffith), but narrativity itself is not specific to a given medium of presentation; and it is a residual narrativity, a narrative competence independent of medium, that allows us to feel our way into the conventions of a narrative medium (silent films, ballet, program music) hitherto unfamiliar to us.

Scholes's analysis of narrativity implies that a successful narrative must be coherent in the sense of not encouraging its audience to translate it into necessarily contradictory chains of events. Different audiences may entertain contrary hypotheses, for example, about what Ishmael's life was like before the events of *Moby-Dick*, but Melville does not provide evidence requiring mutually exclusive hypotheses. Many recent works of fiction (e.g., *The Unnameable, Last Year at Marienbad*) are designedly incoherent; their point is to display the limitations rather than the powers of narrativity as a way of perceiving and ordering experience. We might say that such works are presented as parodies or critiques of narrative rather than as narratives themselves, or that they are ironic narratives insofar as they frustrate our narrativity only by appealing to it with the false promise, however perfunctory, of intelligible sequence. However successful such works may be as parody or meditation, their success as narrative is designedly problematic.

Although coherence is what makes a narrative interpretable, it does not in itself make it tellable, for not every coherent sequence of events is worth telling. If an audience is truly to savor the situations and characters a narrative projects, the narrative must avoid the extremes of overspecification, which renders the audience's narrativity superfluous, and underspecification, which places untoward demands upon it. Overspecified narratives prevent the audience's narrativity from full engagement with the story by specifying too many connections in the story, filling in so many gaps that the reader has too little work to do in reconstructing a story. As Wolfgang Iser has observed, "It is only through inevitable omissions that a story will gain its dynamism," because such omissions give us the opportunity "to bring into play our own faculty for establishing connections— for filling in gaps left by the text itself."[18] Iser speaks of these omissions as inevitable, but in fact every audience has had experiences with stories which seemed to supply too few omissions. Long-winded storytellers can ruin the most promising material by piling on irrelevant details, broadly foreshadowing later developments, and specifying in advance the emotional reactions they intend to arouse. The problem with such stories is not that they are overlong—many of the great stories are extremely long—but that they are pointless: Instead of inviting the participation of the audience's narrativity, they exclude it through overexplicitness. A detective

story entitled "Theodore Witsend, Murderer" would automatically de-
prive its audience of a certain kind of enjoyment, the pleasure in trying to
solve a mystery, although it would implicitly promise another—psychological proximity to a criminal mind, say, or observation of a tactical duel
between criminal and police. Children can spoil riddles—the simplest
form of the mystery narrative, in which what is displayed to be savored is
the gap between witty specification of certain properties and the identification of the object or situation thus specified—by overspecification:
"What's black and white and red all over and says *The New York Times* on
the front?"

Such complete and fatal overspecification is rare in longer narratives,
since no author can plug all the holes in his story, all the opportunities for
the audience's speculation. But everyone has felt at some time resentful of
a more insidious kind of overspecification: the attempt to control an
audience's emotional or psychological reactions too openly. Since narratives commonly manipulate their audiences by engaging their narrativity
along certain lines—that is, by implying certain connections and encouraging certain speculations rather than others—narrative overspecification
usually involves the audience's perception of a failure of tact, as with
Dickens's handling of Little Nell, or hard-core film directors' handling of
sex scenes. Some audiences (not necessarily the same audiences) find Little
Nell pathetically affecting and explicit sex scenes aphrodisiac; others,
accusing them of leaving nothing to the imagination, consider them overspecified. Dickens, they complain, instead of trusting them to draw their
own conclusions about Nell, presses his case too far by contrived hardships
and special pleading; the sexual acrobatics of *Deep Throat* are too explicit
to engage the audience's sexual fantasies. Clearly, a tellable narrative must
accord the audience's narrativity at least the illusion of a modicum of
freedom. The audience must feel it is adding something not explicitly
stated by the narrative, though perhaps required by the circumstances the
narrative conveys.

If an overspecified narrative does not, in Scholes's terms, require the
audience's narrativity, an underdetermined narrative does not adequately
reward the necessary efforts of that narrativity to reconstruct a tellable
story. Consider an example adapted from Boccaccio: "Ser Cepperrello
deceived a holy friar with a false confession, then he died; and although in
life he was a most wicked man, in death he was reputed to be a Saint, and
was called Saint Ciappelletto."[19] This text is not an adequate story—it is in
fact a past-tense version of the summary with which Boccaccio prefaces the
opening tale of the *Decameron*—because it does not engage our narrativity
sufficiently for us to supply the details the story displays: the gratuitous
wickedness of Cepperrello, who "would have taken it as a slight upon his

honour if one of his legal deeds . . . were discovered to be other than false," who always welcomed the invitation to "witness a murder or any other criminal act," and who "often found himself cheerfully assaulting or killing people with his own hands" (70–71); the consternation of the two brothers who find themselves burdened with the dying Cepperrello, whom they can neither get rid of nor secure absolution and burial for; and Cepperrello's spectacularly false confession, in which, concealing his actual sins, he tells the friar that he has often drunk water avidly while fasting and become angry at the iniquitous, that he once spoke ill of a neighbor who beat his wife, made one of his servants sweep Saturday evening, inadvertently spat in church (here the friar reassures him with the news that members of the religious orders spit there continually), and finally, when he was a boy—he is most reluctant to admit this—once cursed his mother.

No one would claim that we could not make sense of Boccaccio's summary without supplying all these details, yet the details are precisely what make the story tellable. If we added more details not required by the story—invented a particularly malicious prank the boy Cepperrello played, for example, or described his reception in heaven—we would be telling a new story rather than using our narrativity to recover Boccaccio's; we would have taken over Boccaccio's role, just as we would have to do to recover the story from its underspecified summary. Evidently the audience's narrativity must be active enough to construct a story according to the cues a given narrative provides but not so active that it transgresses the narrative's guidance. Narratives cultivate an appropriate degree of narrativity, which may vary widely from one story to the next, by avoiding the extremes of over- and underspecification. A tellable story determines the implications of its premise to a degree which makes it unnecessary for the audience to invent new characters and incidents, but at the same time allows the audience the freedom to savor those implications in ways the story does not make explicit. The audience for a tellable story will be able—indeed, will be required—to add connections and interpretations of their own, but will not be able to add just anything.

It is commonplace to say that the most memorable fictional characters are those who premise an existence outside their fictional world, or those who provoke unanswerable questions about their behavior outside the narrative discourse. Although it would be misleading, as L. C. Knights and others have pointed out, to treat fictional characters as independent of their fictional worlds, it does not follow that Huckleberry Finn has no existence apart from the words of Mark Twain's novel, but rather that the novel itself has such a wider existence because it encourages the readers' narrativity to endow Huck with qualities his own discourse never makes explicit, and these constellated qualities have a dimension not strictly constrained by Twain's words. What gives a character vitality is a certain inexplicitness of presentation or analysis which evokes Mr. Pickwick or Dmitri Karamazov in all their immediacy without exhausting their potential for display. All such inexhaustible characters are ultimately products of the audience's imputation, which bridges the gap between analysis and action or speech by positing connections, extrapolations, and ultimately a life beyond what the discourse specifies. This imputation is typically of two kinds, or along two axes, the figurative and the realistic (more accurately the metaphoric and the metonymic). When Henry James presents Mr. Cashmore in *The Awkward Age* as someone "who would have been very red-haired if he had not been very bald,"[20] he invites his audience to interpret this detail both figuratively (Mr. Cashmore's baldness stands for his red-hairedness, with its metaphoric associations of vivacity, unconventionality, and lechery, now supplemented by sterility and advancing age) and realistically (Mr. Cashmore's baldness replaces his earlier red-hairedness, suggesting a definite historical past). Figurative detail, we feel, is chosen with a view toward its figurative meaning, as a trope awaiting decoding; realistic detail, with its suggestion of irrelevance, implies a broader fictional world by presenting itself as typical—instead of this arbitrary detail, we are encouraged to believe, any of a hundred others might have been chosen. Figurative detail invites the imputation of intensive, realistic detail the imputation of extensive, meaning. But the example from James, which displays metaphoric and metonymic significance together, supports Martin Price's argument that "it is not a flounce or a barometer that alone asserts the real; all the details together make that assertion, and all are potentially significant as well. Details do not offer themselves as clearly relevant or irrelevant."[21]

Price is speaking not of character specifically but of what we might call the world of a novel. Since that world is a product, at whatever level of integration, of figurative significance and verisimilitude, we might conclude more generally that the world of a given novel is never asserted by the sum of its details but always imputed by the audience, whose narrativity requires and exploits omissions in narrative discourse in order to make any story tellable. Because what makes a story tellable is something the audience imputes, tellability is normally a function of omission. In films this is true at the simplest level, since feature-length films, with rare exceptions, can present tellable stories only by cutting from shot to shot, encouraging the audience to supply the logically necessary connections.

But narrativity and tellability are still more closely related, for only through tactful or provocative omission can an audience enjoy the latitude it requires to appreciate whatever the story is displaying. In his silent film *Seven Chances* Buster Keaton is required to marry within a few hours in order to receive a legacy his business firm urgently needs. Rejected by his long-standing sweetheart, he goes to a country club, notes the names of the women there he knows, and proposes to each of them in turn. The absence of spoken dialogue provides the dimension of indeterminacy Keaton needs to make this sequence tellable. After the first proposal, the audience knows exactly what Keaton will say to each woman; what the sequence displays is the comedy arising from the number of different ways Keaton can mime proposal and rejection and the way he can integrate this repeated rhythm economically into that of the entire sequence. Keaton sits at a table with a woman and speaks briefly to her; she bursts into laughter. Keaton is walking down a flight of stairs in conversation with a second woman; a third woman passes, going up, and without missing a step (or, evidently, a syllable) Keaton changes direction to walk with her. Rebuffed by all seven of his chances at the club, Keaton looks appraisingly at the hat-check girl; she shakes her head briefly but emphatically. In each case the audience easily supplies the necessary connections, but it is precisely this ability which makes the sequence not only coherent but tellable. Other examples might rely less directly on the wit of the imputation, but in general a story's tellability is based on its audience's narrativity. Put more simply, what stories characteristically display—what makes them pointed, witty, pathetic, profound, or otherwise worth telling—is the way in which the audience supplies the unspecified connections, extrapolations, and resonances they require in order to make sense.

My use of the term *display* has necessarily been ambiguous because of its transactional nature, its dependence on an interpretive audience. Do stories display their own qualities or those of their audience? Is it more accurate to speak of the affecting situation or the audience's sympathy as what a story displays? The transactional nature of storytelling makes both answers the same, for either would be incomplete without the other. The pathos of Little Nell's death is implicit in the text, but only a sympathetic reader can release it. Storytellers who rely on their audience's narrativity engage the audience's thoughts and emotions in order to display some aspect of their stories, but the point of that display is to arouse a certain response in the audience. What is displayed is ultimately irreducible to a quality of the story or its audience, for the story, in a fundamental sense, is successful only insofar as it engages the audience's narrativity—insofar as it is the audience's own story.

This ambiguity in my use of *display* echoes an ambiguity in *narrativity* as it is currently used. Scholes, defining this term as a property of readers, notes that it is also used by such theorists as Christian Metz to refer to a property of narrative films themselves. The ambiguity here is symptomatic of the problematic ontology of narrative, for the narrativity of a given work is in a radical sense the enabling narrativity of its audience. But it suggests the need to emphasize that the audience's narrativity is in turn enabled and constrained by the qualities a given text displays. In discussing Boccaccio's summary of the opening tale of the *Decameron,* I concluded that the audience's narrativity should be active enough to recover a given story according to the cues the discourse provides but not so active that it transgresses that discourse's guidance. We might distinguish along these lines between the audience's narrativity, which *fills in* the connections required to make sense of agents and incidents by establishing the relations and imputing the motives which give them significance, and the discourse's narrativity, which *fills out* a given series of states of affairs by providing the details that make the audience's narrativity necessary and rewarding. The primacy of this distinction may seem difficult to maintain in view of Scholes's own distinction between the "passive or automatic translation of semiotic conventions into intelligible elements" and the "active or interpretive arrangement of textual signs into significant structures" (61).[22] Certainly varying degrees of ingenuity and resourcefulness are involved in different aspects of textual interpretation; but if narratives are tellable because they display their audience's narrativity, then the more active partner in the transaction must be the storyteller. Otherwise, the hyperactive narrativity of an enterprising audience would make every utterance a tellable story. Any utterance is potentially a tellable story, but its narrative potential is released only when a storyteller invites an audience to supply details necessary to establish the story as coherent and tellable.

The foregoing analysis makes it impossible to define narrative in contradistinction to drama: Since narratives are tellable only insofar as they are realized through a given medium of discourse, and since there is no reason to limit the medium to a verbal diegesis which would exclude films, dance, and pantomime, the distinction between mimesis and diegesis becomes tangential to the problem of narrative ontology. In the terms I have established, drama is simply another way of "telling" a story, and Aristotelian tragedy becomes a species of the genus narrative. But defining narratives in terms of the way they display their audience's narrativity has more far-reaching consequences for narratology. John Crowe Ransom once asked, if mathematics was for mathematical interest, what poetry was for, and went on to posit a poetic interest which would not be reducible to moral or ethical interest.[23] If what distinguishes adequate from inadequate stories is the way they engage the audience's narrativity, it seems reasonable to ask what, if anything, narrative as such distinctively displays. This is a reformulation of the question this chapter began with: What view of human experience underlies narrative as such? We are now in a position to answer this question by an analysis of the fundamental properties common to all stories that make them worth telling.

3
The Teleological Principle

Even if narrative is defined in terms of its discursive features rather than in terms of a sequence of actions it presents, narrative still depends on the audience's perception of a discursive sequence, as in an alphabetical model: first A, then B, then C. But this model is misleading in its implications about conclusion or closure. An alphabetical series may stop at D or E or F, but it probably will not continue beyond Z; the endpoint is built into the sequence as a feature of the discourse. But this is not true of narrative sequences, which more closely resemble numerical sequences in this respect. Where does the sequence beginning 1, 2, 3 . . . come to an end? This question is fundamental to the pragmatics of storytelling, for if, as E. M. Forster claims, "a story, *qua* story . . . can have only one merit: that of making the audience want to know what happens next,"[1] each story must provide an ending after which the audience no longer asks this question. Barbara Herrnstein Smith has defined closure as "a modification of structure that makes *stasis*, or the absence of further continuation, the most probable succeeding event. Closure allows the reader to be satisfied by the failure of continuation or, put another way, it creates in the reader the expectation of nothing."[2] A finite sequence like the letters of the alphabet contains its own principle of closure, but an infinite series like the natural numbers does not; any conclusion would be arbitrary unless some further rule were added (e.g., "list the natural numbers from 1 to 10"). Since, as Smith points out, "there is no formal principle which in itself can prevent a poem from continuing indefinitely" (50), all modes of discourse, including narrative discourse, must justify their conclusions by what Smith calls thematic principles: the coming of evening or winter, the death or marriage of the hero, the end of the world.

The importance of closure is more than tactical, for it justifies discursive

sequence as whole, complete, and so intelligible as a totality. Alexander
Welsh has summarized the dependence of narrative on narrative closure in
his Foreword to the special issue of *Nineteenth-Century Fiction* devoted to
narrative endings: "Whereas Aristotle's unities of time and place may be
confidently if variously defined, unity of action evidently depends on what
constitutes a satisfactory denouement. Endings are critical points for analysis in all examinations of plot; quite literally, any action is defined by its
ending."[3] Whether or not narrative is constituted by a sequence of actions,
the logical place to begin an analysis of the narrative transaction is with
narrative endings.

Prosaic Closure

The pragmatic importance of narrative closure is great because there are
no narrative forms which prescribe their own closure. Once we have
recognized a poem as a sonnet, we assume it will conclude after fourteen
lines, and recognizing a poem as a sonnet predisposes us to accept the
terminal force of the fourteenth line. But stories are seldom told in forms
which supply their own terminal force. (Narrative sonnets would be one
exception to this rule.) In folktales, novels, and films the ending must
supply its own authority as the appropriate conclusion of a sequence.
Stories do have their own characteristic terminal tags (e.g., "they lived
happily ever after"), but the power of such mechanical terminal devices
depends to a great extent on their thematic context. In this connection
Kenneth Burke's distinction between "rest as the sheer cessation of motion" and "rest as the end of action"[4] is useful. Walking down a flight of
stairs is an action shaped and determined by its end, in the double sense of
purpose and conclusion; falling down a flight of stairs is not an action but a
series of motions which terminates only because one has run out of stairs.
"They lived happily ever after" can provide the second kind of end, but
not the first; it cannot constitute an action as complete any more than
sonnet form can confer completeness on one hundred forty random pho-
nemes.

As the series of natural numbers shows, the perception of sequence does
not depend on closure, but the perception of unity or wholeness does. A
primary function of narrative endings is therefore to provide or confirm a
teleology or retrospective rationale for the story as a whole, and stories
which lack such endings, whatever their fascinations, are often accounted
unsatisfactory. It is difficult to listen to the long symphonies of Bruckner
or Mahler without some knowledge of musical structure, because there is

no way of telling what is the relation of each part to the whole, or even how
much longer it is till the end. In narrative, too, moment-by-moment
enjoyment, encouraged by Forster's question, "What happened next?", is
ultimately inadequate because a story can be intelligible without being
tellable: The audience wants to know not only what happens next but what
this is all leading to, what it all means. Everyone has had the experience of
listening to a recitation of someone else's dream, told in a series of
apparently inconsequential episodes. The customary response, a politely
anticipatory "Yes?" implies "What happened next?" but beneath that,
"When is this all going to start making sense?" or "So what?", because
dreams, like Mahler's symphonies to a new listener, do not provide their
own formally intelligible grammar.

When Welsh notes the dependence of unity of action on a satisfactory
denouement, he is echoing Aristotle's discussion of plot in tragedy: "It is
the action . . . that is the end and purpose of the tragedy; and the end is
everywhere the chief thing."[5] Listening to accounts of other people's
dreams can be frustrating because they have no end in view, either in the
sense of conclusion or of rational design. ("What happened next?"—"Then
I woke up."—"Oh.") In forms like ritual tragedy which give priority to the
plot, these two senses of ending will be intimately related, for they both
depend on the resolution of the plot. S. H. Butcher makes this connection
when he notes that for Aristotle, poetic unity is manifested not only "in the
causal connection that binds together the several parts of the play," but
also "in the fact that the whole series of events, with all the moral forces
that are brought into collision, are directed to a single end. . . . The end is
linked to the beginning with inevitable certainty, and in the end we discern
the meaning of the whole."[6] The end (*telos*) implies both a line of development for the plot and a rationale which allows a tragedy, unlike most
dreams, to be apprehended upon its conclusion as a unitary whole and for
which, in some sense, the work was written.

The relation between the two senses of ending as termination and
rationale is reflected not only in the English words *end* and *teleology* but in
critics as different as Ronald Crane and Georg Lukács. Crane defines the
whole or form of any literary work from the artist's point of view as "a final
end or first principle of construction, from which he infers, however
instantaneously, what he must do in constituting and ordering the parts.
And there must always be, in any well-constructed poem, drama, or novel,
some one part (in tragedy, the plot) the form of which determines most
completely the form or effect of the whole."[7] And Lukács, arguing along
very different lines that "the selection and subtraction he undertakes in
response to the teleological pattern of his own life constitutes the most
intimate link between a writer's subjectivity and the outside world,"

concludes that "whereas in life 'whither?' is a consequence of 'whence?', in literature 'whither' determines the content, selection and proportion of the various elements. The finished work may resemble life in observing a causal sequence; but it would be no more than an arbitrary chronicle if there were not this reversal of direction. It is the perspective, the *terminus ad quem*, that determines the significance of each element in a work of art."[8]

Lukács's emphasis on the "reversal of direction" implicit in a work's causality is based on his perception of an immanent historical causality in the life of the creator: The teleology of the work is an image of the larger teleology of political history. Crane, who evidently does not subscribe to such a teleological view of history, restricts the teleology of plot as an ultimate end to the single genre of tragedy. Most critics would follow Butcher and Crane in defining the teleology of plot as the final end of tragedy; but then what of narratives whose plot is not their final end? What is the relation between the ends of tragedy and the ends of narrative? Discussions of narrative endings have most often either borrowed Aristotle's analysis, treating narrative as tragedy, or begun by defining narrative structure in terms of a temporal or causal sequence within the story, on the level of the characters. A transactional account of narrative, however, requires an alternative model based on the hermeneutical sequence of the audience's apprehensions.

Action and Knowledge in the Short Story

Because of its brevity and relative homogeneity—short works of fiction generally resembling each other more than novels do—the short story offers an especially promising field of examples which might serve as the basis for an account of narrative structure. The short story has itself, however, proved a notoriously difficult genre to define, chiefly because it is most often considered as a departure from the novel as a narrative of normative length rather than as an independent form. Before the turn of the century, the short story might have been defined in terms of the teleology of action, as Boris Ejxenbaum defined it in 1925: " 'Short story' is a term referring exclusively to plot, one assuming a combination of two conditions: small size and the impact of plot on the ending." In remarking that he is "leaving aside stories of the sketch or *skaz* type," however, Ejxenbaum acknowledges that there is a range of stories not accurately described by his model.[9] From Turgenev, Chekhov, and Joyce to J. D. Salinger, Donald Barthelme, and Ann Beattie, many short stories have presented situations in which action is frustrated, presented incompletely or obliquely, or omitted. Norman Friedman has attempted to incorporate this work into his definition of the short story by ruling that "a short story may be either static or dynamic. . . . An action which is static normally requires fewer parts than one which is dynamic and will therefore be shorter in the telling. A static story simply shows its protagonist in one state or another and includes only enough to reveal to the reader the cause or causes of which this state is a consequence, while a dynamic story brings its protagonist through a succession of two or more states, and thus must include the several causal stages of which these states are the consequences."[10] This account, illuminating as it is, involves the contradictory term "static action." We could rework Friedman's terminology so as to distinguish between stories which display a single mood or effect or situation (static stories) and those which display the relations among a series of events (dynamic stories) instead of distinguishing between static and dynamic action, but in fact the troublesome term "static action" reveals a shrewd insight: that even in those short stories which seem to exclude action, the audience senses a pattern of development. The relation between this sequence and the sequence of intelligible action allows us to get at the underlying structure of the short story.

Ejxenbaum's exemplary writer of short stories is O. Henry, and most readers probably assume as a model or unmarked case of the anecdote or story of action something like "The Gift of the Magi," in which a young wife sells her hair to a wigmaker in order to buy a Christmas gift for her husband, a chain for his treasured watch, only to discover that he has sold his watch to buy her a set of ornamental combs. The action follows the Aristotelian model in which recognition (*anagnorisis*) corresponds to reversal (*peripeteia*) and Kenneth Burke's more detailed model in which the tragic rhythm of action encompasses the moments of *poiema, pathema,* and *mathemata,* translated by Francis Fergusson as purpose, passion, and perception.[11] The story traces a change or development effected by Della Young and her husband, but what constitutes this change as a complete action is their mutual recognition of the ironic way in which their sacrifices have, in effect, canceled each other out. The surprise endings O. Henry so often favors generally embody a similar movement toward reversal and recognition: The hero sees that the situation is not as he had first thought but precisely the opposite (a fortuitous traffic jam has actually been deliberately arranged, the date is Christmas Day rather than the Fourth of July, the halberdier of the Little Rheinschloss is in reality a wealthy young man).

In another O. Henry story, "A Municipal Report," this pattern, though still recognizable, is complicated. The anonymous narrator establishes the relations among the ne'er-do-well Major Caswell, the black cab-driver Uncle Caesar, and the poet Azalea Adair by observing a distinctively mended dollar bill as it passes from one to the other; when Caswell is killed, the narrator conceals his knowledge that Uncle Caesar is the murderer. This plot is placed in a context indicated by the story's title: The narrator is giving a "report" showing what Nashville is really like, interspersing the events of his story with a statistical abstract of the city's location, history, and manufacture, and in the process refuting Frank Norris's claim that no story could ever be written about Nashville. Like "The Gift of the Magi," "A Municipal Report" articulates a coherent plot, but it does not display that plot as such; what it displays is the process by which the narrator becomes aware of the relations among the people he meets and, by extension, among many apparently ordinary people in ordinary places. (The story ends with the sentence, *"I wonder what's doing in Buffalo!"*)[12] The deepest structural affinity between "The Gift of the Magi" and "A Municipal Report" lies in this rhythm of debunking, the movement from the hero's misapprehensions about the world to his or her more inclusive, penetrating, or disillusioned view of the world.

Even this model must be further complicated to include such characteristic O. Henry stories as "The Social Triangle" and "Roads of Destiny." In the three episodes of "The Social Triangle" a tailor's apprentice named Ikey Snigglefritz contrives to shake hands with Billy McMahan, his district leader; McMahan later shakes hands with the millionaire Cortlandt Van Duyckink; and Van Duyckink, on a philanthropic tour of a run-down neighborhood, manages to make himself happy by shaking hands with Ikey Snigglefritz. In "Roads of Destiny" the poet David Mignot, having left his native village in France, comes to a crossroads and cannot decide which path to take. The story allows him three incompatible choices: First he takes one branch, then the other, and finally he returns to his village. In each case the final result is the same, though brought about differently— he is killed by a shot from the pistol of Monseigneur, the Marquis de Beaupertuys. Ejxenbaum analyzes "Roads of Destiny" as "three independent tales . . . without motivational connection"; but in fact the three parts of "Roads of Destiny," like those of "The Social Triangle," are independent only in the limited sense that "the joining is done not on the principle of the consecutive order of the movie's adventures . . . but on the principle of comparison and contrast" (244). Since the connection among the three parts is thematic rather than causal, and the stories in their composite form display thematic points about fate and social climbing rather than the teleology of a single action, none of the individual sections is truly independent. In isolation each is intelligible as a sequence of actions, but none is tellable; only the conjunction of the three episodes makes them retrospectively tellable by endowing them with thematic unity. The movement from ignorance to knowledge, or more precisely from illusion to disillusionment, does not, as Ian Reid has pointed out in another connection, involve "a perceived moment of truth for a character," but is in this case "for readers only."[13]

Another way to put this would be to say that the unity of the stories was not a unity of action, available at the level of agents and incidents, but a unity of hermeneutic sequence, available only at the level of the transaction between writer and reader. We can then distinguish within O. Henry's work two types of short stories typical of other authors as well: those stories which display the teleology of action at the agents' level, and those stories which display a sequence of perceptions at the audience's level. (These would correspond roughly to Friedman's dynamic and static types.) But it is impossible to maintain this distinction on these terms. Since a fictive or discursive action is constituted or completed as action (as distinct from stasis, accident, or motion) by the agent's recognition of it as such, stories which display action are actually stories which display the hero's final revelation as the product of a sequence of what Fergusson calls purpose and passion. Indeed, the very notion of teleology is a gnomic or gnostic conception stressing the climactic revelation of the true order of things, the world as it really is. Every short story is essentially a story of revelation, either the hero's or the audience's. And since the hero obviously never enjoys a revelation to which the audience is not privy, it follows that the underlying structure of the short story is the audience's hermeneutical progression from ignorance (or, more pointedly, from inadequate or misleading knowledge) to knowledge. The story of "dynamic action" is simply a special case of this more general model of "static action," a case in which the author provides a surrogate, a sensitive and perceptive agent, for the audience's own sympathetic engagement, discovery, and final revelation. In this account the epiphanic forms of Joyce and more recent writers are not escapes from plot or alternatives to plot but affirmations of the virtual structure of plot, another means to the authoritative teleological revelations for whose sake plots had traditionally been devised. Stories as apparently plotless as "Ivy Day in the Committee Room" or "Hills Like White Elephants" display, just as clearly as "The Murders in the Rue Morgue" or "The Open Boat," the sequence of the reader's perceptions from fragmentary or incomplete hypotheses about the world the narrative presents to a more complete or authoritative knowledge of that world.[14]

This sequence is, *mutatis mutandis*, as characteristic of novels as of short stories, for the plots novels develop have a pre-eminently teleological force. It is true that the greater length of a novel encourages the audience to assimilate its material diachronically, in terms of what Paul Ricoeur calls a "succession," rather than synchronically, in terms of a "configuration."[15] Even in "static" stories which do not display a sequence of actions, however, the sequence of the audience's responses is as fundamental as in long novels because this sequence is primarily what makes the story tellable in its particular way. The point of O. Henry's gradual unpacking of the revelations implicit among characters in "A Municipal Report" is that a "story" can be drawn out of the most commonplace situation by the proper treatment. Even when the given situation has become a sequence of events developing over many years and hundreds of pages, as in *The Good Soldier* or *Absalom, Absalom!*, this principle still governs the presentation. Critics who decode the novels of Ford and Faulkner in order to present events in their "proper" order are in danger of missing the point that a strictly chronological account of the events would not be tellable, or at least would lack the special kind of tellability conferred by the particular sequence of the reader's revelations. (Compare Forster's "The king died, and then the queen died of grief" with "The king died, no one knew why . . .")

It might be objected here that *The Good Soldier* and *Absalom, Absalom!* are atypical because in them the sequence of events is pointedly subordinated to a disruptive diegetic sequence uncharacteristic of most long narratives, whose diegetic sequence corresponds more closely to the sequence of events they recount. But this difference, as Barbara Herrnstein Smith observes, is only a difference in degree, for "it can be demonstrated not only that absolute chronological order is as *rare* in [such supposedly artless stories as] folkloric narratives as it is in any literary tradition but that it is virtually *impossible* for any narrator to sustain it in an utterance of more than minimal length. . . . By virtue of the very nature of discourse, nonlinearity is the rule rather than the exception in narrative accounts."[16]

Diegetic sequence, which shapes the sequence of the audience's responses to a given narrative, is thus, in teleological terms, what makes a story uniquely tellable whether that story develops the implications of a single situation or traces the development of a situation (or a problem or place or group of people) over a period of several generations. In an essay treating an episode from *Tess of the d'Urbervilles* by turns as a short story and as a chapter from a novel, Suzanne Hunter Brown emphasizes the greater weight the audience places respectively on configuration and succession as patterns of comprehension but indicates that plots of revelation and plots of resolution have ultimately the same teleological force: "Our understanding of Tess's situation is heightened [principally by figurative connections and implications] in reading the short story, but her condition does not change. On the other hand, a sequence governed by the logic of cause-and-effect will lead to a stasis of action in which the conflict is resolved; the final situation is not the cause of any future result in which we have interest."[17] Despite the different ways the reader assimilates "Tess" and *Tess*, both diegetic sequences move toward a comprehension more stable and authoritative than anything which has preceded them. Whether or not the author provides a sequential plot and a surrogate agent who shall comprehend the revelations of that plot, the effect of the diegetic sequence on the audience is essentially the same. Action in the novel, as in the short story, is simply a means to the general hermeneutics of narrative discourse.

Closure and Teleology in Dickens

The novels of Charles Dickens illustrate a broad range of relations between closure and teleology, and by extension between teleology and tellability. Dickens's first three novels provide striking examples of narratives which are tellable more or less in spite of their endings. The conflict between termination and tellability is the more surprising because, except for the unfinished *Mystery of Edwin Drood*, all of Dickens's novels come to coherent, intelligible, carefully planned endings. But these endings are for a variety of reasons not what makes the early novels tellable. In *Pickwick Papers*, the whole idea of an ending is inimical to the characters and the world Dickens had created, and to a story which seems designed to go on forever rather than end however gracefully. In *Oliver Twist*, Dickens's ending provides an appropriate conclusion to the mystery and intrigue he has created around his hero's birth but remains at odds with the thematic teleology he has been adumbrating. The ending of *Nicholas Nickleby*, which supplies an explicit rationale to a plot whose unitary import can be grasped long before the conclusion, is only peripheral to what makes the novel tellable.

Closure is above all a tactical problem in *Pickwick*, for Dickens was faced with the need to conclude within the twenty numbers his publishers had promised a series of adventures which showed no sign of coming to an end. In December 1836, Dickens published at the conclusion of Part X an announcement which indicated that, although he had "every temptation to exceed the limits he first assigned to himself," he did not wish the novel, when it formed "a complete work . . . to contend against the heavy disadvantage of being prolonged beyond his original plan." At the same time, however, he acknowledged the resistance of his material to a unitary conclusion by conceding the possibility of a sequel after the present *Pickwick Papers* had been published: "By what fresh adventures they may be succeeded is no matter for present consideration. The Author merely hints that he has strong reason to believe that a great variety of other documents still lie hidden in the repository from which these were taken, and that they may one day see the light" (xiii).[18] It is not surprising that by the time *Pickwick* was finished, Dickens, in the middle of *Oliver Twist* and about to begin *Nicholas Nickleby*, gave no further thought to a sequel; in the meantime, however, he faced the problem of devising a satisfactory conclusion to an unending story. His techniques over the last three numbers are similar to those which produce the sense of rest or stasis halfway through the novel, at the conclusion of Part X: the retreat to Dingley Dell, a pastoral world of a sort Dickens was always to associate with closure,[19] and the return of several characters the Pickwickians had encountered earlier—the Wardles, Joe the fat boy, and Messrs. Pott and Slurk, the journalists of Eatanswill. Alfred Jingle and Job Trotter, brought by an improbable reversal of fortune to the Fleet and redeemed by Pickwick's kindness, are packed off to the colonies; Mrs. Tony Weller's death puts the Reverend Mr. Stiggins to rout; the Pickwick Club is dissolved by the announcement of its founder's retirement; and the novel ends with a flurry of marriages: Sam Weller's to Mary, Snodgrass's to Emily Wardle, and Winkle's to Arabella Allen. All of these devices provide a sense of thematic closure; in addition, Dickens exploits this last marriage in order to provide a sense of narrative closure by creating and resolving suspense. Benjamin Allen objects to his sister's wedding and has to be won over; there follows a breathless trip in Chapter 50 to the elder Mr. Winkle's in Birmingham; Mr. Winkle's resistance is not broken down until the theatrical scene which concludes Chapter 56. The terminal force of a resolution after such suspension is considerable, even though the inconsequence of the episode makes this force rather factitious.

The situation is different in *Oliver Twist* because the novel is so much more densely plotted. Oliver's alternation between the dark and labyrinthine interiors of Mrs. Corney's workhouse, Sowerberry's undertaking shop, and Fagin's den on the one hand, and the world of love and sunlight represented by the Brownlow and Maylie homes on the other,[20] cannot continue indefinitely; when Nancy attempts to mediate between the two worlds, it is clear that the attempt will destroy her. Given Oliver's extraordinary resistance to assimilation into Fagin's den of thieves—his language remaining as incorruptible as his morals—he is obviously destined for the second world, and the discovery of Monks's plot against him confirms and justifies this destiny. The events of Oliver's life thus have a teleology which Dickens makes explicit in his Preface to the Third Edition (1841) of the novel: "To show, in little Oliver, the principle of Good surviving through every adverse circumstance, and triumphing at last" (vii). What gives the novel its gusto, what makes it uniquely tellable, however, is not this fairy-tale teleology but Dickens's rhetorical effects: the satire of the workhouse where Oliver is born, the stylized dialogue of Fagin and his gang, the hallucinatory intensity of Sikes's flight after he kills Nancy. Dickens's failure to make his good people realistic or engaging emphasizes the journalistic impulse behind the novel: When he is turning his relentless sarcasm against the workhouse system under the New Poor Law, or evoking the terrors of underworld London, or writing more generally against the object at hand, he is more compelling than when he is present-ing Mr. Brownlow or Rose Maylie as an object of admiration.

Commentators on Dickens have long agreed that he is a more effective social critic than social advocate because his criticism has a rhetorical bite his advocacy lacks. This imbalance undermines the conclusion of *Oliver Twist*, for the plot seems to be rescuing the hero from a world more real than he is. Oliver's socio-historical or journalistic status as a figure for the helpless English poor ill accords with his status as the naturally good, because naturally well-born, half-brother of Monks. The devices Dickens uses to secure Oliver's fortunes are consonant with what makes his theme intelligible but at odds with what makes it tellable, for they suggest that Oliver has all along incorporated in his birthright, in his own identity, a principle of deliverance from the social evils Dickens has been dramatiz-ing. Thus Dickens strengthens the sense of closure by weakening the rhetorical power of his indictment. Fagin's resolve to make Oliver a thief is given a rationale (Monks recruits his aid in blackening Oliver's character in order to disinherit him) which makes it far less convincing as a repre-sentative action. Since Oliver is providentially saved, it seems reasonable to expect that every worthy parish boy will be saved too. Only the death of little Dick at the end of Chapter 51 acknowledges the fact that some workhouse orphans are not so lucky. Dick seems to represent that aspect of Dickens's social theme which is not constrained by the intrigue which produces his resolution.

Nicholas Nickleby shows even more clearly the powers and limitations of Dickens's terminal devices in the early novels. Dickens has no trouble inventing incidents, shaping them into compositional units, and bringing them each to a conclusion or revelation which embodies a new and truer perspective. But these incidents rarely entail or even overlap one another. Kate Nickleby enters Madame Mantalini's establishment in Chapter 17; in Chapter 18, Miss Knag turns against her, and by the end of Chapter 21 she has lost her position. Smike, carried off to Squeers's lodgings in London, is immediately rescued by John Browdie. Ralph Nickleby, growing ever more incensed with his relations, hatches scheme after scheme for their ruin, but the schemes have little to do with each other except for their ineffectuality. The looseness of the novel's construction shows Dickens repeatedly creating opportunities for suspense only to squander them because of the brevity and inconsequence of each episode: Once Nicholas leaves Dotheboys Hall, it is impossible to believe that either he or Kate will ever be in serious or lasting danger. For all its vivacity of incident, the novel is constructed less like a chain of events than like a mosaic. Bernard Bergonzi, noting its "fundamental atomism," has aptly pronounced it "theatrical without being dramatic."[21] Hence there is no question of revealing an implicit rationale for a given sequence of events—such rationale as Dickens provides (the optimism, love, and resilience of the Nicklebys are proof against the vicissitudes of chance and the hatred of their uncle) being too obvious from the beginning to supply any terminal force—but simply of providing a final event which shall supply that force by virtue of its greater length, suspense, or complexity. The climactic episode—the rescue of Nicholas's beloved Madeline Bray and her fortune from Ralph Nickleby and Arthur Gride—is far more carefully developed in these respects than the concluding sequence of *Pickwick*. Nicholas has more at stake concerning Madeline's marriage to Gride than Pickwick has concerning that of Arabella to Winkle. The danger is greater because the marriage is threatened rather than desired; the suspense is more skillfully prolonged and better suited to the episodes which have preceded. Even so, this sequence seems in a fundamental way just one more Nicklebean adventure. As soon as Nicholas recognizes the mysterious young woman in the Cheerybles' office, it is clear that she is destined for him; but that certainty is based solely on the intensity of Nicholas's reaction to her, not on the fineness or discrimination of the reaction or on any quality of the young woman herself, for Nicholas's courtship, like his exploits at Dotheboys Hall or among Crummles' theatrical troupe, is presented pre-eminently as an adventure imposed on him from outside rather than an action arising from within him or engaging his nature. Nicholas has no nature to engage, only the qualities (boldness, adaptability, a forthright address) devolving on him by virtue of his position as the juvenile hero. It is only that conventional position, not any qualities implicit in his character, which makes him suitable for any adventures at all.

In a more general sense this is true of all Dickens's early characters: Since they do not as a rule possess any psychological problems or propensities which require an extended action to develop or display them, the actions in which they take part remain largely external to them. The haphazard profusion of incidents in *Pickwick Papers, Nicholas Nickleby, The Old Curiosity Shop,* and even, on the whole, *Martin Chuzzlewit* does not encourage speculation about what the characters are to become, only about what is to happen to them next. Characters like Nicholas and Little

Nell simply go on having adventures until they are towed safely into a
happy ending or shipwrecked in an early death. The characters are not
conceived in terms of a developing action; when Dickens generates suspense on their behalf, as he does with Oliver Twist, he works by exploiting
their situation, not their psychology.

This is not to say that the early Dickens is incapable of creating characters, only to distinguish between two ways of conceiving characters. Most
characters in English novels are conceived teleologically, in terms of future
actions and ends they necessarily imply. Hypocrites like Blifil, generous
spirits like Dorothea Brooke, and morally problematic characters like Lord
Jim reveal their full natures only through a developing dramatic action
implicit in their very conception. They need a chance to be unmasked or to
confront the world of experience or to work out their divided natures.
Other characters, however, need only to be displayed as if onstage.
Characters like Uncle Toby, Becky Sharp, and Buck Mulligan are conceived in terms of histrionic poses and attitudes, habitual scenes or conflicts or voices which immediately make their full natures manifest. They
may undergo adventures, but these adventures are as likely to take the
form of dramatic exposition as of dramatic action.

Dickens's development as a novelist is indicated by his increasing tendency to conceive characters in teleological rather than histrionic terms.
His first characters whose theatrical behavior and whose future development imply each other are in his Christmas books, the first of his major
works which are clearly planned in terms of the ends to which they will
come. Each of the five Christmas books turns on two alternative lines of
development implicit in a given situation. *The Cricket on the Hearth* and
The Battle of Life conclude with authoritative and affirmative explanations
of Dot Peerybingle's and Marion Jeddler's apparent betrayals of love; *A
Christmas Carol*, *The Chimes*, and *The Haunted Man* more pointedly
prophesy disastrous futures for their principals in their middle chapters
but conclude by canceling these prophecies. In telling the stories of
Scrooge and Trotty Veck, Dickens focuses for the first time on the possibility of conversion. Scrooge and Trotty both have gloomy dreams based
on the assumption that they will remain as they are (Scrooge avaricious,
Trotty unassumingly downhearted) but awaken to fairy-tale endings made
possible by their conversion to generosity or self-assertion. In giving
Trotty the dream of a bleak future for his daughter and awakening him to a
reassuring alternative, Dickens raises the same questions he had raised in
Oliver Twist, whose plot implied a teleology so different from that of its
direct social criticism. But now Dickens displays these questions in order
to focus his theme. When Trotty awakens to tell Richard, "You was
turned up Trumps originally; and Trumps you must be, till you die!"

(174), his vision of a harrowing alternative makes his confidence highly equivocal. By inverting the customary logic of dream-prophecies (in the Christmas books, the dreams are unexpectedly grim and realistic; only the ending outside the dream has the quality of a fairy tale), Dickens is opposing his two prophecies programmatically. Just as Scrooge awakens in time to prevent his dream from coming true, *The Chimes* ends with an explicit appeal to the reader to "try to bear in mind the stern realities from which these shadows come" and "endeavour to correct, improve, and soften them" (178) in order to keep Trotty's dream from coming true.

Throughout *Martin Chuzzlewit* and *Dombey and Son*, the novels contemporaneous with the Christmas books, Dickens experiments with characters like Pecksniff and Edith Dombey whose histrionic attributes imply a later reversal, and each of these novels explores the varieties of a particular vice (selfishness in *Chuzzlewit*, pride in *Dombey*) whose effects imply a thematic rationale. The anatomy of pride in *Dombey* encourages particular speculations about the ending of the novel, because pride traditionally implies an ultimate fall. Although Pecksniff, Jonas Chuzzlewit, and Mr. Dombey allow further development, however, the first character who requires such development—that is, the first character who is conceived in terms of his ultimate development[22]—is, appropriately, the autobiographical figure David Copperfield, whose opening address to the reader—"Whether I shall turn out to be the hero of my own life, or whether that station will be held by anybody else, these pages must show" (1)—indicates that he is the first of Dickens's heroes whose personal identity is problematic and that Dickens presents that problem explicitly in teleological terms. But the different versions of David, represented for the first time in Dickens's work (though scarcely the last) by other characters' names for him—his mother calls him Davy; the Peggottys, Mas'r Davy; Steerforth, Daisy; Heep, Master Copperfield; and his aunt, Trotwood, reflecting her earlier desire to have her "niece" called Betsey Trotwood Copperfield—are not different enough, and the education of his undisciplined heart not penetrating enough, to make the novel as insistently end-oriented as the three novels which follow: *Bleak House*, *Hard Times*, and *Little Dorrit*. These novels are doubly prophetic in the same sense that *A Christmas Carol* and *The Chimes* are: They incorporate both diagnostic predictions—that is, pathologies of society through mordant prognoses of its likely development—and prescriptive visions of the future. Dickens's social diagnosis is made manifest through a prophetic plot which shows what the world of English society is by predicting what it is coming to. At the same time, though more subtly than in the Christmas books, Dickens adumbrates an alternative future through his heroes and heroines, who are offered as models to readers who would avert the threatened social apocalypse.

Nowhere is this doubly prophetic movement clearer than in *Bleak House,* whose plot is the most Aristotelian in Dickens. The imagery throughout is eschatological, and the ending, when so many things become literally what they have always been figuratively—the frozen Lady Dedlock dies in the snow, Esther becomes mistress of Bleak House, Richard's decay becomes complete as Jarndyce and Jarndyce "melts away" (863) in costs—foretells the ruin of a social structure defined entirely by legal relations (as Esther, Richard, and Ada are "the wards in Jarndyce" [32]); the perverted charity of Mrs. Jellyby and Mrs. Pardiggle; the unwitting avarice of Richard and the rapacious avarice of Krook, Vholes, and the Smallweed family; and the disease which Jo brings from Tom-All-Alone's to Bleak House. But the genuine charity of Esther, who accepts her community with everyone she meets, from Jo to Lady Dedlock, offers a prescriptive model whereby the prophesied apocalypse may be averted.

The revelatory plot of *Bleak House,* which progresses by revealing social relations implicit from the beginning, allows Dickens to display the teleological implications of his histrionic characters. The delight readers take in Micawber has nothing to do with the expectation that he will change; he gives pleasure by being always himself. When the social implications of Micawber's irresponsibility are made manifest in Harold Skimpole, however, the character's very resistance to change, now a conscious, determined, and self-gratifying resistance, makes him a more profound conception. The social and economic implications of Micawber are essentially beside the point, because his character is referred to, and contained within, the conventions of melodramatic comedy. The revelatory plot of *Bleak House,* however, allows Dickens to display the social implications of an equally static character by changing the context in which he is presented and judged. Skimpole's behavior, without ever changing, grows steadily more shocking as his rejection of social responsibility comes to appear more selfish, more treacherous, and more symptomatic of larger social ills.

In *Hard Times,* whose method, appropriate to its brevity, is that of an eschatological cartoon (cf. *The Crying of Lot 49*), alternative teleologies are dramatized through alternative images for temporal development. The industrial interests of Thomas Gradgrind's Coketown, which spawn a network of "several large streets all very like one another, and many small streets still more like one another, inhabited by people equally like one another" (508), and which propose to "plant nothing else" (489) than a knowledge of Facts in educating children, are associated with the image of fire, which produces energy by reducing its fuel to ashes. Dickens links his critique of industrialism to his critique of regimented education through the image of Louisa Gradgrind attempting to read her future with Bounderby in the fire, "looking at the red sparks dropping out of the fire, and whitening and dying," and concluding "how short my life would be, and how little I could hope to do in it" (537). Against this image, which serves as an analogue to the apocalyptic imagery in *Bleak House*, Dickens sets the imagery indicated by the titles Sowing, Reaping, and Garnering: the image of organic growth, of planting and harvest, an image most closely associated with Sissy Jupe, who would like to have a carpet with a design of flowers because she likes flowers, and whose knowledge of horses, like Esther's knowledge of people, is based only on sympathetic experience. Does the future belong to Gradgrind's image or to Sissy's? Dickens suggests that "Time went on in Coketown like its own machinery: so much material wrought up, so much fuel consumed, so many powers worn out, so much money made" (572). But like the Christmas books, the novel has two distinct endings: the predictive ending at the end of Book II, when Gradgrind sees the catastrophe to which his philosophy has brought his daughter, and the prescriptive ending of Book III, after Bounderby has been exposed and Stephen Blackpool vindicated, and Sissy has been instrumental in banishing Harthouse and effecting Tom's escape. Despite this optimistic progression, the final chapter is equivocal. After presenting Bounderby standing before his fire, "projecting himself . . . into futurity," and Louisa "watching the fire as in days of yore," Dickens makes a detailed prophecy of his characters' future and concludes: "Dear reader! It rests with you and me, whether, in our two fields of action, similar things shall be or not. Let them be! We shall sit with lighter bosoms on the hearth, *to see the ashes of our fires turn gray and cold*" (763–65. My emphasis).

The eschatological impulse in *Little Dorrit* is indicated by Mrs. Merdle's hypocritical remark to Fanny: "If we could only come to a Millenium, or something of that sort, I for one might have the pleasure of knowing a number of charming and talented persons from whom I am at present excluded" (251). The Millenium comes in the form of Mr. Dorrit's accession to wealth and release from prison, Fanny's marriage to Mrs. Merdle's fatuous son, the failure and suicide of Mr. Merdle, and the collapse of Mrs. Clennam's house. As in *Bleak House*, however, these apocalyptic events only make manifest the identities people already had. In particular, release from prison cannot change Mr. Dorrit's identity because he continues to define himself in terms of his role as a prisoner—asserting its domination over him by his obsessive attempts to escape its shadow and ultimately by relapsing into it just before his death—and rightly so, since society itself, as critics have often remarked,[23] is a prison in the novel. People imprison themselves in social relations, Dickens suggests, by their love of power over each other, which defines so many relations (Rigaud-

Cavaletto, Flintwinch-Affery, Miss Wade-Tattycoram, Fanny-Sparkler) in terms of bondage or slavery; by the vanity and snobbery which base all claims to personal identity on an ultimately imprisoning social standing, as in the cases of Mr. Dorrit, Fanny, Pancks, Mrs. Clennam, and the Merdles, all summarized in Rigaud's announcement that "it's my intent to be a gentleman" (11); and by their attempts to change themselves simply by changing their circumstances instead of changing the ways in which their identities are implicated in their past and present actions (Mr. Dorrit and Fanny are the leading examples; another is Clennam determined to improve Doyce's capital by speculating).

Society is a prison because in order to win social recognition and social standing people must give up their own identities and become literally nobody. This situation is reflected in Dickens's working title for the novel (*Nobody's Fault*), in the endless and interchangeable ranks of Barnacles Clennam encounters in the Circumlocution Office, in Clennam's own attempt to divorce himself from his attachment to Pet (in the chapters "Nobody's Weakness" and "Nobody's State of Mind"), and in Rigaud's multiplication of identities (he also uses the names Blandois and Lagnier, and his letter to Mrs. Clennam is signed "Rigaud Blandois"). The attempt to assert a social identity results in a loss of the integrity on which alone a stable identity can be based.

The alternative to being trapped in a social role which makes one nobody is accordingly, and paradoxically, to choose to be nobody—to entrust one's identity to anonymous action, in the manner of Esther and John Jarndyce, instead of an imprisoning name or station. The exemplars of this way of life are Doyce (whose conception of himself in terms of useful activity enables him to accept the prospects of exploitation, neglect, and financial ruin with equanimity), Little Dorrit, and eventually Clennam. Mr. Meagles opposes Little Dorrit's self-abnegation to Miss Wade's self-absorption: "If she had constantly thought of herself, and settled with herself that everybody visited this place upon her, turned it against her, and cast it at her, she would have led an irritable and probably an useless existence. Yet . . . her young life has been one of active resignation, goodness, and noble service" (839). Little Dorrit herself views this loss of self as an exchange of a social and temporal for a divine model of self whose efficacy society cannot recognize when she tells Mrs. Clennam: "Be guided only by the healer of the sick, the raiser of the dead, the friend of all who were afflicted and forlorn, the patient Master who sheds tears of compassion for our infirmities. We cannot but be right if we put all the rest away, and do everything in remembrance of Him" (817). The incarnation Little Dorrit preaches confirms Dickens's attempt, through the single ending he provides for his characters, to link his predictive and prescriptive endings by adumbrating a Christian model which incorporates them both.

The doubly prophetic movement in Dickens's novels reaches a climax in *Little Dorrit*. His next novel, *A Tale of Two Cities*, is a transitional work which stands in somewhat the same relation to the late novels as the Christmas books do to the novels of the 1850s. The form of the historical novel seems at first less ambitious than that of the prophetic novels immediately preceding, but a brief comparison of *A Tale of Two Cities* with Dickens's earlier historical novel *Barnaby Rudge* shows how much more completely the later novel is conceived in terms of a thematic teleology. In both cases Dickens is drawn to a story of mob terrorism, and in both cases the mob, when it finally comes to power, is associated with images of blood, fire, and storm; but in *A Tale of Two Cities* these images, particularly the image of a threatening storm, are prepared from the very beginning. The long prologue to the story of the Gordon Riots establishes the affinities and antagonisms which will shape the behavior of Dickens's characters years later (as Dolly Varden's dismissal of Joe Willet and ridicule of Sim Tappertit motivate later developments in the plot) but without establishing a thematic nexus for the action. By contrast, Lorry's journey with Lucie Manette to recover her father and their chance meeting with Charles Darnay establish the two leading images in the novel—the golden thread of love by which Lucie binds her family together and joins her father's present to his past (and which is parodied in Madame Defarge's remorseless knitting) and the resurrection of which Dr. Manette is the troubled subject. The novel is organized structurally around this second image; not only is Dr. Manette "recalled to life," but Darnay is twice rescued by Carton from a death he seems already to have undergone—at his first trial he is described as "being mentally hanged, beheaded, and quartered, by everybody there" (61)—and Carton is aided the second time by the revelation that Roger Cly is still alive, a revelation made by the "Resurrection-Man" Jerry Cruncher, who had tried in vain to dig up Cly's corpse. Carton describes himself to Lucie as "like one who died young" (145), and the plot turns on whether or not he can put his past behind him and start afresh, as Madame Defarge refuses to do, as Dr. Manette is finally unable to do, and as Darnay can do only at the cost of Carton's life. The presentation of Carton's resolve as a rebirth—first prospectively as his own spiritual rebirth, then as Darnay's literal return to life—looks back to the awakenings in the Christmas books; here again Dickens presents two alternative futures, now incarnated in a double hero who is able both to survive the past and to die in expiation of it.

But the rhythm of death and rebirth which informs *A Tale of Two Cities* looks ahead to the last novels as well. The alternative endings of *Great Expectations* have long exercised critics, most of whom prefer the original ending to the revised ending, in which Dickens acceded to Bulwer-Lytton's request that Pip be allowed to marry Estella, on the grounds that the first version is more consistent with what has gone before. John Kucich has pronounced this problem "less interesting" than the problem of why Pip, disabused of his great expectations, should continue to love Estella.[24] Even this problem, however, is subordinate to the leading teleological question of the novel. Just as *David Copperfield* is organized around the problem of the hero's identity, and the anatomy of society in *Bleak House* and *Little Dorrit* is made to depend on the nature of the heroine's personal identity, the action of *Great Expectations* is focused on the question of Pip's identity. That his identity is not given by his past history but is a problem to be resolved is clear from the first three paragraphs of the novel, whose title suggests Pip's status as a figure for the vanities and pretensions of a whole society. At first unable to integrate the identities imposed on him by the convict, the Gargerys, and Miss Havisham and Estella—whence the scene in which Pip tells reckless and extravagant lies about his visit to Miss Havisham and later confesses to Joe that Estella "had said I was common, and that I knew I was common, and that I wished I was not common, and that the lies had come of it somehow, though I didn't know how" (66)— Pip eventually comes to define himself entirely in terms of his expectations, rejects his past and his family as completely (though not as self-righteously) as Bounderby, and uses his social position (a dependent position, like those of Skimpole and Mrs. Merdle) to insulate himself from the sufferings and judgments of undesirable companions. The revelation that his expectations come from the convict Magwitch, that he is himself the vicarious expression of Magwitch's own aspiration to be a gentleman, completes Dickens's pathology of Pip and of the society he represents. What is most remarkable about the novel's structure, in view of Dickens's earlier work, is why it does not end with that revelation, at the end of the second part of the novel. The problem of the alternative last chapters is less important than the problem of the entire third stage.

Although the appearance of this postdiagnostic or postanalytic third stage may be surprising, its function, in light of Dickens's growing preference for dramatic prophecy over the didactic journalism of *Oliver Twist*, is clear: It is here that Pip gets a chance to outgrow the blighting influence of his expectations. Instead of offering alternative predictions about the future and asking the audience to work toward one in order to avert the other, Dickens shows how Pip can turn one future into the other by abandoning his old conception of himself. The stages in his reform are clear: He acknowledges his community with Magwitch by acting on his behalf, eventually finding in him "a much better man than I had been to Joe" (439); he exchanges forgiveness with Miss Havisham, showing his ability to see his suffering in hers; and he confronts his own most selfish and ungrateful impulses in Orlick, who threatens him with the worst calamity he can imagine—the dread of being misremembered after death (419–20)—and from whom he is appropriately rescued by Trabb's boy. In each case Pip's growth involves a surrender or dissolution of his social identity, and his definition of himself in more active, fluid, or relational terms. By providing an ending which emphasizes not the just reward of the virtuous but the possibility of change for the less virtuous, Dickens emphasizes social prescription over the social pathology which dominates *Bleak House* and *Little Dorrit*.

This progress beyond social pathology goes even further in *Our Mutual Friend,* which again explores the problem of how to create a personal identity based on integrity in a society based on the self-alienating forces of economic power and the vanity of appearances. John Harmon, reported dead in the opening pages of the novel, has actually survived to witness the murder of "a figure like myself" and conclude that "there was no such thing as I" (416). The scene recalls the final confrontation between Pip and Orlick, when Pip responds to Orlick's plan to kill him and burn his body in the limekiln by picturing his own death in "the lonely marsh and the white vapour creeping over it, into which I should have dissolved" (421). In both passages the fear of being outside oneself, of dissolution in the sense of losing one's identity, is the greatest imaginable horror. The difference between the two is that the episode in *Great Expectations* is one of the climactic moments in the novel, whereas that in *Our Mutual Friend,* though presented nearly halfway through the novel, describes its opening situation, the problem with which it begins. Suppose a man were offered the opportunity to cut himself off from the familial and economic ties which gave him his social identity: What sort of identity could he create for himself? What possibilities could such a man find for defining himself outside the traditional roles of a corrupt and corrupting society? Harmon exists on the one hand as a chameleon, a man of disguises (Julius Handford, John Rokesmith) which express different aspects of himself until they collide and reveal his "true" identity, and on the other hand as Our Mutual Friend, as Noddy Boffin calls him (124)—an identity purely relational or purely functional, an identity not in these respects unlike that of Little Dorrit.

Only through analogy with other characters does Dickens reveal the structural basis of Harmon's identity in the rhythm of death and rebirth. Like Harmon, Rogue Riderhood and Eugene Wrayburn are literally saved from drowning, Riderhood to resume his old ways, Wrayburn to become worthy of Lizzie Hexam. Lizzie, inspired by the "old bold life and habit" (790) her brother had urged her to put behind her, rejects instead the new habits Charley had approved to venture onto the river and save Wrayburn's life. And Bella Wilfer, whose betrothal to the wealthy stranger John Harmon has formed in her a horror of being poor and a resolution that "to get money I must marry money" (361), turns her back on the resolution to which she has directed all her plans and energies in order to marry the unemployed secretary Rokesmith, only to find that she is Mrs. John Harmon after all. Boffin and Riah, without ever changing, are revealed under their menacing disguises to be as different, in Jenny Wren's phrase, as the Fairy Godmother from the Wolf each has seemed to be. The literal near-drownings of Harmon, Riderhood, and Wrayburn symbolize the death to oneself and to absorption in one's social role in which alone lies the hope of change and integration for fortunate individuals like Bella and Wrayburn and for the social order represented at the novel's close by Twemlow; characters who glorify their social identities or refuse to relinquish their self-serving desires are marked for death (Riderhood and Headstone) or unmasking and humiliation (Fledgeby, the Lammles, and ultimately, Dickens hints, the Veneerings). Dickens's diagnostic predictions about society function here almost completely as a prologue to the ritual of death to vanity and self-interest and rebirth to a genuinely social identity which Dickens prescribes as necessary to make the social order meaningful and expressive of social interests.

The progression from *Pickwick Papers* to *Our Mutual Friend* shows that Dickens's tactical preparations for the endings of his early novels gradually develop into teleological rationales as the endings come retrospectively to inform the meaning of each novel in all its parts. In short, Dickens's novels become progressively more end-oriented. The early novels close with terminal episodes; the middle novels close with revelations which confirm their status as social diagnoses or critiques; the last novels close with the heroes' development or rebirth presented as an escape from the impasse projected by Dickens's social predictions. Increasingly as Dickens's career advances, his endings incarnate not only principles of coherence and tellability as they become more and more emphatically rationales for the novels they conclude, but ultimately principles of social action which serve as the novels' final end. The very existence of novels like *Pickwick Papers* and *Oliver Twist* which are made tellable not by their teleological impetus but rather despite that impetus, however, demonstrates that some stories may differ from tragedies in having ends distinct from or at odds with their endings. Teleology cannot be the only principle of narrative tellability; it must be complemented by some other principle that makes stories worth telling.

4

The Discursive Principle

In Chapter 2 I distinguished between the audience's narrativity, which fills in the connections required to make sense of the agents and incidents of a given narrative, and the discourse's narrativity, which fills out a given pattern or idea by providing enough details to make the audience's narrativity necessary and rewarding. From an audience's point of view, a narrative represents the first term of a cognitive transaction, and the leading question about stories is how they are recognized as stories, how narrative discourse prepares an audience to interpret it in distinctively narrative terms. The integration of characters and situations—actually words or images—in *Pamela* or *The Rake's Progress* or *The Gold Rush* is based on a series of guesses about the teleology which will make a narrative tellable, the rationale which makes it worth attending to. Hence the teleology of a given story is, in a hermeneutical sense, its leading feature. From a storyteller's point of view, however, a narrative represents the final term in a synthetic process, a construction of materials designed to engage the audience, and the leading question about stories concerns not analysis or recognition but construction: What does a storyteller do to his or her material—an image, an event, a group of imagined people—to make it a tellable story? The teleological principle will give only limited help in answering this question, in part because it cannot always distinguish between tellable stories and alternative versions of those stories which are inadequate even though they project the same teleology, in part because it cannot account for the specifically antiteleological tendency of narratives like *Pickwick Papers*. We need a structural principle whereby a storyteller can make a story tellable—can make potentially narrative material, that is, into narrative discourse.

Stories without Endings

Perhaps the most obvious limitation of the teleological principle is that it fails to account for stories which project no authoritative teleology because they never end. A television soap opera like "As the World Turns" or "General Hospital" can run for years without bringing an end into sight. Failures in ingenuity or in the ratings can bring a given program to a close, but usually against the wishes of everyone associated with it, including its audience. The ideal soap opera, the one that best fulfilled the desires of its creators and audience, would go on forever, outlasting plot twists, cast changes, and set furniture, denying not only the possibility of closure but of coherent teleology. For unlike ritual tragedy and other narratives which borrow a dramatic teleology, the soap opera does not proceed to a determined and determinative end which incarnates the rationale of the whole. What it proceeds to, if all goes well, is more of the same.

It might seem impossible that a soap opera could ever serve as an object of knowledge, for although its audience could discern patterns which developed in a given program over an interval of months or years, they could never discover a pattern which made sense of the whole series with any final authority. Nothing in a soap opera is ever consequential in an ultimate sense—nothing is irreversible, nothing ever happens once and for all. Oedipus is a figure who is unable to escape the consequences of his actions, a figure whose catastrophe gives his life a final, authoritative meaning. In a comic version of this pattern, Jane Austen's heroines find both social and epistemological stability in the marriages which establish once and for all who they really are; for it is a convention of most novels, as Barbara Hardy has remarked, that by their conclusions "everything of moral importance has happened to these people."[1] In soap operas, by contrast, marriage, murder, and revelations about one's past are always multivalent, always gambits implying further development. When the Emmas and Knightleys of daytime television marry, their stability is fleeting; by the end of the week they must cope with Mr. Woodhouse's serious illness, a series of spiteful anonymous letters, or the arrival from Australia of Knightley's plausible but ne'er-do-well brother Robert. Even when characters in soap operas die, their deaths do not normally fix their identities but create mysteries—how did he die? who killed him? is the will a forgery?—which continue the indefinite deferral of teleological significance. Hence no action necessarily entails anything. Happy marriages can always end in divorce, terminally ill patients can hover for weeks between life and death, and characters can disappear with every indication of foul play only to return months later played by a new actor.

And yet, despite the absence of an integrative teleology which presents soap opera experience in its final and authoritative meaning, audiences clearly have no trouble understanding soap operas either on their own terms or as images of a larger world. It is a world in which, in Frank Kermode's phrase, we are always "in the middest," always defining ourselves with reference to an apocalypse which is always receding or, when it arrives in the form of long-awaited marriages or deaths, never settles anything.[2] The audience for soap opera watches not in order to determine the ultimate meaning of the world or its people but in order to spend time in a world which titillates them with the promise of definitive revelations but multiplies complications in the interest of endless suspense. The soap opera can be intelligible even in the absence of a coherent teleology because the audience comprehends characters and experiences in terms of contingent identifications and expectations rather than of purposive ends.

Considering soap opera characters and events as the changing furniture in an essentially unchanging world indicates the soap opera's affinity not only with such endlessly adventurous comic strips as *Dick Tracy* and *Mary Worth* but also with more self-contained strips like *Peanuts* and *Blondie*, and indeed with the situation comedies and melodramas of television. Even though "Laverne and Shirley" may offer a new story, complete with teleology, every week, what makes the story tellable is not the teleological revelation but the resistance of the stock characters, the audience's companions and friends, to any unitary teleology. Whether narrative development is equivocal and multivalent, as in soap operas, or trivial, as in situation comedies, it is not disruptive to the timeless fictive world the story continues to project.

In soap operas nothing and no one has any ultimate meaning. Anything can happen, but since all events are reversible, no teleology is privileged; since no event establishes a pattern of meaning which may not eventually be superseded, all beliefs and expectations are arguable. Even stories which imply a single teleology, however, may not come to a satisfactory end. No writer has ever had, for better or worse, a surer conviction of the meaning of psychological states and events than Sigmund Freud; yet one of the most celebrated of Freud's case studies, his analysis of the patient he calls Dora, was published as a fragment of an analysis, a story without an ending. In his prefatory remarks to the monograph, Freud defines its incompleteness in terms of three patterns. Since no one case history can give insight into "*all* the questions arising out of the problem of hysteria," it is incomplete in terms of its theoretical conclusiveness. Since Freud has "not reproduced the process of interpretation . . . but only the results of that process," it is incomplete in terms of its narrative inclusiveness. Most important, since the treatment "was broken off at the patient's own wish" before the therapist had completely relieved her hysterical symptoms or elucidated all the problems he uncovered, it is incomplete in terms of its therapeutic efficacy.[3] Freud's *telos*, his rationale of the case, is not implicit in his *mythos*, the facts of the case, but is imposed from outside, incompletely and perhaps unpersuasively. This disjunction between event and interpretation, represented within the analysis by Dora's constant resistance to Freud's hypotheses, has given this case study a special fascination for literary analysts.

Although Freud calls this study a fragment, his remarks make it clear that it is to be judged as thematic exposition—that is, in terms of the evidence it offers for the theory that hysterical neurosis is characteristically rooted in infantile sexuality—rather than as history, as a chronological record of a treatment. Obviously Freud was satisfied that despite its several kinds of incompleteness, the study was sufficiently conclusive to publish in the form he gave it. If the analysis lacks the conclusiveness of Freud's other case studies—his papers on the patients we know as the wolf man, the rat man, and little Hans—that is not because the chronological record is imperfect or distorted, but because the treatment, as Freud says, "was not carried through to its appointed end" (VII, 12). In concluding the study, Freud suggests that his failure to explain Dora's transference of the feelings she felt toward her father to Freud himself left her free to cut off the therapy prematurely as an expression of masochism and revenge, without fully accepting Freud's analysis of her case or achieving a comfortable integration into her social sphere. Once again the incompleteness involves teleology in the sense of an authoritative rationale of events. Freud indeed produces such a rationale—incomplete as to details, but clear enough in its general outline—but because the patient resists it, it does not have the power to change her life by giving her more control over her neurosis. As a scientific investigation the study is complete: It offers abundant, though not irrefutable, evidence for a particular hypothesis and a more general psychoanalytic theory. As a therapeutic narrative, however, it is incomplete because it tells the story of a narration—Freud's hypothetical account of Dora's psychoneurotic development—which is itself incomplete, for its completeness could be secured only through its success in curing the patient's symptoms. Formal closure depends in this case on therapeutic efficacy, even as Aristotle would rule a tragedy incomplete unless it enabled its audience to achieve a catharsis.

If the goal of psychoanalysis is the reintegration of the patient with her social milieu, then all case studies may be stories without endings, for a complete integration between oneself and society may well be impossible. Freud, who approached this subject somewhat differently in his later essay "Analysis Terminable and Interminable," concluded that although it was reasonable to expect an analysis to alleviate a patient's specific symptoms and, by uncovering repressed memories and strengthening the weak ego, to prevent their recurrence, it was in theory impossible "by means of analysis to attain to a level of absolute psychical normality . . . which . . . would be able to remain stable."[4] Freud's emphasis in this essay is clinical rather than theoretical, but Philip Rieff, in his observations on Freud's analysis, suggests one reason why absolute psychological normality is chimerical: Since normality is always a socially defined term, a given patient can be pronounced normal only with respect to a particular social milieu. In attempting to prepare Dora for what he took to be her proper role in her immediate social sphere, Rieff contends, Freud overlooks the fact that "it is the milieu in which she is constrained to live that is ill" and recommends for consideration " 'milieu' therapy."[5] From characterizing a given milieu as ill it is only a short step to characterizing society as by definition alienating—a position close to one Freud takes in *Civilization and Its Discontents*. It would seem to follow that not only is mental health entirely normative, but that its norms are based on social structures and institutions necessarily antagonistic to the happiness and fulfillment of any individual. If this is so, then psychoanalytic therapy can hope to achieve no more than a normative dis-integration between the patient's instinctual and communal needs, and the teleology, indeed the closure, of a given analysis can only be nominal and contingent on the particular dis-integration the therapist chooses.

To speak of closure as contingent introduces a much broader and more traditional narrative genre than soap opera and psychoanalytic case studies: the genre of autobiography, specifically the mode of romantic autobiography which properly begins with Rousseau. The traditional justification for autobiography is that the author has gained a privileged perspective on his life which allows him to see it as coherent and whole. In earlier autobiographies like Augustine's *Confessions*, this privileged perspective is the product of a religious conversion which divides one's life in two. Before, one had seen one's life as merely a succession of events (or, worse still, as governed by a false pattern); after, one sees one's life as it actually is, as at once inside and outside time, as God sees it. Autobiographers like Rousseau, who have no God to provide an authoritative teleology for their lives, tend to borrow the structure of the conversion narrative without its teleological authority. Rousseau's *Confessions* accordingly make slow reading because, despite the vivacity of his discourse, there are long stretches in which his life, like someone else's dream, seems constituted entirely by arbitrary events without any tendency to go anywhere.

This teleological incompleteness is again allied to a necessarily contingent conception of closure. In order to write the story of my life, I must still be alive; in order to see my life in terms of an organizing pattern, I must believe that I can see the pattern as complete or approaching completion, and that either nothing in my life after I write will substantially alter that pattern, or that however my life might change, my present perspective will justify itself in the writing. The first of these beliefs—the belief in an inherently privileged teleology—produces spiritual autobiography like Augustine's; the second, romantic autobiography like Rousseau's. Clearly autobiographies must always lack endings in the sense that their stories are incomplete; unless a writer died in completing his last sentence, his endpoint would inevitably be contingent, and his autobiography would become more outdated as he went on living (a problem burlesqued, for example, in *Tristram Shandy*). From a teleological perspective, however, autobiographies which grow outdated grow thereby untrue, because each further day or year the author lives may generate new retrospective patterns. If the authority of a given autobiography depends entirely on the author's arbitrary choice to write whatever he chooses to remember or cares to research at whatever point from which he cares to look back, its teleology will accordingly be limited by decisions and conventions which may have no value outside the time of writing.

It might seem that identifying as stories without endings all those stories whose endings are contingent, whose conclusion and teleology are determined by formal or rhetorical conventions rather than by appeals to external authority, is misleadingly vague, since all endings are contingent in the sense that, whatever their authors' beliefs, they must provide their own formal justification. For an audience that does not believe in a revelatory apocalypse, we might say, any apocalypse is potentially as meaningful as any other. And this may well be true, at least of narrative in general. But it certainly is not true of Aristotelian drama, whose teleology transcends the requirements of formal or aesthetic closure to offer a privileged perspective, a mode of wisdom, concerning the audience's own experience. It is true that dramatic conventions of structural and teleological unity have played an important role, for example, in the development of prose fiction, particularly in novelists like Cervantes, Fielding, and Dickens, who also wrote for the stage. But it is also true that the teleological imperative is comparatively attenuated in narrative. *Don Quixote*, like *Oedipus*, ends with the hero's discovery and acceptance of his true identity; but Sophocles' ending provides the rationale for the entire action he presents, whereas Cervantes' ending is merely a technical device enabling the closure of a narrative which would otherwise, like *Pickwick Papers*, have continued indefinitely. D. A. Miller makes this point when he argues that "the narratable"—that is, "the instances of disequilibrium, suspense, and general insufficiency from which a narrative appears to arise"—

"inherently lacks finality. It may be suspended by a moral or ideological expediency, but it can never properly be brought to term."[6] Although many narratives adopt the formal conventions of a dramatic teleology without Aristotle's faith in teleology as a privileged mode of wisdom, their contingent teleology is to a great extent a contradiction in terms.

Alternatives to Teleology

Few stories, of course, resist closure so resolutely as soap operas: Even Scheherezade eventually brings her stories, and her story, to an end on the thousand-and-first night. Even when stories do reach an ending, however, they are often organized according to nonteleological principles. Sometimes, as in the case of picaresque tales like *Lazarillo de Tormes,* or of Defoe's *Roxana* or *Captain Singleton,* the ending of a story is a rhetorical contrivance which does nothing to make the story more coherent or intelligible as a whole. More often, the ending adds or confirms a teleological dimension which remains relatively unimportant, because stories like *Oliver Twist* can incorporate a teleology without displaying it. The teleology of action is what makes Aristotelian tragedy tellable; other narrative modes, even if they borrow a dramatic framework, are often tellable for quite different reasons.

The most obvious, and probably the most frequent, alternative to teleological display is the kind of histrionic display typical of the early Dickens novels, in which characters give delight by remaining always triumphantly themselves. During his tenure as valet to Mr. Pickwick, Sam Weller does many things to advance the plot (giving information about Jingle's elopement with Emily Wardle, visiting Mrs. Bardell to gather news about the progress of her suit against Pickwick, giving testimony at the trial), but what makes him memorable has nothing to do with his contributions to the plot: his matter-of-fact self-satisfaction, his unfailingly irrelevant analogies, and the agnomens ("young dropsy" and "young brockilley sprout" are two) he uses in conversational address. In the longest story of the *Decameron* (8.7), the scholar Rinieri, tricked by a widow he loves into standing outside her window all night in the snow while she is entertaining her lover, later tricks her into spending a day naked and exposed to sun and insects on an isolated tower on her estate. The scholar's revenge is satisfying in its teleological precision—even the maid who had helped trick him breaks her leg in a fall from a ladder—but what makes the tale uniquely tellable is the emphasis, rare in Boccaccio, on the physical sensations, first of the scholar, then of the widow, and the scholar's long rhetorical speeches about the widow's perfidy and the superiority of older to younger lovers. The plot serves as a vehicle for these descriptions and speeches, as the plot of *Pickwick Papers* provides a vehicle for Sam Weller's histrionic discourse; but in each case it is the discourse, not the plot motivating it, which the narrative displays. The first three sections of Ring Lardner's story "Alibi Ike" are devoted, in formal terms, to the exposition of the title character and his situation; the last three develop a romantic complication which serves as the story's plot. The plot gives the story its teleological structure, but for every reader who can recall the plot, there are a hundred who savor in memory the exposition of a figure who "can't even go to bed without apologizin', and . . . excuses himself to the razor when he gets ready to shave."[7]

The discrepancy between teleological and histrionic display is especially pronounced in film, which offers unparalleled opportunities for the display of spectacle, ranked last by Aristotle among the elements of tragedy. The written sentence, "In order to check her alibi, the inspector drove a motorcycle through downtown Paris and even took a police cutter down the Seine from the place she had been seen to her own house," evokes no particular image and has no import apart from its plot function. In Claude Lelouch's film *Cat and Mouse*, however, these two sequences, filmed by strapping a camera to the handlebars of a motorcycle and the prow of a motor launch instead of by the customary method of process photography, offer a bravura display of kinetic acceleration which provides a high point of the film. The display of physical or camera reality, though not impossible to achieve in written discourse, is more idiomatic to film and easier to make tellable. Hence the problematic exoticism of *Salammbô* finds dozens of more successful analogues in the films of Cecil B. De Mille and other directors of movie spectaculars. The two cinematic genres which place the greatest emphasis on spectacle are the travelogue, which usually dispenses with plot altogether, and the musical comedy, in which the plot is reduced to a "continuity" which motivates the production numbers the film displays. Audiences who watch the musicals Busby Berkeley choreographed, or the films in which Mark Sandrich directed Fred Astaire and Ginger Rogers, for the plot are imposing teleological demands on stories whose display is essentially histrionic or spectacular. Even nonmusical film comedies frequently place little or no emphasis on teleology. Buster Keaton's silent film *The General* motivates its jokes by a plot (Keaton's pursuit and recovery of a Confederate railroad engine seized by a Union detachment) which is itself a primary means of engaging the audience. But in *Modern Times* Charlie Chaplin simply bounces from one adventure to the next; the background situation (unable to accept his role in an industrialized society, Chaplin attempts to create his own counter-society with Paulette Goddard) motivates a series of episodes without providing a teleology for them, and the film ends with a shot of Chaplin and Goddard walking off down the road, presumably to more adventures.

Characters like Chaplin's tramp can go on having adventures because of their exemption from the teleological imperative, but other heroes and their narratives resist teleology more forthrightly. In *The Trial* and *The Castle*, Kafka's heroes are engaged in enterprises—one to ascertain the nature of the charges against him, the other to make his way to the mysterious castle—which are by their very nature impossible to conclude satisfactorily. It hardly matters that of the two manuscripts, both left incomplete at Kafka's death, *The Trial* contains a final chapter and *The Castle* does not, for the final chapter of *The Trial* merely provides a more emphatic version of the failure of teleology which the novel makes explicit almost from the beginning. Narratives like Kafka's are organized iron-ically, by their indefinite deferral of teleological revelations which seem imminent. The Arthurian *Quest of the Holy Grail* ends with a hand appear-ing to Bors and Perceval as it descends and then takes the Grail back to heaven, but not before Galahad has looked inside the Grail and died in ecstatic contemplation. In Kafka's ironic versions of the quest, as in *Waiting for Godot,* the characters' lives and deaths are shaped by an ideal as inaccessible as the Grail, but whose significance is predicated entirely on its inaccessibility. Any authoritative or transcendent revelation would be philosophically suspect.

This ironic principle of display, whereby events are assumed to be meaningful with reference to a teleology which is indefinitely deferred, is exploited most broadly, though not most profoundly, in Alain Resnais's film *Last Year at Marienbad,* which not only refuses to provide an au-thoritative conclusion but presents incompatible versions of the past (so that the audience can never tell whether Giorgio Albertazzi really met Delphine Seyrig last year at Marienbad) and contradictory information about the present (shots are disordered chronologically, and there is no clear principle for ordering them correctly; people walking in the formal gardens cast conspicuous shadows, but trees do not; the large stone sculpture which serves as a focus for the film's imagery changes location repeatedly). Alain Robbe-Grillet, who wrote the screenplay for the film, has argued against those critics who treat its plot as a series of riddles to be solved or questions to be answered, that "such questions have no mean-ing. . . . This is a world without a past, a world which is self-sufficient at every moment and which obliterates itself as it proceeds. . . . The entire story of *Marienbad* happens neither in two years nor in three days, but exactly in one hour and a half."[8] Hence Robbe-Grillet advises the specta-tor who would attempt "to reconstitute some 'Cartesian' schema—the most linear, the most rational he can devise"—instead to "let himself be carried along by the extraordinary images in front of him, by the actors' voices, by the sound track, by the music, by the rhythm of the cutting, by the passion of the characters," suggesting that "to this spectator the film will seem the 'easiest' he has ever seen: a film addressed exclusively to his sensibility, to his faculties of sight, hearing, feeling."[9] The audience constantly and unsuccessfully attempting to integrate the film according to a Cartesian schema is experiencing it as a narrative whose structural principle is ironic; the audience carried along by the visuals and the soundtrack is experiencing it as a kind of static travelogue, in which pictorial display supersedes the promise of teleological display.

A third organizing principle in narrative, closely related to the ironic deferral of teleology, is the principle of digression. Digressions, as their etymological meaning suggests, are usually regarded as departures from (or interruptions of or additions to) a story complete in itself; the interpolated tales in *Don Quixote* and *Pickwick Papers* follow this model, as do the non-narrative digressions throughout the *Decameron* and *Sartor Resartus*. In some writers, however—in Sterne, Woolf, Machado de Assis, the Swift of *A Tale of a Tub*—digressions become hypertrophied and radically disruptive, displacing teleology as the primary structural principle. Just as the film *Monty Python and the Holy Grail* ends abruptly in the middle of a subplot without resolving its main plot—ends apparently because the movie camera is smashed—*Tristram Shandy* ends in the middle of Sterne's thousandth digression, and ends without ever coming to the point. There is no point, for Sterne's essentially digressive imagination has subverted any possibility of an intelligible teleology which would inform his whole work. Sterne's nominal subject, the life and opinions of Tristram Shandy, merely provides him with a linear sequence to depart from.

Works whose structure is digressive differ from those whose structure is ironic in several respects. Although they lack an intelligible teleology, a perspective which endows events with authoritative meaning, ironic works normally have a point—the point that there is no point—and this paradoxical point, or lack of point, is precisely what they display. Ironic works mount a challenge to the possibility of an authoritative teleology; digressive works treat this possibility as irrelevant, or do not raise it at all. Thus, instead of the behavior of the principals of *Last Year at Marienbad*, which can be made intelligible only by postulating a past the film refuses to authorize, or the behavior of Kafka's heroes, which is intelligible in terms of a goal impossible to attain, digressive narratives present the behavior of Uncle Toby or Clarissa Dalloway, easily intelligible in terms of principles of psychology, which prescribe certain kinds of habitual behavior, but not of teleology, which would constitute behavior as a completed action.

Sterne's philosophical attack on the sequential logic of narrative teleology is complemented by his use of the logic of associative psychology. Even in *Jacques the Fatalist,* surely the most insistently challenging digressive narrative ever written—Diderot is constantly taunting his readers with the futility of their expectations—the interaction of Jacques and his master is clearly based on their respective beliefs in fatalism and radical freedom as philosophical doctrines. The example of Diderot shows how closely digressive structural patterns can resemble ironic patterns; indeed the difference between them, as between digressive and histrionic patterns, is largely a matter of emphasis. The point here is not to multiply paradigmatic structures but to place the teleological principle of narrative display within a more comprehensive context.

Digression as a Structural Principle

It might be objected at this point that histrionic, ironic, and digressive patterns of organization, which often defer teleological revelations indefinitely, are not only antiteleological but antinarrative, that they represent not alternative modes of narrative development but exceptions to the rule of narrative development. Just as religious or political excurses are often considered excrescences on the narrative form of a novel or film, ideological interruptions of the story itself, histrionic or spectacular display (for example) might be defined as a more subtly non-narrative mode of development. In one of the climactic sequences in *Strangers on a Train,* Alfred Hitchcock intercuts shots of Guy (Farley Granger) trying to win a tennis match quickly in order to prevent Bruno (Robert Walker) from planting Guy's cigarette lighter in the amusement park where he killed Guy's wife, with shots of Bruno's hand reaching down to recover the lighter from a sewer into which it has fallen. The accelerated tempo of the crosscutting and the graphic contrast of the two compositions—the tennis match brightly lit, the movement within the frame quick, horizontal, and repetitive; the sewer dark, the movement in its frame slow and steadily downward—make the sequence witty and suspenseful. But not only is it unnecessary to the plot (which could easily dispense with it logically), it is illogical in terms of the plot, because dropping the lighter has not really delayed Bruno, who (as Guy had predicted) waits after recovering it for nightfall before attempting to return to the murder scene; because Guy, overlooking the simplest way to finish his match in straight sets, never thinks of losing deliberately; and because Guy, having taken as long as possible to win his match, is in time to catch Bruno anyway. Is the appeal of this sequence then simply pictorial rather than narrative?

The answer to this question is no, for at least three reasons. First, since narrative ontology, as I argued in Chapter 2, is based on tellability, the question of whether a given episode is logically necessary to a causal sequence is less important than whether it makes that sequence as a whole more tellable (as this episode certainly does). Second, if we eliminate ostensibly non-narrative excurses from narratives, it is difficult to say just what will remain and to justify the remnant as *not* non-narrative. (This problem will be considered at length in Chapter 6.) Third, even if the Hitchcock episode does mark a complete digression from the teleology of the film's action, it is still essentially narrative, for digressiveness, whether ideological, psychological, anecdotal, or even geometric (as in *Through the Looking-Glass* and *Finnegans Wake*), is not an exception to the rule of narrative progression but an exemplary illustration of that rule. This third proposition needs to be demonstrated in some detail.

In his "Introduction to the Structural Analysis of Narrative," Roland Barthes, arguing that narrative is fundamentally structural rather than mimetic, observes that "the 'reality' of a sequence lies not in the natural succession of the actions composing it but in the logic there exposed, risked, and satisfied." Since "a narrative can be identified even if its total syntagm be reduced to its actants and its main functions as these result from the progressive upwards integration of its functional units," it follows that stories, unlike (for example) lyric poems, can always be translated or summarized without altering their structural integrity; "the summary of a narrative (if conducted according to structural criteria) preserves the individuality of the message."[10] Barthes's analysis, which distinguishes between cardinal functions, whose interrelations are "both consecutive and consequential," and catalysts, those "consecutive units" whose "functionality is attenuated, unilateral, parasitic" (94), and which can therefore be omitted in summary without affecting the sequence of cardinal nuclei, is essentially teleological: The narrative *praxis* may be expanded by a theoretically infinite number of catalysts, but the logic which constitutes "the 'reality' of a sequence" remains the same.

It is true, of course, that any story can be summarized in a paragraph or sentence without necessarily altering its teleological coherence. What is altered in summary is the structure of the audience's experience, for summaries, even if they preserve narrative structure, are not sufficiently engaging or tellable to allow narrative logic to be exposed, risked, and satisfied. The logic of a summary satisfies logical expectations instantly, without exposing or risking them; the information communicated is the same, but the nature of the audience's experience, which is radically dependent on narrative discourse rather than on any putative series of actions underlying the discourse, is not. Audiences do not go to movies or

World Series games to get information a few hours earlier than they could get it from a newspaper; they go in order to experience a suspension of certainty which makes the resolution more tellable than information alone—a suspension which is itself, as teleological analyses overlook, displayed.

What must be added to summaries to make them tellable stories? It is not enough to say that a story incarnates a teleology which constitutes its action as a significant whole, because many summaries incarnate such a teleology, and some stories do not. Barthes's analysis, which is based on an analogy between the grammar of narrative and the grammar of sentences, predicates a rhythm of aperture and closure: Logic is risked, then satisfied. When Pip discovers that Magwitch, not Miss Havisham, is the source of his great expectations, he could either accept Magwitch as his benefactor, or report him to the police, or leave London and go back to Joe's forge, and so on. By the same token, this discovery could index Pip's priggish naiveté, the radically economic nature of social relations, the cultural equivalence of Magwitch and Miss Havisham, and so on. Although the ending of the novel indicates which of these potential implications are to be confirmed, it is their multiple presence as possibilities which shapes the reader's experience.

According to Barthes, the opening of a narrative implies multiple continuations, actantial and semiotic, among which the ending (of each sequence and of the whole narrative) discriminates, resolving the tension the sequence has aroused. In a sense this formulation is undoubtedly apt: The endings of narratives and sequences are defined by the audience's sense of culmination, resolution, and satisfaction. But it does not account for those stories without conclusive actantial or semiotic endings, or for the resistance of virtually all narratives to any absolutely authoritative teleology, any ultimate semiotic closure. In considering the stories of O. Henry, I described a movement from the audience's perception of an incomplete or misleading order based on discursive sequence to the perception of an authoritative order based on teleological synthesis, a movement based on Barthes's rhythm of aperture and closure. But the example of soap opera and other endless narratives, in which this synthesis or integration is indefinitely withheld, suggests that narrative may be only incidentally a mode of analytic or semiotic knowledge, that hermeneutical revelations may ultimately, like actantial sequence, serve only to indicate some deeper rhythm.

In O. Henry the ending substitutes a true order for the misleading order of the beginning. In more complex narratives, however, the rhythm of penetration or debunking proceeds to revelations far more equivocal. In *Great Expectations* the initial behavior of Jaggers's clerk Wemmick hints at some hidden aspect of his personality, which is duly disclosed when Pip goes to visit him at his home in Walworth. Jaggers's office Wemmick had been dry, reserved, and cryptic; in Walworth, his behavior toward Pip, Miss Skiffins, and his Aged Parent is open, cordial, and affectionate. In O. Henry this second Wemmick would be the real Wemmick; the structural reversal would simply impeach the earlier Wemmick as an assumed social role. Neither Pip nor Dickens, however, characterizes the two Wemmicks this way. For Pip, Wemmick's duality remains irreducible. When he wishes to buy Herbert Pocket a partnership in Clarriker's, he consults with both Wemmicks and acts in cooperation with the Walworth Wemmick. His decision to help Herbert, supported by the Walworth Wemmick, is vindicated or ratified by the qualities (consideration, loyalty, selfless generosity) that Wemmick indexes, but it also in turn vindicates and ratifies those values. In other words, Pip's decision to help Herbert, not any semiotic integration, makes the Walworth Wemmick more authoritative than his counterpart at Jaggers's office.

More generally, since personal identity in *Great Expectations* is based on one's experience of oneself through the world of external appearances and people, as a product of social, cultural, and economic codes, identity is necessarily unstable, irreducible to any single integration. One can be sure who one is not, but never precisely who one is. Pip is not Miss Havisham's protegé, but Magwitch's; and this revelation raises many more questions than it answers. What does it mean for Pip to be Magwitch's surrogate gentleman, to owe his social standing to a social outcast, to find himself chained to a man he has never thought of without revulsion? Dickens's structural ironies here undermine a false model of society without establishing an equally straightforward true model. As Pip's relation to each of his parental figures—Mrs. Joe, Miss Havisham, Jaggers, Magwitch—grows more problematic, it is harder to say just what it means to be the child of a parent, because Dickens's amplification of the pattern introduces complexities which his conclusion does not resolve. In the end Pip has learned who he is not—he cannot, despite his best efforts, be anyone's child—but not who he is, only who he might be. The best he can do is act in full awareness of the circumstances, systems, and codes that have shaped him and then to take responsibility for his actions; and this willingness to assume responsibility for what he does is what distinguishes Pip from Estella, at least in Dickens's original ending. Since only action, whether Pip's or the audience's, can confer authority on any interpretation of a hermeneutic sequence, Dickens's narrative has the effect of affronting the audience's assumptions about Pip and his world without substituting any definite or univocal beliefs. In more general terms still, this principle helps to distinguish between the end-oriented structure of tragedy (the fall of a great person) and the beginning-oriented structure of the narrative *Bildungsroman* (the coming-of-age of a young person).

It would then seem that the debunking rhythm of narrative hermeneutics is less a movement toward an authoritative teleology than a movement away from misleading or incomplete knowledge. Narrative digressions are only incidentally disruptive: What they mainly do is provide an experience whose hermeneutical dimension is antithetical. To put the matter more simply, narratives do not so much teach truth as unteach falsehood; they are less gnostic than agnostic. Critics have often ascribed these qualities and this rhythm to the novel, whose basic convention, as Jonathan Culler has observed, is "our expectation that the novel will produce a world."[11] This expectation distinguishes between stories and their summaries by making narrative an area of experience rather than an object of knowledge. A summary can communicate knowledge, but it does not have a story's power to impugn false knowledge because it does not create a world the audience accepts as a model of their own. Such a constellated world has the power, as Lionel Trilling has noted, "of involving the reader himself in the moral life, inviting him to put his own motives under examination, suggesting that reality is not as his conventional education has led him to see it." For the audience's limited or distorted conventional wisdom, the novel and the film, with their emphasis on the variety and fullness of sensual, social, and circumstantial experience, substitute information "about the look and feel of things, how things are done and what things are worth and what they cost and what the odds are."[12] By impeaching the limiting ideas of conventional education, fully articulated narratives move from *gnosis* to *agnosis*.

Narration as Supposition

Structural models of narrative like Barthes's overlook the agnostic tendency of its thematic organization and the incessant tendency of its action because they place undue stress on its teleology. When Barthes wants to claim actantial or semiotic indeterminacy for a narrative, as in *S/Z*, he smuggles it into the interstices of the action by reading what he takes to be a classic, readerly text as writerly, instead of analyzing the action itself as Sarrasine's unknowing of Zambinella, his movement from illusion to a revelation which makes Zambinella's identity a mystery all the more profound and terrifying—the whole story as an explanation whose explanatory power is almost nil. Instead of using a teleological model of actantial and hermeneutical structure, based on a rhythm of aperture and closure, and treating the digressions and indeterminacies of Sterne and Diderot as exceptions to the structural rule, theorists might better devise an alternative model which would account for the narrative's resistance to closure, its antithetical or agnostic tendencies, and its projection of a world which images our own. The teleological model of narrative structure is based on the geometry of the line segment from A to B, or the rhythm of the proposition *if . . . then*. The digressive model might be based on the figure of concentric circles radiating outward from a stone dropped in water, or the supposition *what if . . . ?* Suppose a man writing the story of his life tried to recall and make sense of every event in his life? How far back and how far afield would he have to go, and what kinds of problems would he get into? This account of *Tristram Shandy* will indicate that although some suppositions project a coherent teleology, many others do not.

In some cases the suspension of teleology feels like a disappointment or a failure because the terms the narrative projects (intelligible action, purposive agents, and so on) imply a teleology which is never made explicit or even recoverable. In a story like Kurt Vonnegut, Jr.'s "Next Door," the mounting complications seem to portend an anagnorisis which will make them intelligible as a complete action, but instead of such a privileged moment, Vonnegut simply provides additional complications, so that his plot eventually runs down instead of concluding. (The image of falling down the stairs is especially apt here.) This structure is typical of Vonnegut's short fiction—even a story like "Harrison Bergeron," which, although it develops a coherent plot, is, like "Alibi Ike," more tellable as exposition than as development—because Vonnegut, like his character Kilgore Trout, is basically an idea man, a creator of situations which have narrative implications but no narrative teleology.[13] Despite occasional exceptions (e.g., *God Bless You, Mr. Rosewater*), the endings of Vonnegut's novels neither pose nor intend to pose as teleologically definitive. Even when Vonnegut has a polemical axe to grind, as in *Slaughterhouse-Five*, the ending of the novel does not make the polemic any more explicit or emphatic. The difference between Vonnegut's conception of fiction and that of structural analysts is the difference between *what if?* and *if . . . then*. Suppose someone invented a chemical reagent that could bring life on earth to an end and, through a series of mishaps, it did. What then? This suppositional account of *Cat's Cradle* suggests how Vonnegut could have accomplished the remarkable feat of writing an apocalyptic novel without committing himself to any particular teleology—without even being able to bring the novel to an end on the terms of its ideological premise.

Like Vonnegut, Donald Barthelme is primarily an idea man, but one whose forms more successfully display his lack of teleological commitment. His characteristically suppositional method of development might be described as the straight-faced examination of manifold aspects of a given outrageous situation. Suppose a thirty-five-year-old man were inadvertently placed in a sixth-grade class (as in "Me and Miss Mandible"). Suppose a giant balloon appeared one night in Manhattan ("The Balloon"). Suppose a dog fell from a third- (or fourth-) floor window and landed on an artist passing below ("The Falling Dog"). Suppose Edward Lear, foreseeing his own death, turned it into a public event ("The Death of Edward Lear"). Instead of being subjected to a single chosen line of development, the hypothetical situation is typically revolved or considered under different aspects, so that Barthelme's stories often assume the form of meditations. In "Daumier," which provides an unusually full exposition and demonstration of Barthelme's method, the title character escapes from his "insatiable" self by postulating or daydreaming "surrogates" who are "in principle satiable" and involving those surrogates in adventures: "Now in his mind's eye which was open for business at all times . . . Daumier saw a situation." The situation Daumier envisions—a surrogate Daumier acting as a scout for an expedition of *au pair* girls, threatened with capture by marauding Jesuits, across "the plains and pampas of consciousness"—implies no particular line of development, and when the Jesuits eventually capture the girls and lead them off to a convent, Daumier merely switches gears to another, "second person" surrogate.[14]

Instead of using teleological structures and digressing from them, Barthelme often employs forms that do not commit him to the idea of an ending. The first part of his novel *Snow White* ends with a series of self-reflexive multiple-choice questions addressed to the reader. Nearly half the stories collected in *Great Days* take the form of dialogues—a most useful form for Barthelme, because, like the question, it posits a situation without committing itself to any implications about it. Even a story like "On Angels," in which a number of propositions are advanced and debated, is described as "impure speculation" on the implications of its opening sentence: "The death of God left the angels in a strange position" (137, 135). The death of God, by depriving angels of any possible meaning, reduces or purifies them to the status of pure phenomenon, a narrative premise which by its very nature can imply no teleology and indeed no significance. The gathering of information about angels—the story cites accounts by Swedenborg, Gustav Davidson, and Joseph Lyons—illustrates what Barthelme calls "the principle of collage," in the sense that "unlike things are stuck together to make, in the best case, a new reality. This new reality, in the best case, may be or imply a comment on the other reality from which it came, and may be also much else. It's an *itself*, if it's successful: [an] 'anxious object,' which does not know whether it's a work

of art or a pile of junk."[15] The persistence of a vast range of information
about angels in a world which has largely fallen away from belief in God
offers an ideal situation for a collage, for the host of angels, unable now to
mean or do anything significant, can be considered simply as an *itself*. "On
Angels," like most of Barthelme's stories, is antiteleological in the double
sense of shunning commitment to any particular plot development and
even to any particular informing idea or attitude. It is not the case, as in
Cat's Cradle and *Last Year at Marienbad*, of a fictional form undercutting
the expectations it arouses about an intelligible plot and revelation: The
possibility of such development simply does not arise.

If Aristotle's rationale for teleological plots is the belief that the relation
between people and their world is most authoritatively established by
purposive action and its moral consequences, what is the rationale for
Barthelme's antiteleological method of development? In a way the question
is unanswerable, for a rationale is as inimical to Barthelme's collages as
teleological closure. But Barthelme hints at one possible explanation in
"Kierkegaard Unfair to Schlegel," a dialogue between Q and A, in which
A quotes Kierkegaard's *Concept of Irony* to the effect that irony frees its
users, negatively speaking, from its object by "depriving the object of its
reality," so that the speaker "is not bound by what he has said," and an
irony directed against "the whole of existence" gives the speaker a correspondingly vertiginous but exhilarating freedom from an unsatisfactory
world. A rejects Kierkegaard's condemnation of Schlegel's wholesale irony
not on logical grounds but because such a rejection is "interesting" (164–
65). Barthelme's fiction, like A's assertion, is clearly intended as an
interesting, ironic, tellable discourse which makes no commitments to the
hermeneutical logic of the speculations it advances. His antithetical or
agnostic method is displayed most economically in "Nothing: A Preliminary Account," which sets out to define nothing by making an exhaustive
catalogue of things it is not: "It's not the yellow curtains. Nor curtain
rings. Nor is it bran in a bucket, not bran, nor is it the large, reddish farm
animal eating the bran from the bucket, the man who placed the bran in
the bucket, his wife, or the raisin-faced farmer who's about to foreclose on
the farm . . ." (245). Despite the unchallengeable accuracy of such observations and the pleasure they may arouse, what they assert about their
subject is precisely nothing.

But are pieces like "Nothing" really narratives after all? The mis-
cellaneous quality of *Guilty Pleasures*, in which it was first collected,
reveals how Barthelme's stories are often based on, and tend to elide into,
forms outside prose fiction: New Journalism, cartoons, book reviews,
interviews, political satire. The special nature of Barthelme's satires indi-

cates the essentially narrative rhythm in all his work, a rhythm less teleological than suppositional. Barthelme is not a satirist arguing from a well-defined corrective viewpoint like Horace or Molière, nor a romantic ironist like Schlegel, but rather a parodist like S. J. Perelman or Woody Allen. A satire like *Tartuffe* operates according to rules prescribing the inflation of a satiric butt to a climactic point at which his pretensions are deflated; satire thus implies a double teleology, a moral belief and a structural principle. In a more broadly conceived satire like *Joseph Andrews*, in which Lady Booby, Mrs. Slipslop, Parson Adams, and numerous strangers all come in for satiric deflation, the moral belief remains constant—pretension and vanity are always bad, even in so admirable a character as Adams—but the deflation or reversal serves as a smaller and less definite structural unit; if it did not, the novel would end with Fielding's first satiric thrust. A parodist like Woody Allen commits himself to no moral belief at all, because he adopts a voice only to display its potential for contradiction and absurdity. The structural unit of parody is the throwaway joke ("Not only is there no God, but try getting a plumber on weekends"),[16] which acts as a deflation in miniature. In all of Allen's earlier films—in *Bananas,* for example, or *Love and Death*—a situation is established or developed only for the purpose of motivating a series of jokes, and the audience is asked to accept the convention allowing Woody Allen to deliver one punch line after another, revealing each time more knowledge than the character he is portraying, without ever stepping decisively out of the character that makes all the jokes possible. Reversals and deflations are structurally incessant in parodies of this sort, and equally incessant in Barthelme; instead of a single, definitive deflation, we are presented with an unremitting and inveterate reduction of everything described.

There is an important structural difference, however, between Allen's work and Barthelme's. In Allen's parodies and films, the basic compositional unit is the joke with its own discrete aperture and closure, a rising and falling rhythm from exposition to deflation, set-up line to punch line, repeated indefinitely. In Barthelme's best stories—for example, "Daumier," "The Indian Uprising," and "Views of My Father Weeping"—the reductive or parodistic impulse has become so inveterate that there are no punch lines and so no stable and discrete compositional units whatever. Allen's parodistic stance commits him, if not to a moral belief, at least to a given series of comic effects: Anyone who failed to find the jokes in *Love and Death* funny could justly claim his expectations had been disappointed. Barthelme, who declines to make this commitment, incurs another one far more difficult to fulfill: His situations must be worth displaying on their own terms, despite their lack of teleological purpose or point. His stories succeed as anxious objects or not at all, since there is nothing else for them to be.

The structure of Barthelme's fiction may be variously described as digressive (because it resists actantial or semiotic closure), ironic (because it not only avoids but sometimes mocks the possibility of an authoritative teleology), or histrionic (because it displays situations for their own sake and presents itself as a series of anxious objects). The incessant quality of Barthelme's irony, however, suggests that his stories could more precisely and comprehensively be described as discursive, because the structural impulse, which in other satirists is expressed in a rhythm of aperture and closure and in the thematic rationale that rhythm projects, is in Barthelme entirely assimilated into the narrative discourse. Barthelme's stories resist summary because the plots that might be extracted from them give no idea of the nature of their appeal; it is on discursive terms alone that they are tellable. The punch line, in effect, has been shifted to the beginning of the story, in the form of a supposition which motivates the ensuing discourse without making it tellable; for the discourse must remain an anxious object which succeeds or fails without reference to any teleological premise. This discursive anxiety, the story's uneasy shifting between the status of work of art and pile of junk, encapsulates, on the smallest possible scale, the characteristic rhythm of narrative by forcing its audience constantly to consider whether its narrativity is worth the effort. By constantly calling into question their own status as tellable stories, Barthelme's stories, like much postmodern fiction, display the audience's narrativity at its most active.

Most stories, of course, are far less resolutely antiteleological than Barthelme's. As a discursive mode, however, narrative is far more digressive than thematic or dramatic modes, not so much because it accommodates the widest array of disruptive remarks and episodes but because these disruptions are to such an extent what make it tellable, and indeed narrative. Narrative discourse is discursive in two contradictory senses. Like philosophical discourse, it tends toward a logical conclusion, but like conversational discourse, it tends to ramble on indefinitely. Despite the end nearly every story predicates, the end which gives it unitary impact and often makes it tellable, a fundamental wish of every storyteller is to create a world without end.

5
The Polytropic Principle

How can we reconcile the genuinely teleological impulse of narrative with its equally authentic (though not always equally strong) discursive impulse? The suggestion that narrative is doubly discursive, though a rhetorically effective chapter conclusion, is too paradoxical to be of much analytical use. It is more satisfactory to define narrative in the terms which Patricia A. Parker has applied to romance, as "a form which simultaneously quests for and postpones a particular end, objective, or object";[1] but although this dialectical formulation aptly describes the rhythm of the audience's experience of narrative, it establishes the discursive principle in fundamentally negative terms, as a resistance (however constitutive of narrative form) to teleological closure. A comprehensive account of narrative ontology would have to honor the claims of both kinds of discursiveness without seeing digression as simply the antithesis of teleology, for such an antithetical structure renders all ontological hypotheses self-contradictory or trivial. Walter L. Reed, defining the novel in such antithetical terms, as "a long prose fiction which opposes the forms of everyday life, social and psychological, to the conventional forms of literature," and noting its "antagonistic stance toward both the literary canon and toward its own precursors,"[2] argues that such a definition makes it impossible to conceive a poetics of the novel. Mark Spilka, however, comparing Reed's antithesis to "the tension between pattern and contingency" other theorists have attributed to the novel, has pronounced it "rich matter for a poetics."[3] To what extent may this antithesis between teleological closure and discursive openness be integrated in a governing principle of narrative ontology?

From Projection to Retrospection

An obvious focus for the problem of how to integrate the teleological and discursive principles is the double nature of narrative time as succession and integration. In novels like *Middlemarch* and films like *Gone with the Wind* which emphasize the contingency of moments in time, experience seems radically temporal; at the end of such stories, however, the apparently contingent and timebound nature of experience is opposed by an explicitly teleological structure into which experience is assimilated. Thus narrative time is evidently both successive and integrative: Events in a story are conditioned, made psychologically and historically distinctive, by their place in the temporal flux, but ultimately incarnate a timeless *telos*. When Northrop Frye identifies the basis of tragedy as "being in time . . . where all experience vanishes, not merely into the past, but into nothingness, annihilation," so that "death is . . . the essential event that gives shape and form to life," and then adds that "tragedy is also existential . . . the experience of the tragic cannot be contained or moralized within any conceptual world-view,"[4] he is acknowledging the doubleness of time in tragedy, the sense in which it makes every event unique even as it shapes events into actions, lives, history. Frye's emphasis in his study of Shakespearean tragedy is properly teleological or end-oriented. At the end of the last chapter I suggested that a more comprehensive model for narrative would be suppositional or beginning-oriented; but this model is unusually difficult to maintain. Patricia Tobin, whose "genealogical imperative" sounds like a suppositional approach to the structures generated by narrative time (the family establishes itself in time with a sense of meaningful destiny but without intending any specific or foreseeing any ultimate end), adopts an essentially teleological approach: "The novel offers . . . not a mimesis of undeliberated, organic life-in-time, but a homologue that enacts a privileged conceptualization of human life as purposeful and therefore imbued with meaning."[5] In general, recent theorists have tended to emphasize the teleology of narrative over its contingent digressiveness, even though, as Tobin notes, a great deal of recent fiction is antiteleological in design, offering instead of thematic coherence "a plenum of unauthorized connections within an indiscriminate inclusiveness" (207).

Tobin's genealogical imperative seems projective but is really retrospective. The meaning of a given life, which lies not alone in its purposiveness but in its purposiveness as mediated by time, is not available until its conclusion, when ends can be read in the context of an authoritative ending. From the point of view of the characters, authoritative insight is always retrospective, for later judgments, made in the light of deeper and wider experience, can overturn earlier judgments, but not vice versa. But the sequence of actions and perceptions within a narrative is less important in this connection than the sequence of the audience's perceptions and judgments. It might seem that comprehension is equally retrospective in discursive sequence, but this is not really so, for just as the genealogical imperative has both projective and retrospective aspects, discursive sequence is informed both projectively and retrospectively. Robert Champigny, noting that although Barthes's analysis of "Sarrasine" proceeds paragraph by paragraph, often sentence by sentence, it "is obviously informed by an acquaintance with the whole," maintains that "to analyze the text as if one were in the process of reading it for the first time can only be a cumbersome and misleading pretence."[6] As Stanley Fish has argued, however, it would be equally misleading to analyze narrative solely from the perspective of later readings, for "everything a reader does, even if he later undoes it, is a part of the 'meaning experience' and should not be discarded."[7] This is particularly true, for example, of detective stories, which display the ways in which incidents and evidence can be misconstrued by projecting for most of their length an incorrect teleology or resisting any teleology whatever. In rereading a detective story, we reassemble the evidence properly, in the light of the detective's final revelation, but also enjoy watching where we went wrong. Since going wrong *before* being set right is largely the point of detective stories (so that most members of their audience *hope* they will be bamboozled), the first, contingent reading is not merely preliminary to the second, informed reading but is the only reading which provides the sequence of experiences characteristic of the genre. For a very large audience, the first reading of a detective story is the only occasion on which that story is tellable.

In more sophisticated narrative forms the distinction is not primarily between a contingent first reading and an informed second reading, because even the first reading of a given work will be informed by a prospective sense of its teleology. Many theorists, going further, have claimed that purely contingent readings are impossible because the mimetic potency of a given work is systemic, not atomistic: The audience never assimilates narrative data except in relation to their place in a teleological pattern; when such a pattern is withheld, as in the opening paragraph of a novel or the first two minutes of a film, the audience's comprehension, formed only by the most speculative imputations of causality, will suffer.[8] It is certainly true that audiences are constantly hypothesizing or projecting rationales to explain, for example, what the two narratives of *Bleak House* have to do with each other, or why *Strangers on a Train* opens with a series of alternating shots of two men's feet. But this projective sense of teleology is itself contingent and timebound—contingent because it is constantly subject to revision, timebound because it is located in the audience's reading or watching time and cannot be adequately summarized in a thematic, atemporal teleology. For its first thirty minutes, *Psycho* looks as if it will be about Marion Crane's adventures after stealing $40,000 from her employer. An audience who believed this, and who projected a corresponding teleology ("Marion will get caught/crime does not pay" or "Sam will get Marion to return the money/love conquers all"), would be making a mistake, but a mistake which is, as Parker and Fish have argued in other terms, essential to the experience the film is designed to provide. E. D. Hirsch has pointed out that a reader's "interpretation is dependent on the last, unrevised generic conception with which he starts,"[9] but virtually any narrative of any complexity plays with alternative generic affiliations before finally declaring its allegiance to a single genre, and some narratives (*Giles Goat-Boy*, *The Black Prince*) remain generically, and so teleologically, problematic even in their concluding chapters. The commonsense model is probably the most useful here: At the beginning of a story, anything is possible; as the story goes on, some developments are more likely than others; finally, a relatively small number of outcomes (typically one) are acceptable as making the whole story tellable. In this model the audience's projective sense of teleology gradually becomes retrospective as more of the story passes into the audience's own past.[10]

Although contemporary theorists have emphasized the teleological dimension of narrative over its suppositional dimension, several recent discussions of narrative have sought ways to incorporate both dimensions, usually by programmatic oppositions. David L. Minter, anticipating Tobin's genealogical imperative, has analyzed the interpreted design as a structuring principle in American prose, a principle incarnated in two heroes, an active, projective designer (Jay Gatsby, Thomas Sutpen) and a relatively passive, introspective observer (Nick Carraway, Quentin Compson) who discovers a teleology in the first hero's life ironically at variance with his original design. Active, optimistic, essentially naive heroes like Gatsby and Sutpen, seeing their world as a place of unlimited personal potential, fail because their suppositions are defeated by the tragic consequences of being in time—a lesson which comprises the wisdom of interpreters like Nick and Quentin. This wisdom has the authority of retrospection, but in its analytical detachment entails an inevitable loss (as in Nick's case) or is secured only through an identification which traps the interpreter himself fatally in time (as in Quentin's).[11] Martin Price, in defining the fictional contract in terms of games and models, seeks to describe the way "the shaping of experience frees it from immediacy as it is given form; we move from immersion to reflection, from temporal anxiety to spatial comprehension."[12] What makes a game tellable or playable is the radically temporal and contingent experience of playing: Retrospective accounts of Monopoly games would be of little interest, and chess players usually resign when the outcome of the game is clear. The value of a model, on the other hand, is retrospective: If a story is to tell us about our world, it is best grasped through its fullest articulation. Hence readers typically pass from experiencing stories as games to experiencing them as models.

Other critics have focused more narrowly on the nature of narrative time. Leo Braudy contends that the two most significant ways American culture assimilates information to a reassuring order are through "catastrophic time" and "soap-opera time." Catastrophic time is millenial or eschatological: "There are beginnings and ends, but no middles; significant moments, but no connecting history; no change or growth, only the possibility of being born again." In soap operas, by contrast, "stories . . . have innumerable crises, but all those significant moments are subordinate to the format of continuity itself."[13] The catastrophic imagination projects an apocalypse based on dogma; the soap-opera imagination projects an unending series of crises which can never be authoritatively understood. In the first case, teleological revelation is imminent; in the second, it is immanent. But both conceptions of time deny the possibility of temporal development, the link between action and consequence, Aristotle took as the basis of dramatic representation. Frank Kermode attempts to link the perspectives of temporality and eternity by invoking Aquinas's concept of *aevum*, the time in which the angels live and act without changing or dying, a time "between *nunc movens* with its beginning and end, and *nunc stans*, the perfect possession of endless life." *Aevum*, suggests Kermode, "is the time-order of novels. Characters in novels are independent of time and succession, but may and usually do seem to operate in time and succession," for *aevum* "is a mode in which things can be perpetual without being eternal," a mode which presents "an image of endlessness consistent with a temporal end."[14]

These attempts to define the relation between a purely linear or successive notion of narrative time and a spatialization of narrative time through some privileged teleology are based on an observation about the nature of our most fundamental interest in stories. Even when we read a story for the first time, as Price points out, we hope "we are not simply following the story but appreciating its development" (19). In playing a game of chess or watching the Super Bowl, we are not normally interested merely in the outcome (teleology as the principle of tellability), nor in a linear sequence of events (discursiveness as the principle of tellability). Our interest is in the process whereby a teleology emerges from apparently contingent events, the evolving shape of a chess or football game as a retrospective pattern emerges from a clash of designs. We wait intently for this pattern to emerge, but as soon as it becomes unmistakable, our interest lapses: Down two pieces, we resign the chess game; seeing a score of 41-7, we leave the stadium in the third quarter. Paul Ricoeur, distinguishing between the two ways in which narratives are recovered— episodically, as a series of events, and configurationally, in terms of an informing teleological pattern—concludes that "the humblest narrative is always more than a chronological series of events and that in turn the configurational dimension cannot overcome the episodic dimension without suppressing the narrative structure itself." Following Heidegger, Ricoeur argues that storytelling is itself constitutive of human time, because it "brings us back from within-time-ness to historicality, from 'reckoning with' time to 'recollecting' it. As such, the narrative function provides a transition from within-time-ness to historicality."[15] This transition is the heart of a narrative's narrativity; it is what all narratives by definition display: the emergence of historicality or teleology from linear sequence by virtue of the audience's projections of causality and intentionality. The nature of these projections, and the conclusiveness with which they are resolved, will naturally depend on the relative importance of teleological and discursive impulses within a given narrative; but a story whose end was immediately and everywhere apparent or which made no commitments, however minimal or frequently disappointed, to an intelligible ending would fail either to arouse or to reward our narrativity and so would be no story at all.

It would seem then that in terms of what stories characteristically display—the intimation of an emergent discursive order rather than its explicit announcement or analysis—the narrative imagination and the integrations it authorizes are projective rather than retrospective; retrospective teleology is a special case (the dramatic case) of the more or less contingent configurational projections audiences make from moment to moment in order to make narratives tellable. This essentially projective quality of narrative apprehension and integration, which follows from the suppositional nature of storytelling, is often obscured by the choice of the novel, with its frequent emphasis on formal closure, as narrative paradigm. But it becomes clearer if we choose as a paradigm autobiography, for example *The Education of Henry Adams*.

In a 1908 letter to Henry James, Adams distinguishes Augustine's *Confessions* from the autobiographies of Cardinal de Retz, Rousseau, Cellini, and Gibbon, on the grounds that "St. Augustine alone has an idea of literary form,—a notion of writing a story with an end and object, not for the sake of the object, but for the form, like a romance."[16] To be sure, the

Education is everywhere informed by Adams's object: "To help young men. . . . react, not at haphazard, but by choice, on the lines of force that attract their world" (314). But Adams's project is far more problematical than Augustine's, for instead of working "from multiplicity to unity," he has to work "back from unity to multiplicity" (xxvii–xxviii). Hence the term *education* incessantly ramifies in meaning as the book progresses, even as its meaning in Adams's own life becomes more obscure.

Adams seeks an education at Harvard, in Washington, at the Court of St. James. His disappointment is the leading note of the first half of his story; the only "useful education" (195) he acquires takes the form of disillusionment with friends, admired models, moral and political beliefs, and himself. After taking a post teaching history at Harvard and editing the *North American Review*, Adams concludes: "Of all his many educations, Adams thought that of a school-teacher the thinnest. Yet he was forced to admit that the education of an editor, in some ways, was thinner still." With this perception, "Henry Adams's education, at his entry into life, stopped, and his life began" (307–8). He tells of meeting Clarence King on a journey to the American West and of his decision to return to Harvard. The following chapter, beginning "twenty years after," passes over the time Adams sought to apply the education he had acquired and resumes when "he had finished, and could sum up the result" (314–15). Instead of describing the actions or work that issued from his education, Adams uses the educational process as a figure for the effort to impose human images of intention and belief upon a world of inhuman force—an effort ultimately unauthorized and futile. Contemplating the relation of the Virgin, who "had acted as the greatest force the Western world had ever felt, and had drawn man's activities to herself more than any other person" (388), and the dynamo displayed at the Paris Exposition in 1900 as a new symbol of "ultimate energy" (380), Adams despairs of establishing any objective scientific or historical authority for the connections whereby he must order his world: "Between the dynamo in the gallery of machines and the engine-house outside, the break of continuity amounted to an abysmal fracture for a historian's objects. No more relation could he discover between the steam and the electric current than between the Cross and the cathedral. The forces were interchangeable if not reversible, but he could see only an absolute *fiat* in electricity as in faith" (381). Given his consequent inability to find authorization for his imputation of causal sequence—"where he saw sequence, other men saw something quite different, and no one saw the same unit of measure" (382)—Adams surrenders the claim of history to objective validity: "If he was bound to reduce all these forces to a common value, this common value could have no measure but that of their attraction on his own mind. He must treat them as they had been felt; as convertible, reversible, interchangeable attractions on thought" (383).

The *Education* is thus doubly a story of unknowing: the story of Adams's own failure to achieve an adequate education except in negative terms, as receptivity to the forces unleashed around him, and the story of the historian's retreat into radical subjectivity as his only authorization for imputing causality and sequence. The self is offered as the only guarantee of historical interpretation even as the historian is dissolved into "the sum of the forces that attract him" (474). Adams's life and mind recede in definition as they grow in importance, for he is simultaneously purposive and reflective, capable of intending and receiving patterns in his education, and reducible to "the function of assimilating and storing outside force or forces" (487). Because Adams's story, though apparently recounting the development of his own capacity for informed action, has as its object a theory of history which would render all action reaction, Adams's consciousness takes other forms: an exhaustion of educational possibilities, an inveterately ironic tone, the example of the second law of thermodynamics, a book called *The Education of Henry Adams*. It may sound paradoxical to say that Adams deconstructs himself as a potency for purposive action only to reconstruct himself as a discursive function, but this paradox, this incessant and incessantly incomplete movement from life-experience as project to life-experience as retrospect, is quintessentially narrative. Always, evidently, at the point of discovering and revealing the pattern in his education, what makes him himself, Adams constantly generalizes the terms on which he poses this question so that the events of his life are gradually made exemplary without ever becoming explicit—without indeed admitting the possibility of any teleology better defined than infinite acceleration and infinite expansion.

What Novels Display

Few autobiographies have the formal elegance of the *Education*, in which the project (to obtain and elucidate an education which would make Adams capable of purposive reaction to outside forces) and the retrospective teleology (all human experience, including Adams's, is shaped by constantly accelerating forces of which intelligence is a product rather than a director) effectively annul or deauthorize each other. This conflict between projective and retrospective orders is, however, the fundamental structural principle of autobiography, a principle aptly described by Michael McCanles's analysis of fictional structure in terms of the chief agent's errant actions or perceptions: "The mythos he generates . . . results . . . from his resistance to the total vision of the system."[17] But the total vision of an autobiographical work, however compelling it may seem to its author, is inevitably less univocal and authoritative for an audience than (say) the total vision of Aristotelian tragedy, for the audience is always aware of the arbitrary selectiveness (the omission of certain incidents as immaterial, the choice of a privileged moment in which to write) which makes the teleology of any autobiography contingent. It is not simply a question, as in *Oedipus* or *Hamlet*, of a true order establishing itself against any false order which the opening of the work presents: Our knowledge about the incessantly retrospective and revisionary operation of memory makes it far more difficult to accept the autobiographer's final order as simply true.

Do narratives more closely resemble autobiography or tragedy in this respect? I have argued that most narratives tend to undermine or attenuate their teleological imperative more radically than McCanles's formula (for example) acknowledges. The conflict between the teleological and the discursive impulses, which produces the suppositional stories of Vonnegut and Barthelme and the contingent patterns in romantic and postromantic autobiography, takes a different form in novels and films. If the philosophical presupposition underlying tragedy is the belief that people have the power through deliberate action to change their relation to the world, novels and films often give equal or greater prominence to the belief that the weight of circumstance on even the most resolute agents precludes the possibility of change. "People can change," Fellini's prostitute Cabiria (Giulietta Masina) tells the man who has asked to marry her, and adds, "I'm going to be happy at last." But even as she says this—in part *because* she says this—we grow more certain that this man too, like all the others, only wants to use her, as indeed he does. In *Nights of Cabiria* the denial of change is specifically a denial of religious conversion. When Cabiria responds with skepticism to Brother Giovanni's assertion that anyone with God's grace in his heart is content, Fellini is implicitly presenting her own natural grace, her wholehearted acceptance of her adventures despite constant disappointments, as an alternative. Her transfiguration, the product of an immanent rather than a transcendent grace, represents the highest value in those novels or films explicitly or implicitly agnostic.

The novel as a form tends to focus on the conflict between an idealistic agent and an agnostic world. Characters like Anna Karenina, Mr. Pickwick, and Dorothea Brooke project certain desires, impulses, and plans onto the world of social circumstance. The world resists these projects, and the resulting conflict leads to the agent's defeat by custom or circumstance (as in *Anna Karenina*), the agent's victory over his circumstance (as in *Pickwick Papers*), or a compromise between the agent and her world (as in *Middlemarch*). Lionel Trilling has traced this conflict, the opposition between an idealistic or visionary hero and a world thick with social appearances, customs, and circumstances, back to *Don Quixote*, which incorporates "two different and opposed notions of reality." From the empirical point of view of the external world, "the world of ordinary practicality *is* reality in its fullness. It is the reality of the present moment in all its powerful immediacy of hunger, cold, and pain, making the past and the future, and all ideas, of no account." Set against this empirical notion of reality is a more idealistic, subjective, purposive notion of reality which implies that "the world of tangible reality is not the real reality after all. The real reality is rather the wildly conceiving, the madly fancying mind of the Don: people change, practical reality changes, when they come into its presence."[18]

Trilling's analysis raises several points important in placing the novel within the general context of narrative. First, the conflict between self and world is for him more properly a conflict between different ways of conceiving the world: externally, as a catalogue of the momentary experiences, conventional manners, and expressive customs which compose our collective experience, and internally, as the projection of idealistic or imaginative impulses toward extraordinary actions or perceptions. Second, the relative strength of these two notions of reality, which varies from one novel to the next and even within a given novel, depends on their formative power, their ability each to impose itself on the other, so that *Sentimental Education* presents an ultimately circumstantial account of Frédéric Moreau's world, whereas *The Charterhouse of Parma* endorses a conceptual or idealistic notion of reality by showing Fabrice's ultimate victory over mundane circumstances. Third, the circumstantial and idealistic notions of reality underlie respectively the discursive and teleological imperatives. Circumstantial reality, as Trilling points out, is quotidian, unremarkable, and relatively unchanging: It is the nature of the external world, social or sensory, to go on forever. Imaginative or idealistic reality, by contrast, is extraordinary, disruptive, and generally purposive and progressive, issuing most often in dramatic action.[19]

Trilling's formulation has been most influential in its application to American fiction. After defining the novel as "a perpetual quest for reality, the field of its research being always the social world, the material of its analyses being always manners as the indication of the direction of man's soul," Trilling concludes that "the novel as I have described it has never established itself in America" because "American writers of genius have not turned their minds to society" (205–6). A great deal of subsequent debate on American fiction has turned on the question of its deviance from the social or empirical norm Trilling establishes.[20] But Trilling's original opposition between self and world establishes social reality not as a norm but as one pole of an actantial and hermeneutical dialectic: There has never been, logically or historically, a single normative treatment of that dialectical opposition. In English novels—in the work of Fielding, Austen, Scott, Thackeray, Dickens, Eliot, and Conrad—the conflict most often results in a compromise, because society is comprehensive and flexible enough to embody the ideals of most heroes and heroines if these ideals can be made less challenging to the social order. (*Middlemarch*, with its programmatic multiple plots tracing the compromise of idealistic impulses in the face of intransigent social reality, is the classic instance of this pattern.) But as Richard Chase points out, "the American novel tends to rest in contradictions and among extreme ranges of experience"; it is "less interested in incarnation and reconciliation than in alienation and disorder."[21] The English novel, which is essentially comic, displays the prospects for accord between the hero and his world, between idealistic and empirical ways of understanding the world; the American novel, which is essentially tragic, displays the impossibility of overcoming or resolving this polarization.

Broadly speaking, English novels place greater emphasis on the empirical, American novels on the idealistic, poles in Trilling's formulation. The real point of my discussion, however, is not to distinguish precisely between the cultural thematics of English and American novels but to indicate their common project: to display the attempt, however successful, to make these two ways of understanding the world, empirical and subjective, consonant with each other by translating empirical details, apparently inconsequential observations, perfunctory remarks, habits of dress or behavior, and immediate physical sensations into an intelligible whole. The novel, which is the most concerned of all literary genres to render the texture of quotidian experience, the circumstantial thickness of ordinary life (so that individual sights and sounds and smells play a much more prominent role in *Barnaby Rudge* than in *The Ring and the Book*) and at the same time to render the formative operation of consciousness, which is constantly shaping empirical experience into intelligible structures, is essentially a problematic mode, for it mediates between two modes of perception on whose uniqueness it continues to insist. But this opposition appears in other narrative modes as well, for example in the pursuit and deferral of a goal Parker finds characteristic of romance or in the agnostic movement away from a false order characteristic of short stories. In ritual tragedy, human experience is displayed *sub specie aeternitatis:* Every word and gesture is significant in what it will lead to, and its final meaning is in

its final consequences. Experience in narrative modes, whether autobiography, saga, film, romance, short story, or novel, is displayed at once
sub specie aetis and *sub specie aeternitatis*, with neither perspective assumed
to be more valid than the other. Narrative takes the long perspective, but
unlike tragedy does not necessarily take it as final.

Odysseus Polutropos

As the paradigmatic narrative structure is doubly discursive, projecting
and deferring closure, the exemplary narrative hero is the person most
open to experience but best able to shape his own actions and ends. In
Eastern narrative the exemplary narrative heroes are Scheherezade and her
surrogate Sindbad. In Western narrative the exemplary narrative is the
Odyssey; the exemplary narrative hero, echoed by such diverse figures as
Aeneas, Don Quixote, Don Juan, and Huckleberry Finn, is Odysseus.

The *Odyssey* has a well-defined goal: the return of Odysseus to his
homeland. It begins, however, by announcing as its subject not an action
or theme like the anger of Achilles and its consequences but a man who has
many adventures after the sack of Troy. From the very beginning, the
action of the poem and its hero are defined in terms of each other. Despite
its clear progress to its goal, the *Odyssey* is so ordered that the very idea of
homecoming is rendered problematic. The opening situation in Ithaca—
Penelope besieged by suitors, Telemachus denied his birthright—clearly
demands the return of Odysseus. But when has Odysseus truly returned?
When Homer first presents him in Ogygia in Book V, he is already
almost home; his arrival on Phaeacia, where he reveals his identity to
Alcinous, who promises to send him home, brings him still nearer his goal.
But when the Phaeacian ship lands on Ithaca in Book XIII, Odysseus is
asleep; awakening, he cannot even recognize the land without Athena's
help. Does the landing, or the recognition, constitute his homecoming?
Perhaps it comes still later, in his revelation of his identity to his son, or his
return to the palace, or his stringing the bow, or his defeat of the suitors, or
his acknowledgment by Penelope, or the night spent with her in the olive-
tree bed. These multiple rituals of homecoming suggest that as Odysseus
approaches his goal, it recedes before him. It is not enough to return to
Ithaca—after he lands there, halfway through the poem, the pace slows
accordingly—he must establish his sovereignty there by compelling the
public acceptance of his authority. In a fundamental sense his homecoming is not complete until Athena sets terms of peace with the suitors'
relatives in Book XXIV, preventing the continuation of an endless cycle of
vengeance.

To say that Odysseus's homecoming depends on his establishing his identity does not make the *Odyssey* a *Bildungsroman* about a middle-aged veteran of a long war who comes of age in the course of the poem. The figure who comes of age is of course Telemachus, who in making voyages, gathering news, keeping secrets, and fighting like his father, displays a younger version of Odysseus. To display Odysseus's identity through such multiple versions (his homecoming, his reputation, his family, his many disguises, his storytelling) is indeed the project of the *Odyssey*. Because Odysseus's return is defined by his displaying more and more clearly the identity he already has, the poem's plot is constantly informed by the question of how it feels and what it means to be Odysseus.

Homer's first epithet for the hero, the word by which he identifies him even before using his name, is *polutropos*, "many-turning," which Homer's translators have variously rendered as versatile, resourceful, wide-ranging, ready at need, and skilled in many ways. The word has two main senses: Like Don Juan and the Wife of Bath, Odysseus is both endlessly receptive to adventures and unusually skilled at turning them to his own ends. The episode in Polyphemus's cave shows that Odysseus is a master of the dangerous situations he courts. Only Odysseus could have devised an escape from his imprisonment—an escape typically dependent on his concealing his identity by calling himself Noman and hiding under a sheep—and only Odysseus, with his boundless appetite for adventure and worldly experience, would have needed to.

When Odysseus's men turn from their ultimate goal of returning to Ithaca, it is because they have forgotten that goal (as in the land of the Lotus-Eaters), or been tricked by others more clever (the Lestrygonians), or given in to their lower impulses (the animal craving for food and sex that makes them vulnerable to Circe's spell). The weeping of Odysseus's companions when they are transformed from animals back into men indicates how hard it is to be a man in Homer's world, how great is the temptation to become simply an animal. As his dalliance with Circe shows, Odysseus himself has a robustly animal nature, but his nature is governed by an abiding sense of means and ends which expresses itself most often in the self-control his companions lack. Before taking Circe to bed, Odysseus, acting on Hermes' advice, is careful to make her promise not to trick or enchant him, for such an enchantment, such a loss of control, would literally unman him. Odysseus's own deviations from his homeward course are most often delays imposed upon him (like his imprisonment by Calypso) or expressions of his desire for adventure rather than lapses into his animal appetites. When he wishes to indulge these appetites—when he shares Circe's bed or hears the Sirens' song—he has been careful to follow the best advice and protect himself in advance from being unmanned.

Odysseus thus incorporates within himself both teleological and discursive impulses in his desire to reach his homeland and his appetite for adventures along the way. Although all the men in Odysseus's world—his companions, his various hosts, the suitors who would supplant him— share certain appetites, the brutish appetite of the Cyclops is much less human than the refined appetite of Alcinous or the love of ritual Telemachus finds in Nestor and Menelaus. Ritual transforms the appetite for food into the enjoyment of feasting because it is more pious, in Kenneth Burke's terms,[22] more intimately in touch with the sources of one's humanity (specifically one's relation to the gods).

The distinction between eating and feasting is like that between the adventures of Odysseus's crew, which are on the whole misfortunes visited upon them by their own appetites, and the adventures of Odysseus, which are a means to a chosen end. Odysseus's companions are incapable of controlling their impulsiveness, their hunger, or their distrustful curiosity: They refuse to leave the island of the Cicones in time to avoid a battle, slaughter the cattle of Helios, and open Aeolus's bag of winds while Odysseus is overcome by the irresistible desire for sleep. Faced with the need to pass either Scylla or Charybdis, no one but Odysseus would have been capable of accepting in advance the lesser misfortune. Odysseus's mourning for the loss of his companions is usually perfunctory because they are literally not worth saving; they do not have the sense of teleological purpose that would affirm their humanity by bringing them home. Odysseus's love of adventure is rooted in his higher appetites, his unquenchable desire for the knowledge of new places. It is this love of adventure, together with his ability to see adventures through to a chosen end, that makes him *polutropos*—that makes him, unlike the children, fools, and beasts his companions and the suitors resemble, fully human.

When Calypso, commanded by Hermes to release Odysseus, asks Odysseus why he wishes to give up an immortal existence with her to return home, he can give no logical answer. Penelope is less beautiful than Calypso, he admits, and some god may have marked him for further disaster at sea. Even so, he longs to return home. This speech, only Odysseus's second in the poem, defines his human identity in terms directly opposed to those in which Homer defines the hero of the *Iliad*. Like the heroes of Athenian tragedy, Achilles feels trapped in his mortality, caught in a position that requires him to choose between a long, ignominious life and a moment of heroic glory. Odysseus's relation to his mortality is rather comic than tragic: Offered the possibility of genuine immortality, he chooses instead, and willingly, an identity defined by his prowess within the mortal limitations he is constantly testing and seeking to extend. In displaying Odysseus as *polutropos*, the complete human being, the *Odyssey* is a celebration of mortality.

It is true that Odysseus is frequently aided by the gods, especially Athena. But his intimacy with Athena is one more sign of the piety that makes him more human than the brutal suitors. The gods' intercession in Odysseus's voyage, whether the storms Poseidon rains upon him or the help he receives from Hermes and Athena, seems designed always to test him to his utmost limit. Hermes orders Calypso to release Odysseus but neither sends him magically home nor assures him a safe voyage—not, surely, because Odysseus needs at this point in his adventures to establish his heroic credentials, but because enduring adversity and turning it to his ends is what makes Odysseus most fully himself, what best displays the mortality in which he rejoices. After Odysseus is shipwrecked off the coast of Phaeacia, Ino gives him a veil that keeps him afloat for three days, Athena stills all of Poseidon's winds but one which brings him to land, and the river god gives him a safe landing. Even so, it is Odysseus, not his divine patrons, who is responsible for his success: Athena and the others have made the voyage just easy enough to be possible for him alone.

Odysseus has been freed from Calypso in order to return home, but in terms of both the meaning of his homecoming and the display of the mortal identity which defines that meaning, it would be more accurate to say that Odysseus is freed to be Odysseus, to display his identity to the poem's audience even as he is establishing it to numerous audiences within the poem. It is in this sense that Schiller is correct in observing Homer's goal as "already present at every point in his progress."[23] The "retarding element" Goethe and Schiller remark in Homer is not a deferral of teleology but an incarnation of teleology, a way of making Odysseus's end immanent. Achilles' dilemma is tragic because his every action is referred to his impending death; although he does not die in the course of the *Iliad*, he comes to see himself as already dead. Odysseus, by contrast, sees himself as always and everywhere alive because his ultimate goal, the goal which gives his life meaning, is not death but homecoming, an end that is his chosen end. It is not merely that Odysseus attaches an absolute value to both his goal and the adventures that retard it. The goal and the adventures are the same, two complementary figures, teleological and discursive, for the world which imposes on him the responsibility, and offers him the opportunity, to be himself. Just as Odysseus is *polutropos*, his world, and the world of narrative in general, is polytropic, requiring and rewarding at once the hero's acceptance and mastery of adventure, proceeding to an end whose authority paradoxically confers an absolute value on contingent experience, arousing the audience's expectation of ultimate revelation only to suggest that the greatest wisdom is to submit to the imperatives of an unending story. Polytropy, the movement which incorporates both senses of the term *discursive,* is at once the general theme of narrative and its distinctive technique.

Two Redactions of Homer

The *Odyssey* is exemplary in its polytropic synthesis of teleological and discursive impulses. Although polytropy is the constitutive technical and thematic feature of narrative, few storytellers integrate these contrary impulses in the same way as Homer because cultural conceptions of human identity vary widely. Epic poets, drawing directly upon Homeric models, are especially likely to correct or improve Homer, writing the epic he would have written given their view of human experience. But even poets whose heroic ethic differs sharply from Homer's, who have the greatest disagreement about what it means to be human, still offer a polytropic account of human experience. Virgil and Dante, though breaking with Homer's view of the relation between self and world, continue to define that relation in polytropic terms.

   In Homer, Odysseus's homecoming is comic because it confirms the identity he has displayed (often by wily dissimulation) all along: His impulses toward home and toward further adventure are essentially the same. But Aeneas is a tragic figure who, lacking his predecessor's paradoxical unity, displays strong impulses both toward and against his goal (the founding of Lavinium, ultimately of the Roman people) which project two identities he cannot integrate. Unlike Odysseus, who is returning to the land of his youth, his family, and his people—that is, to relations which affirm his identity—Aeneas is journeying away from his home to an unknown destination. He tends to define his personal identity in terms of a dead past, in terms of his losses. Instead of emphasizing a motivic return like Odysseus's, Virgil emphasizes the motivic departure from Troy in Book II. This is not to say that Aeneas's journey has no teleology; from the gods' point of view, and the future empire's, the teleological impulse is primary. But from Aeneas's point of view this teleology is obscure. He never knows very far in advance where he is going, frequently loses his way, and is always (first literally, then figuratively) more truly a wanderer than Odysseus. Aeneas's own temperamental affinity for the dead past rather than the unknown future, apparent even in his first speech in the poem, defines his journey in suppositional rather than teleological terms, a story shaped by its beginning rather than its end.

Virgil's critique of Homeric heroism is first made explicit in Book II. The canny resourcefulness of the Achaeans here shows as treachery and deceitfulness; the fighting ability of Achilles' son Pyrrhus, who forces his way into Priam's sanctuary to slaughter Priam's son Polites and then the aged Priam himself, is savage brutality. Homer had provided some precedent for this view of heroic *areté*, for example Odysseus's killing of the spy Dolon and Achilles' refusal to spare his prisoners' lives. In general, however, Virgil takes roughly the same view of Homer's heroes that Homer takes of Odysseus's companions: For all their skill in battle, these men are not men but impious beasts lacking the capacity for piety that would make them human. The contrasting Trojan hero is of course *pius Aeneas* (I.378),[24] a man faithful ultimately to the gods, to his nation, and to his destiny. Although Odysseus's return to Ithaca would be a boon for his family and his people, and although he tries repeatedly to save his companions, he is a fundamentally self-centered hero whose personal welfare happens to coincide with social justice, and whose destiny to return home provides him with the opportunity to affirm his own identity. Aeneas's destiny is external to his nature and antipathetic to his personal desires, but he remains piously loyal to it, giving up the personal relations (to Creüsa, to Anchises, to Dido) which define him as husband, son, and lover in exchange for political relations (to Lavinia, to Evander, to Pallas) which define him as an ally and founder of a nation. Aeneas remains close to his son Ascanius, who will continue the Teucrian succession, but his only speech to him (XII.435–40) defines their relationship in abstractly pious terms as well.

In presenting an epic hero whose personal sacrifices made his destiny tragic, Virgil might have drawn on the model of Achilles, whose overwhelming awareness of his coming death makes him a tragic hero. But unlike Achilles, whose tragedy is existential, and whose life suggests that the curve of any life, of life itself, is tragic, Aeneas has the specific disability of having to act in historical time. Aeneas's historical awareness takes several ironic forms. His wish to marry Turnus's promised bride makes him in effect a second Paris, and he is constantly described as recapitulating the fall of Troy. He is therefore troubled by a recurrent sense of *déjà vu*, a suspicion that what he takes to be his present situation is only a repetition of Troy's doomed past. Virgil presents several detailed historical prophecies, most strikingly on Aeneas's shield in Book VIII, but Aeneas either does not hear or fails to understand them. The glorious future of his descendants is too obscure to give him much pleasure.

The shield presents future events as already in the past; in his account of the fall of Troy, Aeneas frequently presents the past as future, but his awareness of the fate that makes past and future interchangeable is historical rather than existential. When he describes Priam as *moriturus* (II.511), he is not referring to the human condition or saying that war has no real survivors; he is simply reading his retrospective knowledge of Priam's death back into an earlier situation. The specifically historical quality of this irony depends on Aeneas's, but more generally on Virgil's, double vision of events in time: as they appear at the moment they occur, and as they appear from the vantage of a later perspective, when their results are known. This double vision, which is the structural basis of autobiography, is fundamental to Virgil's ironic version of Homer's polytropy. From the temporal perspective of Aeneas's errors, deprivations, and sufferings, he is a pitifully diminished remnant of his Trojan self; from the historical perspective of Virgil and his audience, he is the revered father of the world's greatest empire. Instead of assimilating either of these perspectives, which correspond respectively to the discursive and teleological impulses, into the other, Virgil constantly plays them off against each other by measuring the success of the new Troy in terms of its costs.

The most obvious of these costs are paid by Aeneas's enemies, especially Turnus, who loses his bride and his life to a destiny he understands even less than Aeneas. Turnus is the last of Virgil's Homeric heroes, and in ending the poem with his death Virgil shows the passing of the old order before the profoundly equivocal piety of Aeneas. Originally the unwitting victim of Allecto's firebrand, Turnus has his own brand of integrity: He protests the loss of Lavinia as unreasonable and unjust (IX.136–44). As the fighting continues, however, Turnus is overcome by his own savagery, repeatedly associated with images of wild animals and fire which indicate his calamitously destructive bestiality, and ultimately dehumanized and corrupted to such a point that he sets an ambush for Aeneas in Book XI and flees from single combat in Book XII.

Nor are the Trojans themselves immune from the corruption of fighting. In Book IX, Nisus and Euryalus, on a night mission to warn Aeneas to return from Pallanteum, forget their goal in their lust for spoils and killing and are themselves killed. Earlier, when Nisus had first thought of volunteering for this mission, he asked Euryalus whether the gods put such fire into their hearts or whether each man became his own god (IX.184–85). The question precisely focuses Virgil's polytropic irony. If the gods put the desire for glory into men's hearts, then men in obeying this desire are simply the pious agents of destiny. If men themselves make their desires into gods, they are mere killers like the tyrant Mezentius, who calls his right hand his god (X.773). Does the heroic behavior of warriors in battle make them most selflessly human or most savagely inhuman? For Virgil, both answers are equally true.

Even pious Aeneas is most human when he is least human, especially when he finally joins the battle in Book X. His victory over Lucagus occasions the remarkable line, "With bitter words, pious Aeneas taunts him" (*quem pius Aeneas dictis adfatur amaris*, X.591).[25] Like Turnus, Aeneas is increasingly compared to animals and fire; Virgil finally presents him *furiis accensus* (XII.946) at the sight of Pallas's belt, engraved with a picture of fifty slaughtered bridegrooms. In avenging Pallas and Priam's fifty murdered sons, Aeneas is in fact killing another bridegroom, Turnus himself. The poem ends, not only without a triumphant postlude to Turnus's death, but even without any explanation of what it means for Aeneas to have killed him, whether he has decisively confirmed or denied his humanity. Evidently he has done both. Aeneas does not represent a *via media* which is human in some ways but inhuman in others; he is, paradoxically, each in proportion as he is the other, for just as it is his glorious destiny which makes his personal life essentially void, it is his very piety which makes him savage.

Virgil's critique of Homer's polytropy is an ironic demonstration that the claims of personal responsibility transcend the welfare of the individual and are ultimately irreconcilable with personal welfare: Aeneas is unable to integrate, for example, his passionate wish to remain in Carthage with Dido with the fate that makes him the head of an empire. Dante's critique of Homer is also ironic, but in a different way. Dante does not claim that Odysseus too easily integrates irreconcilable tendencies inherent in human nature, but that his integration is superficial and inadequate. Like Virgil, Dante rules that Homer's conception of Odysseus omits a crucial range of human experience and responsibility. But since this responsibility is to an infinitely wise, just, and unchanging God rather than to his nation or his historical destiny, Dante dramatizes, not the likelihood of his hero's disintegration, but the possibility of a more comprehensive integration than Homer ever considers.

Dante's critique of Homer is of course most explicit in *Inferno* XXVI, when the pilgrim Dante meets Ulysses burning with Diomedes among the false counselors. Dante's Ulysses, who is being punished specifically for having devised the scheme of the Trojan horse, is a man who abdicated from his responsibilities as husband, father, son, and lord to pervert his guile in battle against the Trojans, founders of the empire which prefigured and fostered the Church. What is germane here, however, is not Ulysses' overt sins but the limitations of his virtues, limitations which make them sins as well. Even after he returned home, Ulysses tells Dante and Virgil, he could not restrain his passion for worldly experience. Urging his crew on his ill-fated final voyage not to deny the experience of the uninhabited world, he invoked their human heritage and the brief period of time allotted to them: "*Fatti non foste a viver come bruti, / ma per seguir virtute e canoscenza"* (119–20).[26] In his eagerness to elevate himself above the lower animals, Ulysses overreaches himself; he makes worldly experience an absolute goal and persuades his followers to do the same. Lacking any conception of a teleological order outside his own sensations, Ulysses reduces each new adventure to a new digression whose value is solely that of sensation or spectacle. When a mountain looms in the distant sea, the crew is delighted with the promise of a new adventure because they do not realize that Purgatory represents an order which makes the value of worldly adventure problematic. This mountain cannot be climbed by human will or prowess, but only by integrating the discursive human impulse to adventure with the teleological divine impulse to a moral order, as Dante does at the beginning of this canto when he says he is controlling his own powers more closely than he would like lest they run where virtue does not guide them (21–22).

It might seem that Dante's own example and method would not be polytropic because the need always to bend one's actions to God's authority would produce a poem dominated by its teleology. And certainly the scenes Dante visits, which show the final disposition of souls after death, are resolutely end-oriented. In a sense Dante's method of presentation in the *Inferno* and the *Paradiso* is based not on polytropy but on what might be called incarnational teleology, dramatizing the temporal nature and identity of people by predicting how they will act in an eternal and unchanging afterlife. But just as Ulysses trivializes all experience by treating life as a series of adventures, simply assimilating temporal impulses to a divine teleology would deny the intrinsic value of human action. Dante mediates between these two kinds of devaluation by defining experience polytropically—by overdetermining it, in Freudian terms—as tellable simultaneously on its own contingent terms and as an incarnation of God's will.

This polytropic perspective is clearest in the *Purgatorio*, where Dante is presenting souls not enjoying their final rewards or enduring their final punishments but incessantly in motion, converting from sinfulness to divine love. Just as Odysseus's ability to determine and proceed to an end makes his trials in Homer different from his companions' sufferings, the suffering in the *Purgatorio* is different from that in the *Inferno*: It is chosen, willed, an Aristotelian action (with a beginning, middle, and end which Francis Fergusson has analyzed in detail).[27] Virgil's speeches on love in *Purgatorio* XV–XVIII make it clear that the freedom to act cannot be the freedom simply to follow one's own inclinations because those inclinations are themselves tropisms toward love, whether that love leads finally to God (like Dante's love for Beatrice) or to destruction (like Ulysses' love for adventure and worldly wisdom). To act deliberately entails a constant choice of some tropisms over others; true freedom is possible only to those who know where their inclinations ultimately lead.

In Dante, as in Homer and Virgil, to be fully human means choosing nobler attractions over base appetites, but full humanity is not reserved, as in Homer and Virgil, for the lucky or unlucky few because everyone has the opportunity to choose God's way—every moment of life is potentially a moment of conversion. The immanent possibility of conversion, of turning with shameful recognition from one's sinning self and creating by that act of revulsion an aspiring new self, is of course the subject of the *Purgatorio*, but Dante's narrative taken as a whole is a conversion story, too. Even though the sinners Dante meets in Hell and the saints he meets in Paradise do not change, he changes by virtue of meeting them, and the *Comedia* is the story of Dante's continuous and by no means unvarying commitment to the new life and the new self offered him by God and represented by Beatrice. In her, and in his love for her, Dante sees not the triumph of eternal order over temporal impulse, but rather the eternal order incarnated in a person and an experience that maintain all their individuality. What Dante displays in the *Inferno*, for example, is on the one hand the variety and persistence of the ways in which his sinners go on enacting their sins and damning themselves—this is the first thing most readers of the poem notice—and on the other hand the way their unchanging behavior prepares for his own conversion. The thoroughness and specificity of Dante's representation of sin are matched only by his integration of individual representation into a larger pattern of action.

This proposition might be elaborated by asking when the events of Dante's poem are supposed to be taking place. In terms of the scheme of fourfold exegesis Dante unfolded to Can Grande, they take place at four different times: literally, beginning on Good Friday, 1300; allegorically, during the historical life of Christ, whose own journey to God (here imaged by the ascent from Hell after Christ's burial) Dante is recapitulating; morally, in the indefinite present, as people go on acting out their virtues and vices; anagogically, after the death of Dante. The four senses of meaning Dante employs thus situate his action in two different pasts, in a continuing present, and in the future. Obviously, however, Dante intends that his action be understood as taking place in *all four* of these time frames. The action of the story, like the action of every person's life, is overdetermined, shaped not by an accord between the individual and the social will (as in Homer) or by a conflict between the individual and the historical will (as in Virgil), but by an incarnation of the divine will within the individual will, so that each contingent, freely chosen action necessarily embodies and expresses God's will because it is freely chosen and not imposed from without.

Because Dante presents his own conversion as exemplary, his narrative has a double focus on human experience, as a constant and ongoing activity and as a theological and teleological praxis. But his polytropic perspective integrates this double focus. *Sub specie aetis,* Dante's subject is the incessant potential for free action, that is, love-willed change. *Sub specie aeternitatis,* his subject is the way he changed from prisoner of himself to lord over himself (*Purgatorio* XXVII.142). Dante's presentation of experience as at once irreducibly unique and morally intelligible, of action as at once contingent and intended, of life as at once an ongoing activity and a directed action, makes him the most ambitious and comprehensive storyteller of all, the one in whom narrative polytropy most profoundly images the contingent, ordered, timebound, timeless nature of human experience.

Part Two
Narrative Tropes

6
The Narrative World

Stories engage their audience's narrativity by displaying their polytropy, with a range of emphases running from extreme end-orientation (ritual tragedy) to extreme discursiveness (shaggy-dog stories). But what does it mean, in plain language, for a story to display its polytropy? In Chapter 2 I suggested that the most fruitful approach to the definition of narrative lay in establishing the view of human experience which underlay its forms and conventions. In Homer, Virgil, and Dante, the view of human experience varies widely, but in each case the organizing principle of the adventures (from the hero's point of view) and the discourse (from the audience's) is fundamentally projective, based on intimations of a future goal whose full nature and significance are only imperfectly grasped, but which serves, through the heroes' guesses and doubts and half-formed interpretations about its problematic nature, to inform all their actions.

Even the simplest narratives—riddles or anecdotes, say—display their *intimations* of an immanent yet somehow deferred teleology, imaging a world which is only putatively intelligible. As Shlomith Rimmon-Kenan remarks: "Narrative texts keep implicitly promising the reader the great prize of understanding—later."[1] The special myth of tragedy is that human action is ultimately meaningful in its consequences and that its meaning informs its every stage: The play is addressed to an audience in the middest by a prophet located outside the temporal order who therefore sees beneath its apparent contingencies to the teleology which ultimately shapes them. The more general myth of narrative is that the order of the world is always followable but seldom demonstrably teleological: Stories are addressed to an audience in the middest by an *ad hoc* prophet also in the middest who sees the world as always hypothetically intelligible, even though the patterns that make it so may change from day to day, or

moment to moment. Many stories, including tragedies, make their teleologies explicit, but within the context of narrative generally, this emphasis is a special case, like the complementary case of the soap opera.
The more typical case is that of a world which carries intimations of
intelligibility which are never fully articulated; as soon as they become
explicit, the audience's enabling narrativity can no longer be engaged. A
useful model for narrative is therefore economic, with the storyteller and
the audience competing for time and attention. The audience demands
that the story provide a rationale which will guarantee its tellability; the
storyteller provides enough intimations of such a rationale to keep the
audience's attention without making it explicit and so losing the audience's
interest. Even so, the audience's desire for a teleology which would release
them from their fascination with the story is not wholehearted, for they
want the story both to establish its tellability and to continue indefinitely,
providing them with the assurance that their own lives, which seem
endlessly discursive, make sense, though not the definitive sense conferred
by death.

Stories maintain the audience's interest and faith by displaying their
polytropy, but surely most audiences would never use the word polytropy,
even if the term were more widely known, to explain the appeal of stories.
In addition to displaying their polytropy, most stories display their plots
and characters in the sense that most audiences read novels and watch
movies for the plot and the characters, and often for something else as well:
the pleasures peculiar to a particular medium like pantomime or comic
strips, the thematic development that seems to have some bearing on their
own situations, the sense of a particular location or setting. To explore the
characteristics of particular narrative modes in any systematic way is
outside the scope of this essay, but in this second part I shall consider the
ways in which each of these other principal elements of narrative establishes its appeal. Plot and character, as analysts have long recognized, are
leading tropes of narrative, figures for the nature of human experience in
stories. But they depend on a more fundamental trope. Leo Braudy,
attempting to account for the specific appeal of cinematic narrative, asks,
"What does the filmmaker and the cameraman love the way the writer
loves words?" and answers, "The potential of objects to create a world, the
potential of technique to become meaning."[2] Braudy's observation is
surely pertinent to noncinematic narratives. What novels display (sc.,
"what . . . the writer loves") is not words as such, but the potential of
words to create a narrative world which is intelligible or followable but
somehow inexhaustible, because it cannot be reduced to a set of schematic
principles. The narrative world is at once a universe of possibilities
demarcated by the features of a specific mode of presentation—a land-

scape, setting, or arena within which many (but not any) different things may happen—and a system of rules which determine what may or may not happen within a given story. Like the plots and characters it enables, the narrative world is in its fullest articulations a world ever just at the point of making the authoritative sense that would simultaneously reward and supersede the audience's narrativity.

Just Before the Apocalypse

In *The Genesis of Secrecy,* Frank Kermode takes the synoptic Gospels, especially the Gospel of Mark, as exemplary narratives because of their accretive method of composition, whereby hermeneutical functions are progressively transformed into narrative functions, and because of their appeal to spiritual interpretation, which deliberately affronts and excludes merely carnal or secular readings. Several other texts, however, have these exemplary characteristics and others as well, for the Gospels are not essentially polytropic; in their present form, they are teleological in orientation, the crucifixion and resurrection standing as both climax and revelatory end. The Gospels are organized dramatically, according to a pattern which finds the true meaning of a human life in its end—in this case, in death and resurrection. For a polytropic narrative with Kermode's other characteristics, a text which displays a polytropic world obviously intended as a figure for the audience's own world, we may turn to another biblical text: to Genesis, to Ezekiel, or to the Acts of the Apostles. This last example may seem surprising, as Acts is generally considered a sequel to Luke's gospel by the same author, who refers to the earlier work as his in the opening sentences of the later. The movement from Luke to Acts is a movement from a teleological to a polytropic order, and more generally from a teleological way of thinking (to what definite conclusion will this lead?) to a polytropic way (what are the prospective implications of this situation?). Luke's gospel is given form and meaning by Jesus' climactic vindication of his identity; Acts is given its much more problematical form by its opening events, the ascension of Jesus to heaven and the descent of the Spirit on the apostles on Pentecost. This double movement, which establishes a structuring absence (Jesus is taken up to heaven) and a project (to preach the gospel of Jesus) without any preordained conclusion, is teleologically coherent yet open-ended; the apostles know what to do and why, but not how it will turn out. If the Spirit has indeed come, what then? Acts poses the polytropic conflict of intending self against circumstantial world with exemplary sharpness, for its heroes are at once inspired and mediocre, spiritual and carnal people.

In the Gospels the exemplary Christian hero is Christ, who seldom falters in accepting his identity and his temporal mission. In Acts the notion of the Christian hero and Christian identity is rendered problematic by the nondivinity of its principals (who are Christian without being the Christ), by the incompleteness of their achievement (they do not win the world for Christ, at least not by the end of the story), and by the questions the text raises about the very nature of action. Like the *Poetics*, though with a different bias and different answers, Acts has at its heart questions about what it means to act and what the relation is between action and identity. When Peter cures a lame man (3.1–7), who is really doing the curing? To put it differently, in what sense does the story recount the acts *of* the apostles?

The nature of the apostles' acts depends first on the kind of acts they are. What the apostles are most obviously *not* doing is celebrating the Eucharist—a strange omission, given the eucharistic emphasis of Luke's gospel. Instead, they give themselves "to prayer, and to the ministry of the word" (6.4),[3] to preaching, to healing, and more generally to converting sinners to Christ. The process of conversion is marked throughout Acts by an *agon* of challenge or confrontation. After the apostles miraculously address the Pentecost crowd in tongues, and Peter has announced the Christian aegis of this event, he is asked, "What shall we do?" and replies, "Repent, and be baptized" (2.37–38). The call to repentance as the basis of Christian conversion marks a peripeteia which explicitly rejects one's old identity for a new, spiritual identity. The terms of this conflict are made clear in the apostles' defense to their jailors of their preaching: "We ought to obey God rather than men" (5.29). In this clash of God against oneself, of spiritual versus temporal identity, there remains the question of who is doing the acting. Readers of Acts frequently complain that the apostles' conversion leaves them less free, indeed makes them puppets, both because their actions typically substitute suffering for initiative (so that they are arrested, intimidated, beaten, rescued, killed) and because their apostolic mission is established by the similarity of their behavior to Jesus' own (so that Peter cures a cripple and raises a dead friend, and Stephen preaches fulfillment of the covenant and dies forgiving his enemies). Evidently the ideal Christian acts in such a way as to assert his identity with Christ.

This conclusion is homiletically satisfying but psychologically disturbing. The possession of Euripides' Bacchae by Dionysus renders them lunatic, their situation literally explosive. Their displacement of personal identity by the incarnated divinity surely makes them less free and less human, as Agave shows when she awakens from a dream to find herself holding her son's bloody head. Peter seems to reveal a similar attitude when he says, "We cannot but speak the things we have seen and heard" (4.20), but this attitude is not problematical for him, for he has willingly surrendered himself to the Spirit. The problem would be more acute if Peter were a disciple *malgré lui* like Jonah or Flannery O'Connor's Hazel Motes, a prophet who struggled against his own prophetic mission. But this is precisely the situation of the central character of Acts, Saul, who on his way to Damascus to persecute Christians is knocked down, struck blind, and commanded to obey the Lord. In this conversion, which is so effective that the convert never again has doubts about his vocation, we find again the characteristic agon of divine against human will: When Saul asks, "Lord, what will thou have me to do?" he is told, "Arise, and go into the city, and it shall be told thee what thou must do" (9.6). Later, in the same verse in which Saul is "filled with the Holy Ghost," it is mentioned that he "also is called Paul" (13.9), a name which remains as a sign of his new identity.

Conversion must have been a deeply troubling concept for the author of Acts and his audience, for he tells the story of Paul's conversion three times. One reason for such unusual emphasis is that it insists on the importance of the question of who Saul (or Paul) really is. We see the miraculous conversion that makes him Paul, but there is also a surprising amount of discussion about the factors that made him Saul in the first place: physical humanity (as when Peter tells Cornelius, "I myself also am a man" [10.26], or when Paul and Barnabas are mistaken for Mercury and Jupiter [14.11–18]), private concerns and prejudices (as when Peter remarks, "God is no respecter of persons" [10.34]), civil status (as when Paul insists on his Roman citizenship in 22.25–28 and elsewhere), and kinship in a chosen people (the intimacy assumed through heirship to Abraham's covenant). These criteria all confer a given identity on a person; someone like Saul does not need to do anything to be human or Roman or Jewish, and his identity in these respects is stable and continuous.

What is surprising throughout Acts is that these quite ordinary marks of identity are equally problematical. There is considerable debate over whether Paul is a human being or a god, a Roman or a foreigner, and the central ideological debate in Acts concerns the special intimacy the Jewish people have always enjoyed with God. Should salvation be available only to the Jews? Instead of emphasizing the family relationships within the Jewish people, Paul proposes a more radical community of all people in the family of God (17.28). In answer to the question of who can receive Christ's salvation, of who can be a Christian, Acts poses a notion of identity not given, received, assumed, or continuous, but conferred only through conversion and requiring constant reaffirmation through faith.

Hence Peter concludes of his first cure that "faith in [Jesus'] name hath made this man strong" (3.16). Without this faith, healers are in danger of failure and defeat, as when the evil spirit tells the vagabond exorcists, "Jesus I know, and Paul I know, but who are ye?" and the possessed man overpowers his would-be healers and drives them away (19.15–16). The carnal identity each person takes for granted is no more stable than the spiritual identity to which he is called; Paul's identity is as freely established as Saul's, and more clearly understood.

Another reason for emphasizing the story of Saul's conversion is its political and ideological implications. Each time the story is told, God specifically says that Paul's mission will be to preach to the Gentiles (9.15, 22.21, 26.17). The decision to preach to the Gentiles was a crucial and troublesome step for the early Church, for it aroused Jewish hostility and entailed the loss of official Roman sanction as a branch of Judaism. The author of Acts clearly wants to justify this decision by putting it in the strongest possible way: The apostles had no choice; God Himself commanded them to go outside the Jewish community. Peter defends his baptism of the Gentile Cornelius by describing his prophetic dream (10.10–16, 11.5–10) and concluding, "What was I, that I could withstand God?" (11.17). This question seems to suggest that the apostles' actions and identities were not their own after all, and in a sense this is true. Unlike Aristotle, the author of Acts does not define human identity in terms of freely chosen action, for no one is ever *a priori* free. Still, the crucial choice, the decision whether to accept a call to action, is ultimately free. When Paul tells Agrippa, "I was not disobedient unto the heavenly vision" (26.19), he implies at least the possibility of disobedience, either at the point of conversion or afterwards. The primary issue for Paul and his chronicler is not the degree of psychological constraint but rather the divine provenance of the vision.

Given this provenance, the Spirit acts as a Virgilian fate, a call to personal action and ultimately to group action. What makes people human in Acts, as in the *Aeneid*, is not doing what they please, acting in accord with the rational will, or maintaining an integrated ego, but acting for the greater good, the larger vision, of community, history, God. In the *Aeneid* this vision is secular and, in narrative terms, ironically foreshortened; the victorious note is consistently elegiac. In Acts the vision is divine and eternal; hence the process of conversion, though operating through history, is incessant. Aeneas can never reach or understand his people's goal, but Virgil is already looking back on it; the author of Acts is looking back on a broadening of the apostolic mission only to look ahead to a goal attainable in history but not yet attained. Although the apostles' freedom to act is bound by God's command, this discipline, instead of abolishing human freedom, transforms it, since God's command is simply that all people might have access to the Word. The apostles' individual freedom, like Aeneas's, is abridged for the sake of the community's greater and more radical freedom to hear, to accept, to believe. And this hearing, accepting, and believing is the everlastingly incomplete action which makes each person human, giving everyone an identity which, however recognizable and distinct, would be absolutely stable only in the event of the Second Coming or the conversion of the world to Christ. It is precisely these two historical events toward which Acts looks, and which would make its narrative, written by and addressed to those in the middest, unnecessary.

For this reason it is in some sense misleading to call Acts open-ended, for although neither the apostles nor their audience know how this conversion story will end, the apostles are not shown wondering how, and the audience is not encouraged to wonder. The stance the author of Acts adopts toward his story and its audience leaves no room for speculation; it is not told as a narrative whose hermeneutics are inconclusive (how will this turn out?) but as a conversion story in the additional sense that it is intended to convert its audience. Whether or not it is effective in the telling is what finally determines its status as narrative: Unless it leads to a series of conversions which ultimately win the world for Christ, it is incomplete. It seems then that the very possibility of narrative tellability is incommensurate with the final end which the narrative has been designed to secure. The world of Acts, more explicitly but not otherwise differently from that of other stories, is a world defined as operating just before the apocalypse it constantly portends, an apocalypse whose arrival would put an end to all stories because the audience's wondering how a given story would turn out would be superseded by another kind of wonder altogether.[4]

Worlds and Rules

The world of Acts is in intention the world: Its author takes as his goal nothing less than the extension of his worldview to include that of every possible audience. Most narratives are considerably more modest in both their pretensions and the inclusiveness, even to specification, of the world they create. What does it mean to say that more minimal narratives create a world?

The concept of a narrative world indicates first the subgenre within which the storyteller refers the audience's expectations, for example jokes about strange visitors to bars, which informs the following story:

> (1)   A gorilla sat in a bar drinking a double scotch. The bartender
>   said, "We don't get many gorillas here." "At these prices," said
>   the gorilla, "you won't get many more."

The point of this joke depends, of course, on our finally accepting as
normal the outrageous premise with which the joke begins. The gorilla's
reply forces us to redefine the conventions within which the story operates,
endowing the bartender's remark with a new significance. The audience's
anagnorisis, which makes us move from the expectation of one generic
world with its attendant rules to that of another, thus forms, as so often,
the structural basis of the story.[5]

Considering another similar story will allow us to focus on another sense
of the narrative world:

> (2)   A gorilla walked into a bar and asked the price of a double
>   scotch. What does a gorilla know? thought the bartender, and
>   said, "Ten dollars." After serving the drink, he added, "We
>   don't get many gorillas here." "At these prices," said the
>   gorilla, "you won't get many more."

Although longer than (1), (2) is a more economical story because its
climactic twist is more carefully motivated.[6] The gorilla's original question gives his final remark a more thoroughly logical justification and also
makes the bartender's own remark more plausible, as the continuation of a
series of associations about how rarely gorillas come into his bar. One way
of describing the difference between (1) and (2) is to say that (2) uses up
the material of its world more thoroughly; even though more details are
presented, each of those details is motivated by the logic of the generic
world the audience first assumes and which in turn motivates the climactic
surprise.

Jokes frequently provide pleasure by supplying details which issue an
implicit challenge to the audience to predict how they will motivate the
ending, as in

> (3)   René Descartes walked into a bar. The bartender, eager to serve
>   such an illustrious patron, asked, "Can I get you something,
>   M. Descartes? A brandy, perhaps?" "I think not," replied Des-
>   cartes—and vanished.

Here our pleasure depends on seeing the figure of Descartes as potentially
meaningful (why him, of all people?) but not quite foreseeing the way in
which the joke will pun on his most famous observation. The success of
the joke is based on the way in which it uses up or exhausts the particulars
of a world which seems too narrowly specified for the kind of story being
told.

The primary purpose of a narrative world, then, is to provide rules within which a given story can operate. Even if those rules are eventually superseded or overridden, as they are in a great many narratives, the process of superseding itself, the way in which the audience has been misled, will be tellable. What a narrative displays will in any case be implied by the rules it adopts, as a few examples from Boccaccio's *Decameron* will demonstrate. In the story (9.2) in which the nun Isabetta, caught by her abbess with a man in her cell, realizes that the abbess has inadvertently put on a man's trousers in place of her bonnet, she uses her observation to escape punishment; but the story might have ended differently, for example with the abbess magically transforming the trousers into a bonnet. Boccaccio uses magic in a few other tales (e.g., in 10.9, where Saladin's physician spirits Messer Torello back to his native Pavia), but never without some logical preparation (magic might well flourish in Saladin's court), and never simply to resolve a tale's complications (for Messer Torello, returning just before his wife's remarriage, determines to test her loyalty to him). Since magical resolutions are allowed in some stories (the adventures of Superman) but not in others (*Barchester Towers*), each story evidently establishes its own decorum; nothing in the story of Isabetta and the abbess authorizes a magical resolution.

Boccaccio treats a similar premise differently in the story of Masetto (3.1), who pretends to be a deaf-mute in order to get a job as gardener in a convent and allow two novices to seduce him. Eventually the other nuns discover this liaison and insist on a share of Masetto, and finally the abbess makes such demands on him that he pretends to regain his speech in order to beg for relief, which comes in the form of a more equitable and moderate distribution of his resources. The story might have ended earlier, with Masetto's success in arousing the first two women. In this case it would still have fit the rule for Day 3 (people who by their own efforts have achieved an object they greatly desired) but would structurally have more closely resembled 8.5 (in which three young men pull down the breeches of a judge sitting at his bench), for the emphasis would be on chastening the pretenses of a hypocritical institution. Still, Masetto's ingenuity would be a slender thread to bear the weight of the story, and Boccaccio wisely complicates his opening situation so that Masetto, having achieved his goal, finds himself at such risk that he is in need of a new stratagem. A rule frequently adopted in stories involving the pursuit of a goal, whether or not they are by Boccaccio, is that at some point the principal agent must be in danger of losing more than simply the hope of his goal; pursuing the goal must threaten the loss of even the relative stability he enjoyed at the beginning of the story. King Arthur's knights, in accepting commissions from their ladies, risk not merely the possibility of failure, but consequent ignominy, perhaps death. A detective who failed to identify the criminal would put the community at risk. When Boccaccio overrides this rule, as in 3.8 or his stories of Calandrino, he is displaying not the inaccessibility of the goal but the imaginative means to secure a readily accessible goal like cuckolding a foolish man or gulling the simple Calandrino.

We might summarize and extend the rules implicit in Boccaccio's tales, and in classical narrative generally, in broader terms. The minimal condition for narrative discourse is *the rule of tellability: A story should be worth telling.* This rule in turn implies three subsidiary rules. The first is *the rule of display: A story should display some aspect, implication, or conse-quence of a situation or state of affairs which is (or is made) tellable.* The second is *the rule of economy: The given state of affairs should itself imply some line of development.* In Aristotelian drama, the opening situation implies not only certain lines of development but, at least in retrospect, a certain resolution; but since stories like soap operas and autobiographies can get along without any resolution at all, an economical or coherent resolution cannot be made a defining condition of narrative. What this rule suggests is that how a story develops should be more or less closely connected to what it displays; a story which serves mainly as the pretext for denouncing the Church (or pleading for peace and brotherhood, as in Chaplin's *The Great Dictator*) suffers to that degree as a story, though perhaps succeeding better as a homily or jeremiad. The third rule is *the rule of suspense: Although a story's development (and perhaps its resolution) should be implied by the state of affairs which is first displayed, they should not be predicted in every particular.* The point of this rule is to avoid the extremes of underspecifica-tion (failure to reward the audience's narrativity) and overspecification (failure to engage the audience's narrativity) I considered in Chapter 2. Narrative logic requires that the development of a situation be implicit in the situation—a just man may turn to crime because he is weak, or badly in need of money, or corrupted by society, but not for no reason at all— but prescribes a difference between a situation and its development. This difference is best described in terms of the audience's perceptions; the characteristic movement from false certainty to disillusionment or en-lightened ignorance demands that an audience's experience of a story be sequential. If the opening of a discourse predicts its development in such explicit detail that the audience grasps its form and rationale from the beginning, then that discourse is expository or ritualistic, not narrative. This is not to say that stories cannot foreshadow their endings in more or less detail. Each of Boccaccio's hundred *novelle*, after all, begins with a summary by the author. In cases like these, the audience is kept in suspense by wondering how the promised end will be brought about;

when the audience has already been informed of this as well, the story loses its ability to provoke a narrative sequence of responses and becomes simply gnomic or thematic, like illustrative fables or moral exempla whose rationale is designed to be grasped at once from the beginning. An interesting transitional genre is the news article, part narrative and part expository, which begins with the most important information and proceeds to less and less important detail. Such articles, although they usually imply a story, display the information they provide rather than its narrative form; a reader scanning them may stop at any paragraph without violating their logic, and unlike other stories they may be abridged to any length by removing their endings.

The rule of tellability establishes a minimal criterion for stories, but each of its three subsidiary rules (display, economy, suspense) is more narrowly conceived than the last, and each successive rule excludes more narratives than the last. The second general rule, which is still more tendentious, is *the rule of coherence: A story should make sense in narrative terms.* The first of its subsidiary rules is *the rule of closure: A story should fulfill in some logical (though perhaps unexpected) way the expectations it arouses; it should satisfactorily resolve the implications of the situation it displays.* It might be argued that radically open forms like soap operas and psychoanalytic case studies do make good on their promises, because what they promise is an indefinitely deferred resolution or ever more penetrating insights and successive readjustments. Nonetheless, this rule in its present form, which requires that stories come to an end in order that they may be grasped as intelligible wholes (and might just as easily, but more pointedly, be called the rule of unity), would exclude all stories that could not be grasped as a totality. Only by arguing that narrative unity requires a premise or point of departure rather than a dramatic teleology can we recover interminable stories. The final subsidiary rule, the narrowest of all, is *the rule of significance: The states of affairs presented with their implications should, viewed as a whole, display some general pattern or point.* This pattern need not be a gnomic teleology. *Tristram Shandy,* which violates so many rules of relevance and closure, establishes its unity and significance as a project long before it is over (and the kinds of unity and significance it establishes are perfectly consonant with its going on forever). Just as the pattern in a braided rope does not dictate the rope's length, or even its need to come to an end, a narrative may establish a pattern of significance—the philosophical issues in Dostoevsky's *Notes from Underground,* the color scheme of Antonioni's *Red Desert*—without reference to its conclusion. Still, this last rule implies more strongly than any of the others a teleological imperative, and in general the five subsidiary rules prescribe a narrative logic ever closer to the teleology of Aristotelian tragedy. This is hardly surprising, since classical narrative characteristically borrows the teleological impetus of tragedy. A more comprehensive analysis of narrative, however, yields a different conception of narrative logic, a conception based on the peculiar nature of the narrative world.

In *The World in a Frame*, Leo Braudy, following Heinrich Wölfflin, distinguishes between open and closed cinematic narratives: "In a closed film the world of the film is the only thing that exists; everything within it has its place in the plot of the film—every object, every character, every gesture, every action. In an open film the world of the film is a momentary frame around an ongoing reality" (46). In closed films, for example in the work of Hitchcock and Fritz Lang, meanings and relationships are defined predominantly through an expressive (often studio-built) mise-en-scène and a fully articulated plot; in open films like those of Jean Renoir and Roberto Rossellini, outdoor settings and a freer handling of plot emphasize the arbitrariness of the audience's perceptions. Braudy points out that films are rarely completely open or completely closed; instead they combine the tendencies toward aperture and closure in different ways. These tendencies correspond to the discursive and teleological impulses in narrative, the tendencies toward and away from a final vision whose authority is absolute. But there are other polarities with which they are associated as well. "Lang teaches us about ourselves; Renoir teaches us about the rest of the world," writes Braudy (50). More generally, narratives like the novel, with their emphasis on the empirical cataloguing of circumstantial reality, tend to be more extroverted than closed narratives, which present a thematically concentrated image of human experience through direct identifications. Aristotelian tragedy, which defines experience in terms of consequential actions, is the prototype for closed narrative. Open narrative, which tends to define experience in terms of an endless series of adventures or an incessant and ultimately inexhaustible consciousness given over to assimilating circumstantial reality, has no such distinguished formal exemplar, though the novels of Tolstoy and Virginia Woolf, the soap opera, and the comic strip offer some models. As the frame in an open film is always provisional, the meanings it generates always contingent, the realm of experience open narratives explore is the unformed potential of wishes, desires, impressions, and escapist fantasy. Experience in closed narratives is by contrast what is actual and univocal, a matter of public record. Open films emphasize the subjective, closed narratives the objective, quality of the worlds within their frames. In practice, however, the oppositions sketched here are so often complicated that Braudy describes open and closed cinematic forms in figurative terms, as "a revolving door of visual meaning" (55).

Braudy contends that, "more than novels or paintings, films have the capacity to present an enclosed world of total meaning at the same time that they offer the possibility of another reality outside these momentary limits" (77) because of their unique ability to present things in the frame as at once meaningful parts of a closed composition and irreducible objects whose ultimate significance is that they simply are. And it is true that films like Renoir's *Rules of the Game* make agents and their experiences thematically coherent while preserving at the same time their sensory and psychological uniqueness. But this ability seems due more to narrative polytropy than to any properties specific to the cinematic medium. There have been, after all, not only open and closed films but open and closed theories of film, each claiming that only open or only closed films were truly cinematic and faithful to the distinctive properties of the medium.[7] Even though the audience typically begins by perceiving novels as open and ends by perceiving them as closed, there have also been open novels (*Tristram Shandy, Mrs. Dalloway*) and closed novels (*Pride and Prejudice, The Secret Agent*). The novel as a form is neither open nor closed, but can be either, and also has the potential Braudy ascribes to film of being open *and* closed (*Lost Illusions, Our Mutual Friend, V.*)—that is, to create a world at once orderly and contingent. The worlds of novels, films, epics, and comic strips typically have a fullness or density of reference which is not merely an attenuation of teleology but rather a distinctive trope. The amplitude of detail in the great nineteenth-century novels figures a world in principle inexhaustible because, however tightly its metaphoric structure may be organized, its metonymic frame remains open. The attempt to translate the particulars of an open world into the rules of a closed world without losing the sense of openness—to see the world as finally open-and-closed—is simply another definition of narrative polytropy.

No-Frills Narrative

To see the narrative world as open-and-closed is to acknowledge that there is nothing which some narrative, depending on the rules it establishes, cannot incorporate into its world. But this inclusiveness renders the narrative status of that world problematic. If narratives are defined in terms of the worlds they project, rather than the plots they develop, what parts of those worlds are properly narrative? Traditional wisdom has singled out certain kinds of digression—political propaganda, moral sermonizing, sometimes even philosophical discussions—as extraneous to narrative form. When Ivan Karamazov has a dream about the Grand Inquisitor, that dream reveals his own nature more fully and has its place in what Barbara Hardy might call the "dogmatic form"[8] of *The Brothers Karamazov;* the political theories of Plantagenet Palliser, by contrast, seem to be interrupting rather than deepening the story of *The Prime Minister.* Are Dostoevsky's digressions somehow more narrative than Trollope's? What counts as a digression from the logic of the narrative world? Finally, is there such a thing as a narrative without such digressions, a pure or no-frills narrative?

Hardy addresses the question about narrative digressions by arguing that "the novel holds us by its story and informs us by its moral argument, but it moves us by its individual presences and moments," and that its form should be defined in terms of its effort to tell the truth about our lives. Novelistic form, in Hardy's view, automatically entails a considerable amplitude and verisimilitude, for although "the truthful detail may look irrelevant if we see form in a merely skeletal way, as the form of the story or the form of moral categories," the concept of novelistic form "must be enlarged to include the individual life which is the breath of fiction and of a real response to fiction" (2–3). Particular incidents whose effect is to enlarge the audience's sense of life, to arouse their recognition or shock them into authentic new perceptions, participate in the novel's form; those which serve to urge a given moral or metaphysical view at the expense of particular rendered experience are digressions from that form.

Against this mimetic analysis may be set the semiotic analysis of Roland Barthes. As Barthes begins the task of distributing the 561 lexias of "Sarrasine" among his five codes or categories, he observes that "without straining a point, there will be no other codes throughout the story but these five, and each and every lexia will fall under one of the five codes."[9] A brief consideration of the codes explains Barthes's assurance on this point, for two of his five codes (the semantic and, to a lesser extent, the cultural) are in essence catch-all codes which, by assimilating any possible information Balzac could possibly give about his own or his characters' opinions, or incidents which bore no direct relation to the story of Sarrasine and Zambinella (or of the narrator and the marquise), effectively guarantee the relevance of every detail in this or any story. Relevance here does not suggest an intimate or organic relation to the rest of the narrative, for except for the remark that "actions . . . form the main armature of the readerly text" (255), Barthes simply waives the question of relative degrees of formal relevance or digressiveness. Every detail can be recovered under the five codes; none is more salient formally than the others. In this account "Sarrasine" has no digressions; neither does *Tristram Shandy,* since there is no such thing as a digression, only details whose disruptive force remains hidden in the readerly text.

Although Hardy's position may seem the more unexceptionable of the two, it is in fact the more problematic. Even granting the considerable point that narratives like the novel have as their ultimate responsibility the full and truthful representation of particular experience, it is difficult to determine precisely what elements in narrative are *not* more or less digressive. Information about the characters' partisan beliefs is mere propaganda; information about their sexual escapades is mere pornography; information about their particular manner of speaking (Titus's self-justification to Sophronia's relatives, for example, in *Decameron* 10.8) is mere rhetoric. Each of these has its own value, but none of them is properly narrative. Most critics would stop here, but it is logical to go further: Information about the characters' personalities is mere psychology, not narrative; information about the thematic import of the plot is mere ideology, not narrative; information about the possible causes for a given set of effects is mere metaphysical hypothesizing, not narrative. With a little effort we can erase narrative altogether and leave only a set of unmotivated, uninflected, and untellable states of affairs. Clearly tellable narratives require certain ramifying imputations which may take the form of thematic generalization and psychological explanation, or may invoke rhetorical, sexual, or ideological contexts as well. The point is not that it is impossible to distinguish between relatively salient and relatively digressive details but rather that there is no essential or unmarked process of narrative formation which cannot itself be perceived as digressive. To narrate, as I observed in Chapter 4, is automatically to digress.

This position is close to Barthes's own, but I do not wish to go as far as his five codes in authorizing any potential information whatever. Just because narrative by definition admits of a great deal of rhetorical (ideological, cultural, psychological) elaboration does not mean that it has no logic of its own. The logic of narrative is the logic of implication, in the double sense of chronological or teleological implication (A causes B) and hermeneutical implication (A means B). The second rule of tellability stipulates that the situation a story displays should itself imply some line of development. Judgments about individual elements will vary among audiences, but in general an audience who feels that a given digression is implied, in either of these two senses, by the world a story displays will accept it as authorized by the story—that is, as a narrative digression.

More generally, the dramatic axiom *post hoc ergo propter hoc* does not necessarily apply to narrative, since narrative sequence may not imply causality. In closed narrative forms like the detective story, sequence does imply causality (the detective is finally able to identify the criminal because of the evidence he has collected; this evidence both "means" that the culprit is guilty and causes his identification); the more closely hermeneutical sequence is identified with causality, the more closed the form.

But even a thriller like Martin Cruz Smith's *Gorky Park* employs many implications more digressive though still logical and followable. One of Smith's most characteristic devices is the illustrative anecdote. Instead of merely describing his detective Arkady Renko's attitudes toward his wife, his neighbors, his co-workers, and his counterparts on the KGB, Smith is always ready to translate his predicates into short narratives. We know how repressive the political regime is because we hear stories about the political misfortunes of minor characters; we understand Renko's dislike of Major Pribluda because Smith recounts the episode in which it is rooted. Smith's habit of rendering categorical predicates (passionless, angry, corrupt) in terms of retrospective narration is akin to the tendency Tzvetan Todorov has found in the *Arabian Nights* to turn predicates (Sindbad likes to travel) into actions (Sindbad takes a trip) instead of developing them psychologically (Sindbad struggles against his restlessness, Sindbad neglects his affairs, etc.).[10] Smith's characters, like Scheherezade's, are "narrative-men" (70), but in a broader sense: not because everything about them—their existence, their qualities, their feelings and desires—is automatically turned into actions, but because Smith recounts so many illustrative incidents that he creates an authentically narrative world based on the audience's habit of defining characters with reference to their putative backgrounds, a world in which, we assume, narratives could be adduced to support any belief or judgment without exhausting its significance. Despite the aptness of the term "narrative-men," Todorov's application of it is somewhat misleading, for if Sindbad feels restless, struggling with his restlessness is just as "narrative" as going on a trip; the comic strip is no more narrative than the soap opera.

The audience's ability to follow a narrative, or even to predict its future development, without necessarily grasping its thematic implications—the fact that an audience can often follow an Ingmar Bergman film, for instance, without understanding or grasping it as a whole—illustrates the fundamental difference between teleology and the logic of implication. Stories do not necessarily promise (although they may) that conflicts will be definitively resolved or the truth manifested once and for all; they promise only that something further will happen, or that there is something else to learn. Any event or situation implies an endless network of other events, relations, meanings, viewpoints, and possible developments (or hypothetical antecedents, as in *The Sacred Fount* and *Absalom, Absalom!*), none of them inherently more narrative than the others. The only obligation every story incurs is to make some of these implications tellable. The other rules for stories simply indicate the ways this obligation is most often discharged.

Stories normally end more definitely than "General Hospital," but their implications and the worlds they create do not end in the same way. Sherlock Holmes can be resuscitated by Conan Doyle and later imitators; horror movies which end in the destruction of the monster can send the audience home to restless dreams. A story never implies an ending as strongly as it implies a world in the middest, a world whose logic resists endings. Even the most closed narratives manage to undermine their meanings somehow, either by presenting alternative endings or by questioning the meaning or formal potency of any ending. Few films come to an end as emphatically as Hitchcock's *Psycho*, when Norman Bates is unmasked in the attempt to kill again and the motive for his crimes is set forth in detail. Although the motivation and rationale for the incidents are clear, their thematic teleology is highly equivocal. However assured the psychiatrist's explanation of Norman's madness may be, it seems utterly inadequate to the episode that follows, in which we see that Norman Bates has submitted to his mother's identity not in order to escape his own but in order to assert it—that Norman is simultaneously his mother and himself. Any explanation rhetorically strong enough to end the film would necessarily be unfairly reductive. Because Norman's true horror escapes the psychiatrist, it continues to frighten us outside the frame of the story, and the only satisfactory ending is to pull us out of the film as if from an ongoing world, precisely as Hitchcock's final shot (Marion's car being pulled toward the audience out of the swamp) does.

Critics of the film have often reenacted the psychiatrist's reductive interpretation by recasting the plot in moral terms: Marion is killed because, in stealing forty thousand dollars from her boss, she has placed herself outside the human community and left herself vulnerable to violation and death. This Jansenist account of the film's plot, like the psychiatrist's explanation, overlooks the gratuitous ferocity of the violence and is morally inconsistent as well. If Marion is killed because she is guilty, then what is the detective Arbogast guilty of, or the women Norman is said to have killed earlier? It seems equally reasonable to say that Marion is killed because everything else this weekend has already gone wrong, or because the windshield wipers of her car slashing through the rain have portended the manner and place of her death, or because Norman's hobby is taxidermy, or because people often get killed in Hitchcock movies. In each case the murder is implied but not required by some earlier potential pattern—a convention, an image, a moral design. And in each case the murder is recognized as a fulfillment of a promise, an implication made explicit. But since narrative worlds thrive on incomplete patterns, implications which engage our narrativity precisely because they remain potential, any pattern of implication and realization may be simply that, a pattern, which may have no moral or thematic valence whatever. This is true not only for particular patterns but for the story as a whole, for stories can be intelligible and tellable without meaning anything. Although *Psycho* is replete with action, the action is all consistently motivated, and the story is readily followable, it does not necessarily follow that *Psycho* has any plot in Aristotle's sense. Hitchcock's story is committed to no plot, no teleology, nothing the pattern authoritatively implies except success in manipulating the audience by encouraging and rewarding their narrativity.[11]

Hitchcock's remarks to François Truffaut about *Psycho*[12] suggest that it is designed to do nothing but engage and satisfy the audience's narrativity, and that its effects are achieved through purely narrative means. A story which was all story and nothing but story—that is, which employed the minimal narrative logic to be followable without being thematically coherent—would presumably be pure narrative, unadulterated by other genres or discursive modes. But *Psycho* is not such a narrative. Its characters act in terms of consistent psychologies, and its pattern of impotent predators (the stuffed birds, simultaneously powerless and threatening, which define Norman as both their analogue and their victim as he talks with Marion about the "traps" people are born or step into) has thematic implications for an account of human nature. The relative thematic coherence of *Psycho* is more readily apparent in contrast to a somewhat purer and more minimal narrative, *Dressed to Kill*, Brian De Palma's homage to Hitchcock's film.

Dressed to Kill stands in somewhat the same relation to *Psycho* that the Physician's Tale in Chaucer stands to the episode in Livy on which it is based; in each case incidents are borrowed from the older story without that story's teleological intimations. Chaucer's physician claims to be demonstrating "how synne hath his merite,"[13] but his tale illustrates this moral poorly, for it displays the suffering of Virginius and his daughter rather than the sins of Apius. Over a third of the tale comprises a description of the daughter's impregnable virtue and an exhortation to governesses and parents to foster this sort of virtue. Hence the scene between Virginius and his daughter represents a triumph of virtue at its most perverse. When Livy's Virginius kills his daughter, he is expressing a tragic contradiction in the Roman code of honor; when Chaucer's Virginius kills his daughter, he seems only monstrously peevish.

Dressed to Kill does not borrow so directly from its original, but its indebtedness is plain: the grisly and shocking murder committed in an unlikely but confining and so dangerous place, the importance of voyeurism and sexual deviance, the reliance on visual narrativity and the corresponding paucity of dialogue, the motivic confusion of hero and villain, and the final discovery that the criminal is again a man dressed as a woman (now a transsexual rather than a schizophrenic). For all De Palma's departures from *Psycho*, he supplies close analogies to the original in matters ranging from the manner of death (now slashing with a razor rather than stabbing with a knife) to the emotional and hermeneutical rhythm of the film (beginning with a misleading subplot designed to misdirect the audience by establishing a strong identification with the victim, proceeding to an unexpected murder which destroys this identification, following the subsequent investigation to the unmasking of a murderer whose identity we had mistakenly thought we knew, and concluding with an unnerving coda which indicates how ineffective rational explanations have been in allaying our fears). Yet the logic of *Dressed to Kill* is far less thematic, far more purely narrative, than that of *Psycho*. Morally speaking, Kate Miller's death is more gratuitous than Marion Crane's. The police act as if she had been killed because she picked up a man in an art museum, but in fact the murderer, her psychiatrist, had already decided to kill her earlier when he felt threatened by what he took to be her sexual advances (advances unworthy of the name). She has done nothing to deserve such a sudden and brutal death. It would make more sense to see her death, like Marion's, as the final insult in a day when everything else has gone wrong (she has felt alienated from her husband, son, and psychiatrist; the man she left the museum with had venereal disease; she left her wedding ring in his apartment and had to go back for it; a girl in the elevator stared disconcertingly at her moments before she was attacked and killed).

De Palma's imagery forms coherent patterns, but patterns without any clear thematic significance. The film is full of people watching other people, usually through a looking-glass: The cab driver adjusts his rear-view mirror to watch his passengers' lovemaking; Kate's son Peter spies on Dr. Elliott with a camera and later watches the climactic scene through his rain-drenched glasses and Dr. Elliott's window; De Palma's heroine, Liz Blake, sees Dr. Elliott as Bobbi watching her in a bathroom mirror. These images are in turn organized around the central image of the film, the heroine's glimpse of Bobbi in an elevator mirror. And their implication is consistent. The observer or spy is always at a disadvantage, usually because anyone she can watch in a mirror can be watching her at the same time, so that looking becomes a profoundly dangerous activity. But this implication itself remains simply a pattern of images whose consistency justifies each one (and produces a shock of recognition with the final image in the pattern, the sight of Bobbi's sunglasses reflected in the bathroom mirror) without encouraging any further thematic generalization. In the same way, De Palma uses formal devices like Hitchcock's long sequences without dialogue or his manipulation of the audience's response through appeals to their voyeurism less for their thematic value than to display the penetration of his homage, to display the narrative and stylistic resources of his world.

Displaying these very resources prevents *Dressed to Kill* from being a pure narrative, since it displays not only its narrativity but its intertextuality and its pictorial design as such. Indeed there is no such thing as pure narrative even in principle, because since narrativity is itself a transaction rather than an ultimate end, any story, from *Dressed to Kill* to the Acts of the Apostles, must always display something besides its narrativity: its verbal or plastic resources, its use of themes whose significance reinforces its tellability, and all the other aspects academic critics analyze in their readings of individual stories. Even a narrative as thematically reticent as *Dressed to Kill* implies a certain thematic coherence by the causal and logical order of its events, for, as Hayden White notes, "every narrative . . . is constructed on the basis of a set of events which *might have been included but were left out*," and a specific and ascertainable "notion of reality authorizes construction of a narrative account of reality in which continuity rather than discontinuity governs the articulation of the discourse."[14] All narratives are to a greater or lesser extent governed by a dramatic teleology in which each event further limits the range of acceptable developments. Detective stories may end with the capture of the criminal or his escape, but not with the detective's confession of utter perplexity or his transformation into a dolphin.

The pervasiveness of what White calls the rule of continuity and what I have called the teleological imperative can be dramatized by considering an alternative model for narrative, the novel Jorge Luis Borges describes in his story "The Garden of Forking Paths":

> "Fang, let us say, has a secret; a stranger calls at his door; Fang resolves to kill him. Naturally, there are several possible outcomes: Fang can kill the intruder, the intruder can kill Fang, they can both escape, they can both die, and so forth. In the work of Ts'ui Pen, all possible outcomes occur; each one is the point of departure for other forkings. Sometimes, the paths of this labyrinth converge: for example, you arrive at this house, but in one of the possible pasts you are my enemy, in another, my friend."[15]

The logic of this hypothetical narrative is based on the comprehensive fulfillment of causal and hermeneutical implications. The garden of forking paths simply fulfills every implication it presents. Such a narrative could only be infinite—a maze with a beginning but no end, or a billion—

and indeed Ts'ui Pen's novel is based on a nonlinear view of time wherein multiple versions of the same event, and contradictory events, are simultaneously possible. This arresting concept of narrative as an endless labyrinth finds expression in some form in a number of programmatically modernist or postmodernist works: in encyclopedic fictions like *Bouvard and Pécuchet, Finnegans Wake,* and *Gravity's Rainbow;* in Borges's own parables, "Tlön, Uqbar, Orbis Tertius," "The Babylonian Lottery," and "The Library of Babel"; in the suppositional fiction of Robert Coover (e.g., "The Babysitter") and Donald Barthelme; and in the *nouveau roman* of Nathalie Sarraute and Alain Robbe-Grillet.

Of all these cases, Robbe-Grillet's is perhaps the most challenging to the assumption of narrative continuity or linearity, because his world is so ordered that alternative versions of events are sharply contradictory. Have Giorgio Albertazzi and Delphine Seyrig met before (in *Last Year at Marienbad,* which Alain Resnais directed from Robbe-Grillet's screenplay) or not? Is there a mirror over the mantelpiece in Seyrig's room or not? Does Serge Pitoeff kill Seyrig or does she go off at the end with Albertazzi? Robbe-Grillet's comments on these problems discourage any authoritative resolution of events: "The universe in which the entire film occurs is, characteristically, that of a perpetual present which makes all recourse to memory impossible. . . . This man, this woman began existing only when they appear on the screen the first time; before that they were nothing; and, once the projection is over, they are again nothing. Their existence lasts only as long as the film lasts. There can be no reality outside the images we see, the words we hear."[16] But this line of reasoning is fallacious, because a spectator who lets himself be carried through *Marienbad* purely on the basis of its sensory appeal, without speculating about the "real" relationships among the principals, would find it, however logical, distinctly less tellable than Borges's labyrinths. *Marienbad* is a handsome film whose auditory and visual design is intriguing, but not intriguing enough to sustain the audience's interest for ninety minutes without the promise, however completely thwarted, of teleological development. The effect of *Marienbad* depends not on its declining to engage the audience's narrativity through a net of implications, but on systematically engaging and frustrating its narrativity. The structure of *Marienbad,* though Robbe-Grillet seems to consider it purely narrative, is antinarrative, and *therefore* quintessentially narrative.

Why may pure narratives be antinarrative? Robbe-Grillet's second novel, *The Voyeur,* indicates the relations between the two forms and shows why an audience will perceive pure narratives as antinarrative. The novel turns on the question of whether the watch salesman Mathias raped and murdered the young girl Jacqueline in between the first and second parts of the novel (in effect, in the white space between the two parts). There are three ways to answer this question, on which depend three different readings of the novel. In the first reading, which most readers probably accept, Mathias did kill Jacqueline and is insane, as his obsessive memories and speculations suggest; the alternative, often contradictory versions of events in the story (references to Mathias's calling on houses before his boat has docked on the island he is visiting, inconsistent versions of his success in particular calls, rapidly contradictory reports about his bicycle's mechanical condition) represent different stories he is rehearsing to himself. The novel presents a recoverable chain of events rendered more obscure by its discourse, which displays its temporal and logical lacunae in the same way that a detective story displays the pains taken to conceal the criminal and the indirect means of identifying him; and the voyeur of the title is Julian, the boy who attempts to construct a univocal sequence of events for which Mathias shall be held responsible.

Against this first, hermeneutical or ratiocinative, reading may be set a second, humanist reading. Here it is ambiguous whether or not Mathias killed Jacqueline, but he probably did not, for his obsessive and contradictory reveries about rape and murder, like his obsessive calculations concerning how many watches he can sell in how many minutes, represent the psychopathology of everyday life, whose social and economic pressures are so alienating and ironically distorting (the watch salesman is utterly unable to control time and so is late for his boat) that Mathias, a normal bourgeois, might as well be a maniac. The novel displays a critique of normative psychology and capitalistic culture, an attack on the statistically normal, from a perspective like that of R. D. Laing. The voyeur is not Julian but Mathias himself, who, never acting but only speculating and fantasizing about possible actions in the past and present, sees his own life entirely from outside. The reader recovers the novel as a coherent metanarrative which creates designedly incompatible chains of events in order to render more accurately the quality of Mathias's bourgeois madness.

In the third reading, which seems to be Robbe-Grillet's own, Mathias neither kills nor fails to kill Jacqueline, nor is Robbe-Grillet committed to an ambiguity about her fate. Indeed he is committed to nothing at all except to make his story tellable, and he does this by imagining alternative versions of the same events which are simply alternative, manifold rather than contradictory. Such manifold possibilities neither require nor encourage a limiting choice in any ultimate sense; the novel which proposes them is like Borges's garden of forking paths, or like a multiple choice exam in which all answers are equally possible. Lacking a coherent teleology or its attendant thematic resonances, the novel operates as pure narrative, engaging and rewarding the reader's narrativity without providing as a bonus any teleological wisdom whose manifestation would make it more than minimally narrative. The voyeur is the audience ourselves, spying on Mathias through the peephole afforded by his obsessive concerns (the images of a gull, a figure 8, the nape of a girl's neck) as if we could make out by inference the whole area of his physical or mental experience, an experience Robbe-Grillet declines to reveal authoritatively. This reading of *The Voyeur* makes it at once antinarrative and virtually pure narrative, narrative without the frills of psychological or teleological generalization, a story which displays nothing but the world or worlds it projects and so qualifies as narrative without aspiring to any other goal. The failure so far of Robbe-Grillet's pure narrative to displace the impure narratives of classical storytellers from Homer to Hitchcock suggests that pure narrative is from the storyteller's point of view a vertiginous theoretical ideal and from the audience's point of view decidedly an acquired taste. Most audiences continue to prefer narratives incorporating such formal excrescences as plot and character. I wish now to examine the circumstances under which each of these tropes is displayed and to consider the range of relations they project with the narrative world.

7

Plot

I argued in Chapter 3 that the constitutive feature of narrative development is the sequence of the audience's perceptions, projections, and reintegrations of the story, typically following a line of development from illusion to disillusionment, and for this purpose plot in the sense of a temporal or causal sequence of events is clearly not necessary (whence the minimal plots of Joyce, Hemingway, and Woolf, and the antiplots of *Last Year at Marienbad* and Robbe-Grillet's short fiction). Story is possible without plot. The great majority of stories, however, not only contain diegetic sequences of events, but display those sequences in a way that constitutes the plot as a distinctive trope for human experience. The audience's experience of narrative plots is polytropic, since the ideal plot, imaging our conscious experience of the world, would be followable but endless, portending at every moment a teleology which never became explicit. Since many stories present events without displaying their teleology, we might describe Dickens's first three novels, for example, as eventful but plotless. To use *plot* in this way, however, would sever it almost completely from its long-standing association with event-sequences as such. Given the formative influence Aristotle's assertion that plot (*mythos*) is the soul or first principle of mimetic poetry[1] has had on narrative theory, I shall use plot in this chapter in its Aristotelian sense, as a sequence of events or actions (*praxis*) which display a particular end (*telos*). The concept of *telos* is essential to plot, for not every sequence of events constitutes a plot. Plot is properly that aspect of narrative which displays the teleology of action, an image of human experience as a series of rational actions with a necessitous end.

How Plot Means

The fundamental paradox of plot is that it adumbrates a universal or detachable wisdom having implications outside the particular represented situation through a dynamic process of development. A plot shows us something about the narrative world by changing that world in some important way: It alters or reorders the world even as it provides an interpretation of it. How can action and plot simultaneously gloss and transform the narrative world? Which world are they glossing—the world defined by the relations at the beginning of the story or at its conclusion (often a very different world, as in *One Hundred Years of Solitude* or *Gone with the Wind*)? Aristotelian dramaturgy solves this problem by displaying a certain moment in the presentation—the peripeteia, the anagnorisis, or the catastrophe—as alone indicative of the true state of affairs. Oedipus seems to be successful and justified in his authority, but he is actually living in wretched sinfulness and appalling ignorance. Physically blind and stripped of authority at the end of the play, Oedipus has been implicitly blind, his authority equivocal, from the beginning. To an audience wondering which of these contrasting figures was the real Oedipus, we could reply that they were identical; the action of the play simply made the character's implicit qualities manifest. As long as we agree with Aristotle in regarding dramatic action as a privileged trope, this answer will be correct. But few narratives are as dominated or fully constituted by their plot as *Oedipus*. *A Christmas Carol* also presents the transformation of its principal, but here the transformation is privileged in some ways (we assume Scrooge has reached a final stage of development and will not turn back) but not in others (when we call someone "a regular Scrooge" we are not referring to his surprising and prodigious generosity). For most audiences, the "real" Scrooge is the miser constrained by a plot which remains external to the character we remember; Scrooge does not contain the seeds of his transformation in the same way Oedipus does.

This paradox can be illuminated by considering briefly the range of relations between action and the narrative world. The most familiar relation is an opposition in which the principal's action functions as an affront to a given social order. The hero wishes to oppose or transcend the limitations of his world; the world generally compromises or defeats this proposed action; the rhythm of opposition shapes the audience's perception of the action. The heroes of such stories are often described as being in their world but not of it: Don Quixote, Thomas Sutpen, and Dorothea Brooke (whom Eliot begins by presenting as a latter-day Saint Theresa) are typical. When an affronting hero has closer affinities with the social world, as in *The Red and the Black* or *The Princess Casamassima,* the resulting action, whereby a representative of society destroys himself by setting himself against the social order, tends toward tragedy—a pattern Erich Auerbach finds characteristic of the great nineteenth-century novels.[2]

But the world need not oppose the principal's planned action; even if it does, this adversary relationship, which displays the conflict between self and world, may be subordinate to another kind of display. In the film version of *The Wizard of Oz* the conflicts between Dorothy and the figures of authority in Kansas generate a dream in which Dorothy is constrained by the wizard's commands and the witch's threats. These conflicts shape the action of the film, but the point of the action seems less teleological than spectacular—that is, it provides a thread which motivates a scenic presentation of the land of Oz. When action has a primarily scenic valence, the world provides a theater, setting, or foil which displays the action as spectacle without determining its ending or meaning. Hollywood musicals, which commonly reduce plot to the continuity which separates and motivates the production numbers the audience has come to see, treat action as spectacle; but even when the movie presents an intricate plot like that of Hitchcock's *To Catch a Thief,* the audience may well consider that plot essentially a pretext for a decorative pictorial survey of the French Riviera. When Cyril Hare observes that the most effective way to give a detective story distinction is to provide an unusual background (a brewery, a traveling circuit court, a burlesque show),[3] he is assuming that the plot of crime and detection is so formulaic that it can be made tellable primarily by serving as a catalyst or spectacle in an unusual new world.

To go still further, the relation between action and the narrative world may be genuinely collaborative: The world may allow the opportunity for incipient spiritual or imaginative values to become manifest. The paradigm is the synoptic Gospels, in which Jesus' divinity can be displayed only through his conflict with the temporal world, but there are many other examples. Early Christian theologians read the necessity of the Savior's coming back into Adam's fall to produce the doctrine of *felix culpa:* only by sinning could man be saved. In Dante, action similarly functions as incarnation rather than affront; Hell, Purgatory, and Paradise offer souls the opportunity, by being and doing as they desire, to act themselves out. The Franklin's Tale, which seems initially to turn on the conflict of wills between Dorigen and Aurelius, ends by displaying the extraordinary generosity of each of its male principals, a generosity the story has clearly been developed specifically to display. These examples will suggest how closely the idea of action as incarnation is linked to the idea of action as affront, how spiritual and imaginative powers are rarely manifested except through conflict. The difference is one of emphasis:

Does the narrative display the dynamics of conflict, or the nature of the values emerging through conflict? In his Preface to *The Portrait of a Lady*, James describes "the germ of my idea" not as a plot or "set of relations" or "situations," but rather as "the sense of a single character," Isabel Archer, whom the plot was designed to display. How can a character be conceived except in terms of specific situations and dramatic conflicts? James proposes several answers to this question, beginning with a non-answer. His "grasp of a single character" was "an acquisition I had made . . . after a fashion not here to be retraced." In order to answer the question, "If the apparition was still to be placed how came it to be so vivid?" James would need "to write the history of the growth of one's imagination." Finally, however, he suggests that to the degree that a figure has assumed a given form in his meditations, "the figure has to that extent . . . *been* placed—placed in the imagination that detains it, preserves, protects, enjoys it."[4] Here the conflict between Isabel and Osmond and the larger conflict between American and European values are invoked as a way of focusing, projecting, and displaying the heroine's moral intelligence.

A fourth relation between action and the world, which all the other three imply, is Aristotle's figural relation, in which action functions as trope. In detective stories, if Hare's analysis is accepted, the conventional plot has no formal relation to the background which makes it tellable; murder is equally at home among Georgette Heyer's obsessively witty juveniles and Emma Lathen's world of corporate finance. In most nondetective cases, however, the relation is far more intimate: The narrative world implies an unchanging system of means, values, or relations, which the action develops sequentially. Any narrative whose plot can be analyzed thematically is using plot as a figure for its theme (sc., Aristotle's *dianoia*, "thought"). In allegories like *Pilgrim's Progress*, the plot is intended as a transparent vehicle; once the theme has been read through it, it has no residual interest, at least not for the author. *Joseph Andrews* begins ("It is a trite but true observation that examples work more forcibly on the mind than precepts")[5] as if the plot were equally transparent, but it is not; and in general action is no simpler in its relation to its ostensible subject than other tropes like metaphor and irony are in relation to theirs. Kenneth Burke has called the way in which action expresses a timeless system of relations sequentially "the temporizing of essence."[6] His analysis suggests that the thematic essence thus temporized is no less fictive or more authoritative than the plot which unfolds it; narration and exposition simply represent different, necessarily interdependent, tropes.

Action can serve as affront, spectacle, or incarnation, but it is only in its status as trope that it can mean anything, in hermeneutical terms, at all. Don Quixote may oppose every standard of decorum his society prescribes, but if he did not also express some of that society's fundamental wishes and beliefs, the collision would be pointless. Since the narrative world is never simply given or directly imitated but created in part as a function of its plot—since the world and the plot of a story necessarily imply each other—the complex relations possible between action and the world suggest that action can have several valences as a trope. A formulaic plot may act as a conversion or ritual whose outcome is definitive and more or less predictable from the beginning. In the classical detective story, for example, it is given that some member of a closed circle must be the criminal, and that he must have acted for some intelligible reason. Hence the detective plot assures us implicitly that the world is ultimately knowable because we trust that the puzzling events of the plot will function as clues to its resolution.

Frequently, the conventions of plot work to make agents and events typical of particular historical forces or theories rather than of human nature or the world in general. In *The Historical Novel,* Lukács treats the plots and characters of Scott's novels as synecdoches figuring the rise of the unheroic English bourgeoisie. Readers of detective stories can predict from the beginning how an ideal world must turn out; the audience for historical novels like *The Charterhouse of Parma* treats the narrated incidents as representative figures offering a way of understanding the historical past. A plot can be prophetic in the hortatory sense, like the plot of *A Christmas Carol,* whose relation to the world is governed by a wish: If only this would happen! (Readers who remember Scrooge as a type of meanness are attesting the difficulty of endowing an exhortation with the same authority as an observed type.) Or it can be prophetic in a diagnostic sense, as in Dante: This is what must become of people, because it follows from their present behavior. (Compare the later detective novels of Ross Macdonald: This is what must have happened in the past, because only it can explain what we observe socially and culturally in the present.) Finally, plot can be a hypothesis or supposition, as in Borges's garden of forking paths: This is how things could be; after all, the world may well be like this.

The valence of a plot's meaning, the authority its assertions command, will vary depending on whether it functions as ritual, historical analysis, exhortation, diagnosis, or simple hypothesis. Whatever its function, however, plot operates as a trope cognate with, and to a great extent convertible to, the tropes of character and world. Consider for example the affinity between the California landscape and the hard-boiled detective. Herbert Ruhm has demonstrated[7] how the hard-boiled detective grew out of hard-boiled adventurers like Natty Bumppo, Deadwood Dick, and Buffalo Bill. For all his analytical intelligence, Dashiell Hammett's Continental Op is essentially an urban cowboy, the bringer of violent justice to a lawless world. California, originally acclaimed by frontier myth as the garden of the world, later developed an equally symbolic reputation as a place of glamor and disillusionment, of instant fortunes and shady histories. Just as the imaginative landscapes of Hardy and Faulkner seem implicitly to predict their own futures, the California landscape implies the urban cowboy—the rough hero in search of an ideal of truth—and the two together invite, indeed require, a plot which will incorporate a movement from the celebration of superficial glamor to the discovery, through violent action, of universal guilt—the plot of the hard-boiled detective story. The mythic California landscape, the figure of the private eye, the hard-boiled plot of crime and detection—each of them is a trope for the fallen world urgently in need of therapeutic truth which the genre projects.

Narrative plot is then a trope which, in concert with other tropes, helps project a world; it can be (as in Aristotelian tragedy), but need not be, a privileged trope, and its claims to authority may, but need not, be displayed in its ending. Far from being simply a natural sequence, narrative plot depends on its status as trope for its mimetic potency. One way to analyze the nature of plot as a trope is by considering two genres seldom considered primarily narrative in order to examine the relation between plot and the teleology of action.

Acting and Action in Shakespearean Tragedy

In his lecture "From *Henry V* to *Hamlet*," Harley Granville-Barker applauds *Hamlet* as "the triumph of dramatic idea and of character over plot";[8] we may concur in this observation while taking exception to its terms. Granville-Barker's description of *Henry V* as "a play of action," whose hero is "the perfect man of action," but whose action lacks "any spiritually significant idea" (144, 146), suggests that not every human action is dramatically significant. Audiences who categorize films like *Bullitt* or *The Green Berets* as action movies are defining action in terms of its significant consequences, but action on the screen (and, Granville-Barker might add, in *Henry V*) is often better described by Kenneth Burke's contrasting term, motion, or by Shakespeare's description, sound and fury, signifying nothing. Loaded pistols, pitched battles, and the constant threat of death are not necessarily indications of what Aristotle means by action. Action is after all a trope, not a given quantity of events or relations in one's life or in historical chronicles. Granville-Barker contends that the triumph of Shakespearean tragedy is a triumph of character revelation over the "external action" in which the drama once "formally" inhered (152). I would suggest instead that Shakespeare's gradual mastery of tragedy is precisely a more authoritative grasp of the nature of plot.

It is a commonplace of Shakespearean criticism that Shakespeare began with his sources (Plutarch, Holinshed, and so on) and developed them with increasing freedom. But Shakespeare's sources are chosen, not given, and chosen, as *Romeo and Juliet*, *Hamlet*, and *Othello* indicate, from a wide variety of material. What Shakespeare was given, what he could not help but choose, was a theater, a set of acting and staging conventions and a concomitant set of assumptions about what was theatrically effective. The tradition of Elizabethan theater from Sackville through Marlowe is essentially a tradition of rhetorical declamation whose influence, or whose earliest fruits, may be found in the Elizabethan translations of Seneca. T. S. Eliot, contrasting the Elizabethan Seneca with Kyd, has commented: " 'Plot' in the sense in which we find plot in *The Spanish Tragedy* does not exist for Seneca. He . . . interested his auditors entirely by his embellishments of description and narrative and by smartness and pungency of dialogue; suspense and surprise attach solely to verbal effects."[9] The events in *Thyestes* or *Hercules* do not incarnate a teleological rationale which the ending makes explicit; they are a succession of horrors which motivate a series of rhetorically effective speeches. The great theatrical events in Elizabethan tragedy—in *Gorboduc*, in *The Spanish Tragedy*, in *Tamburlaine*—are speeches. It is of course possible for tragic action to develop rhetorically, as it does in the theater of Racine. But in *Phèdre* each speech advances the action of the whole play and displays the anguished conflicts within the principals, so that speech has become action, whereas in English tragedy before Shakespeare speeches tend to coagulate into setpieces that interrupt the action by expatiating on or from a particular unchanging attitude, as the production numbers might be displayed in a musical tragedy. This is less true of Kyd than of Seneca, less true of Marlowe than Kyd. Even in *Edward II*, however, the image of fortune's wheel whereby Mortimer figures his own end (V.6.59–63)[10] shows how completely he conceives the rhythm of tragedy as something external to himself as an individual.

Marlowe's heroes see action either as something entirely within their control or, in their decline, as something that happens to them. Faustus, the exemplary Marlovian hero, spends the last hour of his life wishing he could escape the consequences of his pact with Mephistopheles; his very panic makes the conversion he longs for impossible. What makes Marlowe's heroes compelling is their voices, their command of a rhetoric less expressive than impressive. So too are Shakespeare's early heroes figures of speech rather than figures of action; or, to put it more accurately,

Shakespeare's active heroes are paired with Marlovian rhetoricians like Aaron the Moor and Faulconbridge the Bastard. The heroic role in the early plays is divided between relatively inarticulate figures like Talbot, in *1 Henry VI*, whose personal identity is so completely a function of his generalship that he can tell the Countess of Auvergne, "I am but shadow of myself" (II.4.50),[11] and relatively inactive figures like Henry VI who move the audience by commenting pathetically or ironically on actions external to themselves.

A crucial feature in the development of Shakespearean tragedy from 1592 to 1600 is the fusing of figures capable of action with figures capable of reflective and expressive speech in order to display action theatrically. Already in *Richard III* Shakespeare's rhetoric is more flexible: Richard's delight in his villainy and his coldly self-conscious grasp of *Realpolitik* are far beyond the range of the earlier histories' verse and even further beyond the indiscriminate ranting of *Titus Andronicus*. Through Richard's sense of himself as a character, Shakespeare can present his murders and betrayals as part of a pattern of action which can end only with his death. In *Richard II* he goes still further, making Richard's command of language a fatal facility which substitutes for the action necessary to oppose Bolingbroke, or even to accept his fealty (e.g., in III.3.194–95). In *Romeo and Juliet* the hero begins with a less impressive rhetorical range—his complaints about Rosaline are conventionally euphuistic—but his ability finally to see his own experience as at once uniquely personal and part of a larger pattern (e.g., in V.3.88–100) gives his voice a much wider resonance; his voice and Juliet's are the first which develop such a resonance in the course of an English tragedy. The rhetorical range of the play is further extended by the prose of Mercutio and the Nurse, but not until Prince Hal does Shakespeare create a hero who demonstrates his capacity for action (here, his fitness to serve as king) through his deliberate mastery of different rhetorics and the worlds whose values they express. The Marlovian ranter of *1 Henry IV*, Hotspur, realizes to his inexpressible chagrin that by defeating him Hal has at once mastered everything significant in Hotspur's rhetoric of martial valor and annexed the glory of his earlier victories.

Rhetorical characters—characters whose personality is a function of their speaking voices, and who act only by speaking—reappear in *Julius Caesar*, but, as Granville-Barker notes, Shakespeare "now relegates rhetoric to its proper dramatic place. Cassius is rhetorical by disposition; Antony because it suits his purpose" (148). His interest is rather in the problematical relation of Brutus to the assassination of Caesar—the relation of Brutus the contemplative stoic to Brutus the agent of violence and misrule as he struggles to comprehend the meaning of his action. If *Julius Caesar* is indeed the turning point in Shakespeare's career as tragedian, that is because it is the last tragedy in which the two senses of acting are split between two characters. Brutus is an agent like Talbot, Bolingbroke, and Prince Hal, a man whose identity is defined by the actions he undertakes. Antony is a figure like Richard III, Mercutio, and the Bastard, a figure whose identity is shaped by the roles and the corresponding rhetoric he self-consciously adopts. Shakespeare's theater presented him with a fundamentally histrionic or rhetorical conception of action: The development of Shakespearean tragedy toward *Hamlet* is shaped by an attempt to unite that conception with an Aristotelian conception of *proairesis*. It is an attempt on the one hand to make dramatic action theatrically effective, on the other to disclose the deeper meaning underlying the declamatory plays of the earlier Elizabethans.

Hamlet dramatizes the relation between action and acting by making it the subject of the play. Its hero, though temperamentally histrionic, is far more introspective than Antony or his theatrical forbears and more reluctant to take any definite action against Claudius. Throughout the first two acts of the play, Hamlet's predominant note is one of metaphysical petulance at having to act in a way apparently at odds with his own nature and prescribed solely by external forces (I.5.188–89). Not until he hears the Player's very Senecan account of the death of Priam, whose unjustly slain king and "mobled queen" so strangely recall his own parents, and whose principal agent Pyrrhus he identifies simultaneously with his uncle and himself (for he too has acted "like a neutral to his will and matter"), does Hamlet chide himself, first for not acting the avenger's theatrical part (II.2.560–93), and then for trying to act that part in purely theatrical terms, as if for its effect on an audience rather than a more direct end (594–99). His resolution is characteristic: He will act by acting, confirming Claudius's guilt by having the murder of Gonzago played. What he cannot yet know, but will ultimately realize, is that action is more consequential than acting, and that in a world as deceptive as Elsinore, action necessarily involves the kind of acting, or "seeming," he had once proudly disdained. Hamlet begins with a confident sense of his own identity in his integrity and his superiority to his fickle mother and her satyr-like husband; by the time he kills Polonius, he is enmeshed in the guilt inevitable in a world of appearances. No longer able to define himself in theatrical isolation from the world, he must accept the identity his actions imply. The conflict between his resistance to and acceptance of such an identity informs the movement of the soliloquies, Shakespeare's greatest rhetorical set-pieces, and the action of the play as a whole.

In one sense Hamlet's uniquely histrionic temperament makes the play a tour de force, an unrepeatable solution to the problem of how to display action. But the method of tragedy is to dramatize this problem, not to resolve it, and Hamlet's self-consciousness about acting a role requiring purposive action is a key to all the later tragedies. Iago goads Othello by persuading him that his wife and lieutenant are playing roles: Othello's revulsion becomes so great that, like Hamlet, he cannot accept even his own sexual identity. Lear, in divesting himself of his roles as father and king, brings calamity to his family and kingdom and leaves himself unaccommodated, a man whose personal identity has been stripped away by his own action. Macbeth, drifting through the murder of Duncan as if playing a part, finds that part increasingly determining his nature. In each case the theatrical rhetoric which asserts a fixed and independent identity, but which makes that identity tellable (or showable), is tempered by a growing awareness that identity as a function of action is never independent and never fixed except in death. As in *Hamlet*, the conflict between the assertion of the individual voice and the demands of action is what makes Shakespeare's dramatic action theatrically effective, or, to put it the other way around, what consecrates the rhetorical posturing of his heroes as significant action.

Plot in the English Sonnet

Shakespeare's early histories and tragedies mark a progression from the presentation of striking events and rhetorically accomplished speeches to the grasp of the teleological and psychological motives that display events as a plot: What begins as one kind of action eventually becomes a trope for the conscious awareness of human experience. The history of the English sonnet (that is, the sonnet as written in English, not the sonnet adopting the form of three quatrains and a closing couplet) describes virtually the opposite pattern. The earliest sonnets in English, generally translations or close adaptations of Italian and French models, already display a high degree of formal and thematic integrity—that is, the sequence of ideas and images has a unity and consonance absent from many Elizabethan tragedies. Although the English sonnet depends formally on a teleological rationale, however, this teleology is seldom manifested through a sequential plot. As Shakespearean tragedy begins with events and moves toward a fuller teleology, the English sonnet begins with a teleology and gradually adds events.

The following sonnet by Fulke Greville offers a representative example of Renaissance formal structure:

Farewell, sweet boy, complain not of my truth;
Thy mother loved thee not with more devotion;
For to thy boy's play I gave all my youth;
Young master, I did hope for your promotion.
While some sought honors, princes' thoughts observing,
Many wooed fame, the child of pain and anguish,
Others judged inward good a chief deserving,
I in thy wanton visions joyed to languish.
I bowed not to thy image for succession,
Nor bound thy bow to shoot reformed kindness;
Thy plays of hope and fear were my confession;
The spectacles to my life was thy blindness;
But, Cupid, now farewell, I will go play me
With thoughts that please me less, and less betray me.[12]

We could easily find contemporary sonnets having more or fewer features of a sequential plot. This one uses a number of preterite verbs, though they describe habitual past behavior, not a particular course of action, and display a conflict without resolving it. The surprise of learning the boy's identity would be more in the nature of a narrative resolution if the poem had hinted more strongly that his identity were in question, but that would have made the point too obvious, and even so the poem would have functioned less as an anecdote than as a riddle, a popular form for Elizabethan sonnets. (For more openly anecdotal sonnets, compare "Lucifer by Starlight" and "Leda and the Swan.") The formal unity of Greville's sonnet and of sonnets generally is based on their structure. Since a fourteen-line poem cannot be divided evenly into quatrains, the sonnet form is unbalanced: Italian sonnets are normally divided into an octave and a sestet, English sonnets into three quatrains and a couplet. The turn before the sestet or couplet corresponds roughly to the anagnorisis of Aristotelian tragedy, except that the revelation is the reader's, not the character's. (Greville's speaker does not suddenly realize at line 13 that he is addressing Cupid.) Mario Praz, writing of the Italian sonnet, has traced this structure to the sonnet's roots in song: "Its very musical structure postulated this: the second part represented the conclusion, a conclusion which was the culmination. . . . By its very structure . . . the sonnet asked for a *concetto*, a witty invention, at the end; in the same manner in which the two premises of a syllogism are summed up in the conclusion."[13] The tendency toward wit is still greater in sonnets which, like Greville's, end with a couplet, for, as Paul Fussell has pointed out, "The very disproportion of the two parts of the Shakespearean sonnet, the gross imbalance between the twelve-line problem and the two-line solution, has about it something risible and even straight-faced farcical: it invites images of balloons and pins."[14]

Although the concluding couplet of an English sonnet is likely to depend on paradox or wit, it does not follow that readers of sonnets integrate them only as rhetorical exercises or sentimental riddles, for even sonnets with as little sequential action as Greville's invite integration at several different levels. Most obviously, the sonnet can be recovered as a gnomic form, two lines of conventional wisdom motivated by twelve lines of circumstantial preliminaries. To reverse these terms, the reader can integrate the poem as an argument leading to an unexpected yet logical conclusion. Why did Greville's speaker hope for promotion? In what sense was the boy's blindness the speaker's spectacles? A reader considering the poem retrospectively can appreciate the aptness of its conclusion, but to a reader considering these questions as he reads the poem offers another possibility of integration: the integration of the reader's own experience as interpreter, based on his constant reinterpretation of what he has read in the light of what he is reading. Just as my last sentence seemed at first to require one grammatical integration ("as he reads the poem") but actually requires another ("the poem offers"), Greville's sonnet seems at first to be addressed to a loved friend; by the time he reveals it is addressed to the god of love himself, the reader, who has treated this patron as the object of the speaker's affection, has mistaken devotion to love itself for devotion to a loved one, a confusion essential to the emotion Greville is representing (for example, in his concluding line). This confusion in turn indicates a final level of integration, the placing of each sonnet within the sonnet tradition. Stephen Booth observes that "more than a writer in any other genre, a sonneteer depends for his effects on the conjunction or conflict of what he says with what the reader expects. Like the basic courtly love convention from which it grew, the sonnet convention is one of indecorum. . . . [It] relies upon a reader's sense of the frame of reference in which the writer operates and the writer's apparent deviation from that pattern in a rhetorical action that both fits and violates the expected pattern."[15] The success of Greville's poem depends on the existence of an alternative subgenre (poems addressed to departing friends or lovers) to which, until the couplet, it could plausibly belong. The reference to "thy mother" (1. 2) would then be a merely rhetorical comparison, the references to "thy boy's play" (1. 3) and "thy wanton visions" (1. 8) recollections of particular activities, not a kind of activity. The retrospective summary, "I've given you the best years of my life," is a plausible overstatement; when Greville identifies "you" as love itself, the sentiment, however hackneyed, is no longer exaggerated. This reading is supported by the position of this poem as the last secular love poem, and nearly the last sonnet, in *Caelica*.

My point in describing all these ways in which sonnets may be integrated is not to claim great complexity for Greville's unassuming poem, but simply to emphasize the fact that, although it has no definite plot, it has a principal agent: the reader who makes sense of the conclusion in terms of the argument, of the argument in terms of guesses about its conclusion, about each figure by reassessments of the poem's developing pattern, and of the poem as a whole in terms of the sonnet tradition. Greville's poem contains a turn after line 12, but like most sonnets, the poem itself is a turn as well, an unexpected but appropriate addition to a universe of paradoxical discourse.

Evidently the addition to the sonnet of a plot in the narrow sense of a sequence of events embodying conflict, suspense, and resolution does not materially affect the reader's experience of the poem or the poetic form. The reader is the principal agent in any sonnet, whether or not it has this sort of plot. An examination of some sonnets with a more fully developed plot—the opening poem of *Astrophel and Stella*, Drayton's "Since there's no help," *Amoretti* 75 ("One day I wrote her name upon the strand"), Milton's "Methought I saw my late espoused Saint"—does not reveal them to be any more dramatic than sonnets without plots; indeed it is difficult to remember which sonnets have plots and which do not. The English sonnet in general did not evolve toward the anecdote, but it did evolve toward a fuller accommodation of anecdote (Herbert's "Redemption" being an early example). In this respect it developed in the opposite direction from the short story, which begins as an anecdote and gradually dispenses, as in Chekhov and Joyce, with plot in the sense of a sequence of represented events. The relatively slight dependence of the sonnet on a sequential plot is illustrated by the vogue of sonnet sequences, which imply a plot without displaying its events. As C. S. Lewis has observed: "The sonnet sequence . . . is not a way of telling a story. It is a form which exists for the sake of prolonged lyrical meditation. . . . External events—a quarrel, a parting, an illness, a stolen kiss—are every now and then mentioned to provide themes for the meditation."[16]

Plot in the sonnet, as in Shakespearean tragedy, is not simply a representation or selection of a natural, chronologically ordered sequence of events; the sense of plot instead grows slowly out of a highly sophisticated system of prosodic and thematic conventions. Unlike Shakespeare, who works from historical events to their dramatic rationale, the Elizabethan sonneteers work from a formal and rhetorical rationale to the possibility of including more elaborate sequences of events. In neither case, however, is human behavior assumed to be inherently meaningful, or action a natural or privileged or unpremeditated trope. To the degree that we can speak of plot at all, it is always a conceptual category, not a natural sequence.

Action and Existence

Action is a trope for human existence: It equates being alive with a sequence of purposive, discrete, consequential, morally significant decisions. Except in Aristotelian tragedy and works modeled on Aristotelian principles, however, it is not a privileged trope; that is, it is one way among others of imaging human experience. What valence does action have in narrative? Its range of implications is indicated by its range of uses or formal effects, which is surprisingly wide. Broadly speaking, stories which display the potential of human agents to change their world do so by means of fully articulated plots; as plot becomes marginal or fragmentary, the power of human subjects is correspondingly reduced or takes the form of consciousness rather than the potential for action.

1. Action can cohere in an expressive plot and teleology, as in *Oedipus*. Here the plot as trope reveals the essential nature of the hero and his definitive relation to his world. Modern plots of this sort are rarer than are sometimes supposed, but they persist in works like *The Ambassadors* (in which Strether learns about himself and Woollett, Massachusetts, by learning about a world he has never known), *Rules of the Game* (in which the climactic shooting of André Jurieu brings to the surface tensions implicit in the social order and prophesies the end of that order), and *Potemkin* (in which the sailors' mutiny is vindicated as an episode in the revolutionary dialectic through its acceptance by the people of Odessa and the rest of the fleet). The distinctive feature here is the intimacy and fullness with which the plot expresses the constitutive features of the narrative world.

2. More often, action coheres in a plot presupposing a conventional, and largely unexamined, worldview; that is, plot is grafted onto a world whose assumptions it treats as unexceptionable or irrelevant. In this category belong Dickens's early novels, the formulaic plots of most Hollywood westerns and thrillers, and most folktales and collections of stories like *The Thousand and One Nights* (except in its frame-tale) and the *Decameron*. By the end of the story the tensions of the plot are resolved, but the world remains the same, for it serves only as background for the plot, not as its figurative tenor. As Nick Charles tells his wife at the end of *The Thin Man*, "Murder doesn't round out anybody's life except the

murdered's and sometimes the murderer's."[17] Critics who claim that formulaic works like *The Searchers* or *The Maltese Falcon* transcend the limits of their genres are usually claiming to see an expressive function uncommon to most formulaic plots.

3. Action may cohere in a plot designed to display character, thought, or spectacle. This form, which has become increasingly common in the twentieth century, corresponds to Ronald Crane's plots of character and thought.[18] Crane's definitions make character and thought subordinate to plot; the point at issue is whether the plot displays the dynamics of change or reveals, however gradually, a relatively unchanging person or way of thinking or visual or verbal technique. Plots displaying character include those of *A Portrait of the Artist as a Young Man, The Last Laugh,* and *Citizen Kane;* plots displaying thought (much rarer) include *The Magic Mountain* and most of Shaw's plays and Godard's films; plots displaying spectacle include Hollywood disaster movies like *The Poseidon Adventure* and musicals like *Singin' in the Rain* which seek to integrate production numbers closely into the plot. Movie epics like *Lawrence of Arabia* also belong in this category, though it is hard to say exactly where.

4. Revelation can displace plot as the focal point of the story, or, to put it differently, revelation can serve as plot. This is the characteristic method of the modern short story, whose teleology is predicated on the audience's comprehensive vision rather than a character's completed action or resolved dilemma, and in which often nothing seems to happen. Many examples could be drawn from Turgenev, Chekhov, Joyce, Sherwood Anderson, and more recent storytellers. This is also the method of Browning's dramatic monologues, whose convention is that a character's habitual speech will give him away completely within a hundred lines or so. At the end of "Caliban upon Setebos," Caliban has completed no action and undergone no change, but the audience knows everything there is to know about him; if the poem continued, there would be nothing more to learn. The distinctive feature of this category is the adumbration of a coherent teleology in the absence of a sequence of events.

5. The opposite configuration is possible: A sequence of events may be elaborated without embodying an expressive, or even a formulaic, teleology. In Busby Berkeley musicals the plot, however fully developed, has little relation to the numbers the film displays. This tenuous relation is thematically developed in French New Wave films like *Breathless* and *Shoot the Piano Player,* in which the principals are involved in gangster plots that seem to have nothing to do with them, even if they are the gangsters. (Compare Charlie Kohler's relation to the villains in *Shoot the Piano Player* to Roger Thornhill's relation to the villains in *North by Northwest;* each is drawn into the plot accidentally, but Thornhill suc-

cessfully adapts to his involvement.) The point here is not the absence of action but its irrelevance, so that a backstage musical like Warner Brothers' showcase *Thank Your Lucky Stars*, or any of the Marx Brothers' movies, can seem to have too much plot for its own good.

6. The plot can be open-ended, intelligible but inconclusively developed, with teleological implications which remain unresolved. This is the method of *The Counterfeiters* and *A Passage to India*, and of such open films as *Red Desert* and Mel Brooks's *History of the World, Part I*. Most comic feature films are more or less episodic; if comic sketches have thematic connections without definite teleological consequences, as in *Modern Times*, we speak of the comedy as open-ended (cf. *The General, Bringing Up Baby*, and *Dr. Strangelove*). In *Rashomon*, Akira Kurosawa presents four incompatible accounts of the same events. The film has what might be called a metateleology, but its conclusion depends thematically on irresolution; the film is a faithful representation of an unfollowable world.

7. Instead of being unfollowable, the world can be all-too-followable, with no allowances for the variables of chance or human will. Hence the plot may be claustrophobic rather than open-ended, as in the work of such naturalists as Zola, Norris, and Dreiser. Here characters act out their destinies under the illusion of freedom but in unwitting accord with social, political, or economic determinants. *McTeague* and *An American Tragedy* do not display the teleology of action (there is no action in the Aristotelian sense) but rather the way in which circumstances preclude action; hence their thematic implications are not for theories of individual action but for theories of sociological reform. Works in this category differ from works in the first category in the predictability of their teleology. Not only the most likely outcome, but its causes and rationale, are known from the beginning rather than dramatized through moral decision, and plot becomes a trope for an oppressive external environment, not for the interaction between people and their world. The strongly fatalistic cast of such works sometimes risks failure to engage the audience's narrativity very completely. One compensating pleasure they offer is the thoroughness with which oppressive forces can be discerned within a large and complex social organization. Successful works of this sort therefore tend to run to great length (hence the American naturalists excelled in novels rather than short stories, and Erich von Stroheim attempted to film *McTeague* in 23 reels as *Greed*). There are many borderline cases like Hardy's novels and Ibsen's plays. The best-known Hollywood examples are the gangster films of the 1930s and the *films noirs* of the 1940s in which the criminal protagonist is eventually trapped by his complicity in previous crimes. The teleological motifs of such works are indicated by the titles of Hardy's *Satires of Circumstance* and Jacques Tourneur's *Out of the Past*.

8. The action may imply a plot which is ultimately unrecoverable: The story's effect, that is, may depend on frustrating the audience's expectations rather than satisfying them. This is the characteristic strategy of postmodern works like *The Crying of Lot 49* and *Last Year at Marienbad*, which explicitly raise hermeneutical problems they do not resolve. But the inconclusiveness of such works need not be hermeneutical; it can be based instead on an indefinite extension of Scheherezade's trick of deferring the conclusion, as in soap operas. In this form it goes back in European literature at least to *Tristram Shandy* and *Jacques the Fatalist*, each of which pointedly implies developments and a conclusion which never come to pass.

9. Instead of raising the expectation of a coherent plot directly by devices like Diderot's addresses to the reader, a work may imply a more tentative promise through its generic status or through residual conventions of significance. We expect novels and films to tell intelligible stories because most of them do. For this reason it is difficult for a film to disorient an audience very completely in its first five minutes or so; the audience *expects* to be disoriented at first, because they assume the deferral of any explicit teleology. *A Sentimental Journey* seems to challenge its readers less openly than *Tristram Shandy* because its narrator does not keep raising questions about his project and his competence to complete it. (The full title, *A Sentimental Journey Through France and Italy*, is one of the few places in which a specific promise is made about the scope of the work, but the reader has to finish before realizing that Yorick has never reached Italy.) More recent examples include *The Confidence-Man* and *Jealousy*, both of which make their projects explicit only in their titles—if Melville had titled his novel *Confidence*, how long would it have taken his readers to notice that all those swindlers were the same person?—and *Dead Souls*, the greatest of all shaggy-dog stories.

10. Finally, the action of a story may be so minimal, episodic, or incoherent that no plot whatever is implied. Episodic action does not guarantee incoherence, for a story's events can display a thematic pattern without coalescing into a unified plot. In Rossellini's war films, for example, the conjunction of episodes projects certain themes—the simultaneous impossibility of political resistance and surrender, the clash of cultures in an occupied country, the unexpected depth and fragility of emotional commitments—in expository terms, without providing a formal teleology. Robert Flaherty achieves somewhat the same effect in *Nanook of the North*. At this point narrative begins to turn into something else, usually turning toward lyric or thematic modes. *Nausea*, perhaps the classic example of minimal narrative, is incoherent as narrative, but can be recovered, like Beckett's novels, as an extended meditation on the relation

between experience and the categories whereby it is apprehended. We might round out this category, and the entire survey, by mentioning the more openly confessional modes of recent literary criticism.

The variety of relations between action and meaning, which ranges from action as a maximally effective or privileged trope to action as inconsequential, irrelevant, futile, or philosophically invalid, corresponds to a range of attitudes toward the human subject: from person as agent to person as object or spectacle or person as consciousness. Evidently narrative plot can serve as the vehicle for philosophical beliefs from Platonism to determinism and existentialism: The world it images can be a rationally ordered world in which human purpose itself incarnates a higher order, or an intelligible world whose order is determined by laws beyond the individual will, or a purely contingent world made tellable only by frankly subjective observation. Narrative polytropy characteristically treats plot as a way of mediating between such different conceptions of human experience by presenting events as both contingent and inherently ordered, people as at once free to act and constrained by circumstance, the political order, or their own biology. Just as polytropic narratives present human life both *sub specie aetis* and *sub specie aeternitatis*, they present plot as a contingent trope which defines a relation (in different stories, a wide range of relations) between doing and being, action and existence.

8
Character

As plot is a trope for human experience, character is a trope for human identity. Just as plot is constituted as a trope by the way a story's action is displayed, we can speak of characters, as against plot functions, to the degree that an agent's identity is displayed polytropically, as intelligible but never entirely predictable, and above all as interesting in its own right. Like plot, character has become unfashionable in postwar criticism—Martin Price's recent study *Forms of Life*, like W. J. Harvey's earlier *Character and the Novel*, has the distinct cast of a rearguard action—but the grounds for suspicion toward character have been different. No one denies that people have experiences, and no one writing since Sartre is likely to confuse those experiences with the plots which represent them, but the tendency of poststructuralist critics like Jacques Derrida and Jacques Lacan to question the authority of the human subject has rendered the philosophical basis of character suspect. Putting aside the question of how stable and discrete one's personal identity can be, a question treated in suggestive detail by René Girard and Leo Bersani,[1] this suspicion of character seems based on a confusion, or at least too close an association, between characters and people.[2] Even if it became generally accepted that people did not function as authorizing agents, the concept of action would retain a certain historical currency, representing a way of thinking, if not an existing reality. So too the debate over the status of the human subject is largely irrelevant to character as a trope or conceptual category. In this chapter I wish to examine some of the conditions, historical and technical, under which characters (and character) have been displayed in an era which may well be approaching its end.

Before Character

Since character, as Price points out, is "an invention,"[3] it should be possible to say something about the conditions under which it was invented. Like the concepts of democracy and private property, character has been invented repeatedly, and repeatedly fallen into neglect, by different cultures, but the most important invention of character for our purposes was in fifth-century Athens, and its primary inventors were Sophocles and Euripides. This is not to deny the existence of characters before *The Women of Trachis* and *Antigone*, not only because generalizations about Athenian tragedy can never take account of lost plays, but because even Homer's epics abound in personal agents who are called, *faute de mieux*, characters. But Homer's characters seem more properly plot functions. As William H. Gass remarks, "Achilles is what Achilles does,"[4] and Achilles is certainly the most problematic figure in the *Iliad*, the one the poem most clearly displays. When Homer wishes to display a character like Odysseus more fully, he multiplies versions of his hero as seen, remembered, or imagined by others (his wife and son, his colleagues, his hosts, his enemies). The modern notion of character, by contrast, is nuclear in structure, implying some residual quality neither required by nor expended in the action, some resistance Todorov's narrative-men lack to exhaustion by their situation, plot function, or public action.

This nuclear or residual conception of character is antithetical to Aristotle's definition of character as "that in virtue of which we ascribe certain qualities to the agents";[5] indeed there is no single term in the *Poetics* which corresponds to the modern notion of character. Butcher notes that *ethos*, which is usually translated as "character," has the more narrowly focused meaning of an ethical disposition or incipient moral action, and needs to be supplemented by the intellectual or rational concept of *dianoia* in order to approximate our idea of character.[6] Aristotle's terms allow us to discuss the character of Achilles and Ajax and Hector, but these characters have no residual life, no qualities not expended in action, no capacity, as Erich Auerbach observes, for change;[7] they are never displayed as a distinctive trope for human identity.

In the Introduction to his translation of the *Oresteia*, Richmond Lattimore discusses the difference between Aeschylus and Sophocles as a difference between "lyric tragedy" and "actor's tragedy": "Sophocles turned tragedy inward upon the principal actors, and drama becomes drama of character. . . . *Agamemnon* is a play about the Trojan War, but *Antigone* is not a play about the Theban War, though that lies in the background."[8] Of the playwrights whose work has survived, Aeschylus provides the best illustrations of Aristotle's rule that tragedy is possible without character, but not without plot (VI.11:1450a). In his earliest extant play, *The Suppliant Maidens*, the principal character is a Chorus necessarily without psychological individuality; in *The Persians* and *Seven Against Thebes*, both structured as dialogues between the Chorus and a series of individuals about an ongoing offstage battle, the emphasis is on lyric ritual rather than dramatic action. This ritualistic emphasis persists even in *Prometheus Bound*, which might to a modern critic seem to offer the perfect opportunity for displaying the dynamics of individual character (cf. *Samson Agonistes*).

In the three plays of the *Oresteia*, especially in *Agamemnon* and *The Libation Bearers*, the dramatic action is more immediate, the agents more sharply focused as individuals. The audience does not merely hear about a conflict of wills but sees it unfold onstage. Even here, however, Aeschylus has not created what Lattimore calls actor's tragedy. In the first play, the psychology of the victim Agamemnon is perfunctory, that of the agent Clytemnestra obscure. What Aeschylus is displaying is the enactment of past bonds of kinship, loyalty, and hatred in the present, the determinative power of historical and legendary antecedents which his agents focus without grasping their implications, and which are much more interesting than they are. Anyone who has graded freshman essays on the *Oresteia* knows how much less a "character sketch" of Clytemnestra or Agamemnon illuminates the play than a study of any of its leading images (blood, serpents, nets, the soil), and how perverse and irrelevant it is to impute a personality to Cassandra. The principals define themselves with constant reference to formative past events—the slaughter of Thyestes' children, the abduction of Helen, the sacrifice of Iphigeneia—whose interplay determines and exhausts their dramatic vitality.

In *The Libation Bearers*, Aeschylus again emphasizes conflicting moral issues over individual psychology. Orestes' doubts about killing his mother are expressed in one line of verse (899) and immediately quelled by Pylades, who, in his only speech of the play, reminds Orestes of his duty to Apollo. Thereafter Orestes' dialogue with Clytemnestra has the flavor of a harrowing legal debate which both parties know will change the mind of neither. Orestes' concluding assertion to Clytemnestra—"You killed, and it was wrong. Now suffer wrong" (930)—although the pivotal line of the play and the *Oresteia* as a whole, focuses all the moral problems of the trilogy (was it wrong to kill Agamemnon? is it wrong to kill Clytemnestra? how can any act of vengeance be distinguished from the chain of atrocities which preceded it and be justified morally?) without at all illuminating Orestes or Clytemnestra as characters. The lines of conflict are sharp, but they are moral and ideological rather than psychological.

By *The Eumenides* Orestes, the title character of the trilogy, has all but vanished as a character. As his action in *The Libation Bearers* did not seem to be particularly his (cf. Oedipus's actions as King of Thebes), here his persecution and suffering do not seem particularly his. The debate between Apollo and the Chorus of Furies, a more civilized echo of the debates between Clytemnestra and Agamemnon (no open debate, but a treacherous murder) and between Orestes and Clytemnestra (a debate ending in murder), bears little relation to Orestes' individuality. The relation is almost entirely metaphoric and ritualistic, a preparation for the establishment of courts which will institutionalize and morally sanction the impetus to revenge. For this reason Orestes' acquittal and immediate departure neither resolve the play's problems nor significantly reduce its dramatic tension; he has been simply a token in the struggle between Apollo and the Furies. The Chorus of Furies-turned-Eumenides, which incarnates the transformation from vengeance to justice, is again, as in Aeschylus's earlier work, the true hero of the play.

A brief look at Sophocles' and Euripides' treatments of the story of the house of Atreus will show how much more fully they display their agents as characters. The middle play of Aeschylus's trilogy is aptly called *The Libation Bearers* because it displays a ritual (pouring libations on Agamemnon's grave) which marks a transition between staining the ground with Agamemnon's blood and sending the Eumenides underground as household gods and protectors of Athens, and incidentally emphasizes the bonds between Electra and the Chorus of foreign slave women. Both Sophocles' and Euripides' treatments of this material are called *Electra*, marking a shift in focus from ritual to the psychology of a character helpless to act. In Aeschylus, Orestes identifies himself to his sister less than a quarter of the way through the play; Electra's complaints are all addressed as prayers to her father's spirit, and most of them are made together with Orestes in active preparation for killing Clytemnestra. In Sophocles, Orestes conceals himself from Electra first by Pedagogus's false report of his death, then by entering with an urn he claims is full of his own ashes; he does not reveal himself until the play is three-quarters over. In the meantime Electra has the opportunity for bitter personal attacks on Clytemnestra, a memorable confrontation in which she asks her mother if the sacrifice of Iphigeneia justifies engendering children by Aegisthus (a scene for which there is no Aeschylean precedent), and an outpouring of grief and despair when she hears the news of her brother's death. Sophocles gives Electra a sister, Chrysothemis, whose counsels of prudence, like Ismene's to Antigone, focus the defiant attitude of her sister—here, the resentful frustration of Electra's forced inaction. Even when Sophocles' interest turns briefly from Electra, it is still an interest in character. His Clytemnestra, on receiving the report of Orestes' death, asks:

> Zeus, what shall I say? Shall I say "good luck"
> or "terrible, but for the best"? Indeed,
> my state is terrible if I must save
> my life by the misfortunes of myself. (765–68)

This speech displays a conflict of psychological impulses quite outside Aeschylus's interests. In Aeschylus conflict is always external: The guilt that Orestes might be assumed to feel over killing his mother is made palpable in her avenging Furies, and the issues her death raises are finally resolved in an open debate between the Furies and Apollo. In Sophocles we find characters whose nature is divided, so that their actions do not exhaust their moral and intellectual impulses. Of the Athenian tragedians whose work survives, Sophocles is closest in his handling of character to Aristotle's analysis: Character is subordinated to plot, but not translated so completely into action that it is not a distinct trope or locus of display.

In Euripides' version of the material, character takes precedence over dramatic action. Again Electra is given a confrontation with Clytemnestra during which she presents the moral case against her mother. But by this time Aegisthus has already been killed—stabbed in the back during a sacrifice—and Electra has already taunted his corpse in defeat; her speech to Clytemnestra, another ironic taunt, is designed more to vent her feelings than to direct or vindicate any action. Euripides' Clytemnestra expresses some regret for her crime; so do Orestes and Electra, though none of them feels threatened with retribution. Orestes is in fact so reluctant to kill his mother that he expresses doubt that Apollo's oracle was morally authoritative or even genuine: "O Phoebus, your holy word was brute and ignorant. . . . A polluted demon spoke it in the shape of god" (971, 979). When Electra in turn accuses him of cowardice, the relation between divine justice and psychological impulse has become so attenuated that it is impossible to tell whether she is right. Indeed, there is something in Euripides' characters, and in his whole conception of character, which Aristotle's ethical and intellectual terms (*ethos* and *dianoia*) do not comprehend, some impulse more purely emotional and histrionic, a need to act out one's feelings even if they are neither morally or logically efficacious, or even necessarily pleasurable. In Aeschylean tragedy, dramatic conflicts always turn on moral issues; since every agent acts in accord with the wishes of his or her patron deity, the plays, especially *The Eumenides*, have the quality of a divine psychomachia. The behavior of Aeschylus's characters is ethical and rational because no one ever does anything he or she believes to be wrong. But in Euripides characters like Phaedra and Medea constantly act against their own ideas of right and their own best interests simply because they cannot help themselves. Euripides sometimes attributes their passions to the work of the gods (Cypris in *Hippolytus*, Dionysus in *The Bacchae*), but more often his gods appear as pointedly irrelevant, *dei ex machina* whose function is to provide divine sanction for an action already completed, as Athena does in *Iphigeneia in Taurus* or the Dioscuri do in *Electra* (a construction and attitude Sophocles anticipates with the appearance of Heracles in *Philoctetes*).

It is not just the individual's ties to the divine order which Euripides loosens, but his ties to ritual and family as well. John Jones has noted already in Sophocles a weakening of "family solidarity" and "ritual forms" in favor of "personalising of consciousness" and "the pressure of individual will" and concludes that in Sophocles' *Electra* "the pious individual conceives his ritual activity in a new way, instrumentally."[9] Sophocles' characters are less pious than Aeschylus's—less loyal, in Kenneth Burke's phrase, to the sources of their being, less unquestioningly defined by their allegiance to divine justice, religious ritual, and ties of kinship—and Euripides' characters are less pious still.

Here then is a formula for the historical emergence of character: When the bonds joining the individual to the larger communities and ideals of worship, religious belief, and kinship have become tenuous enough to make piety a matter of choice rather than a requisite of personal identity, then it becomes possible to speak of character as a distinctive trope for human identity. Character is not to be confused with identity; people always and everywhere have an identity, whether or not they consider themselves individuals, and there is nothing necessarily more authentic, or even more individualistic, about defining people with reference to their emotional and sexual desires than with reference to their pious allegiances. Moreover, piety remains a constitutive element in all characters, even those in which it is partially eclipsed; if it did not, we could not make sense of any characters whose emotions and whose immediate situation were different from our own. Character is always defined with reference to piety, but it is only when pious allegiances offer the possibility of attenuation or abrogation that character becomes more than a function of ritual or plot. This historical process, as I suggested earlier, is not unique to fifth-century Athens; we find it again in seventeenth-century England, when, as Paul Delany has shown,[10] the growing importance of the individual quality of experience set down in journals and autobiographies reflects a similar diminution of religious and cultural piety which ultimately prepares the emergence of the novel, the literary form most closely concerned with the problematical nature of the individual's pious allegiances.

What Are Characters Made Of?

Like little girls and little boys, characters are an amalgam having properties distinct from those of their components. In criticism before the twentieth century, for example in Johnson's essays on Shakespeare, the question about what characters are made of or how they happen takes the form of a question about where they come from, and in Shakespeare's case at least the answer is clear: They are drawn from life. William H. Gass has offered a salutary corrective to this view: "Stories . . . and the people in them are made of words."[11] Although Price points out that "it is precisely because words differ from wood and cloth that they can be used to produce stories" (56), he agrees with Gass that characters are constructed from material that cannot simply be equated with life. A *via media* between the extreme arguments in favor of imitation and construction (themselves both sufficiently problematical concepts) might be indicated by the question of what the audience's sense of a given character is based on, what kind of information induces the perception of a character.

The most obvious and superficial way to render characters is in terms of external details. Aspiring novelists often overload their introductions of characters with precise physical descriptions, but the technique of external description plays a leading role in successful novels as different as *Père Goriot* and *Buddenbrooks*. The majority of silent comedians apart from Chaplin and Keaton—Chester Conklin, Snub Pollard, Larry Semon, Mack Swain, Harry Langdon—were essentially funny-looking people on whom gags were inflicted, and the use of actors as physical types persists in the casting of such character actors as Sidney Greenstreet and Wally Cox. Characters can be defined primarily in terms of a social function or role. Dan Seymour, who plays Abdul in *Casablanca*, is a well-known character actor, but an audience who does not recognize him from his other roles will perceive him simply and adequately as the doorman. Price suggests that this is the way we perceive most people in our own lives: "When a conductor approaches us in the railway car, we don't look to see if he has legs" (56). To go further, our knowledge of a character can be based on the presentation of his or her routine behavior, a presentation which may have little to do with the plot with which character is normally interdependent. By the end of *Nanook of the North*, the audience has a strong sense of the representative quality of Nanook and his family, in much the same way that Walt Disney's *Beaver Valley* presents what amounts to a character sketch of the beavers that live under particular conditions. Some of the Maysles brothers' documentary films (e.g., *Salesman*) create a similar sense of character based on habitual behavior. Finally, a character can be defined primarily by his voice, either in the sense of the physical timbre of his voice (the actors Eugene Pallette and George "Foghorn" Winslow), dramatized voice (such Dickensian creations as Alfred Jingle, the Artful Dodger, and Flora Finching), or narratorial voice (Huckleberry Finn, Holden Caulfield, Augie March). All these indications are based on external details, the kind of details we are most often in a position to notice about the people we encounter outside stories.

Another category to which we often refer our sense of character is a range of *topoi* or general truths different characters are felt to embody. The limiting case is that of Aesop's animals, whose individuality is shaped and exhausted by the gnomic morals they illustrate. A more complex case is the scholar Rinaldi in *Decameron* 8.7, whose plot function is gradually eclipsed by his denunciations of women's love for young men, speeches whose rhetoric defines him. Rinaldi lives for the audience not primarily for his role as avenging lover, still less for the originality of his thought, but for his passionate but formal mastery of rhetoric, an element which also plays a prominent role in the characters of Titus (10.8) and the unfortunate lovers of Day 4. Still more complex, though more purely rhetorical in conception, are the characters in *The Importance of Being Earnest*, in which even Algernon's butler is a master of paradox, and no one ever speaks except to prepare or complete a witty remark.

Wilde's characters already imply those figures of Shaw in which rhetorical mastery as such is subordinated to ideological analysis. In Shaw's comedy of demagoguery, characters like John Tanner, Andrew Undershaft, and Saint Joan deliver themselves of opinions which, while not submerging the play of ideas in ideological debate, give the characters a quality of commitment they do not have in Wilde. From Shaw it is only a short step to characters who are defined entirely in terms of their beliefs; here the limiting cases are the revolutionary characters in Soviet silent films like *Mother* and *Potemkin*. This ideological approach is not new. It is already implicit in Aeschylus's Orestes, whose actions seem motivated so little by personal animosity and so much by divine command.

But characters conceived in purely ideological terms are rare. A far more common presentation of character in terms of mental attitudes involves Jonsonian humors, those habitual and limited emotional dispositions whose name gained currency through Jonson's plays but which clearly influence such Shakespearean figures as Malvolio and Polonius. The delineation of character in terms of a humor or ruling passion reaches an unprecedented concentration in Pope's Moral Essays, but it survives today in movie comedians like Abbott and Costello and Bob Hope (particularly in his early films), who always play the same kinds of characters thrust into new situations and nominally into new identities, and in the characters of situation comedy, who reappear on television each week to act out new jokes based on the same premises of character: Ricky will never let Lucy have enough money, Lucy is always willing to try a new scheme to surprise him, Fred and Ethel spend all their time waiting for the return of vaudeville. Humorous characters tend to be objects of ridicule (hence the comic connotations of the word *humorous*) on account of their mechanical inflexibility, as Bergson demonstrates in *Laughter*. Polonius, in essence a comic conception, is early marked as a sacrifice by his inadequacy to the thoughtful responsibility his world demands; like Malvolio, he seems to act as if he were in the wrong kind of play, and he is clearly out of his element in Gertrude's bedroom. Pope's powers of generalization, which present Atossa as both larger and more limited than her world, make her the exemplary tragically humorous character, rivaled only by a few figures from Dickens—Edith Dombey, Steerforth, Miss Wade, and Miss Havisham.

Characters apprehended in terms of external details or of mental attitudes can be defined, like the figures in Landor's *Imaginary Conversations*, in relative isolation from any dramatic or actantial role. But our sense of most characters depends at least in part on the situation which defines their relation to the plot and to other characters. This dramatic role is not, like that of Price's railroad conductor, habitual, but, as Kermode's analysis of characters as plot functions demonstrates, it may not be unique either, for the messengers in Athenian tragedy (for example) are assimilated as nothing but agents of a plot, and agents whose role (to give bad news, usually of offstage deaths) is formulaic. On the other hand, a sufficiently obscure or compelling situation will transform an agent into a character even when no "characteristics" have been supplied, as in " 'Childe Roland to the Dark Tower Came,' " whose narrator, though technically a function of his landscape and dramatic situation, seems far more complex in conception. Browning's poem is a tour de force which creates a compelling character from the barest materials analytically proper to character. But such examples of what Kenneth Burke calls the scene-agent ratio[12] could be multiplied. Early in *Citizen Kane*, the reporter Thompson goes to the Thatcher Library to examine the late Walter P. Thatcher's reminiscences of Charles Foster Kane. The library is gloomy and inhospitable; a statue of Thatcher, shot from below, seems impressive and threatening; the librarian who helps Thompson is authoritarian, condescending, and humorless. The audience subliminally transfers all these attributes to Thatcher himself, who has scarcely appeared so far, and who will be onscreen for only a few minutes.

Most definitions of character in terms of role involve Burke's act-agent ratio (15–20) and are more straightforward. Alatiel (in *Decameron* 2.7), like the young couples in the pastoral romances of Longus and Xenophon, is like an empty ship set adrift in a sea of exciting and improbable adventures; Aeschylus's Prometheus lives only to suffer. Characters can be defined in terms of their past by means of a determinism either genetic (as in the case of Oedipus, who was from birth the man destined to kill his father and marry his mother, and then the man who, despite his ignorance, definitively had done so) or circumstantial (as in much of Balzac and Ibsen and in the fiction of Zola, Crane, and Dreiser). They can be defined in terms of their implicit teleology, like Dante's saints and sinners. Or they can be defined by an authoritative transformation which definitively reveals them and retrospectively makes their previous behavior a foreshadowing of their true behavior. This is Ovid's method throughout the *Metamorphoses*, in which the movement of individual episodes is marked by the tendency of characters like Narcissus, Procne, and Baucis and Philemon to become more purely themselves through transformation to nonhuman shapes. Dickens borrows this use of metamorphosis in the episodes involving freezing and decay in *Bleak House* and rebirth in *Our Mutual Friend* in order to impute a greater depth to characters whose actions indicate a change in heart without a change in nature. Kafka's ironic use of the trope in "The Metamorphosis" displays the contradictory ways in which Gregor Samsa is and is not like a gigantic insect; at the end of the story, his sister stretches out like the butterfly she has aspired to be all along.

To define characters in terms of their external appearance, their mental attitudes, or their relation to a role (whether a plot function, a circumstantial determination, or a teleology) is to define them ultimately in terms of a group of assigned traits, in the sense in which Seymour Chatman uses that term.[13] But defining characters as collections of traits raises several problems. It has the apparent effect of reducing the resonance and indeed the mimetic potency of any given character, for character cannot operate as a distinctive trope if it can be reduced to a series of predicates. Characters who seem irreducibly complex or unfathomably deep are of course illusions, but they are not mere combinations of traits, however numerous or contradictory. Archie Goodwin, to take a simple instance, is ebullient, resourceful, extroverted, physically attractive, susceptible to women, flippant, and devoted to his employer Nero Wolfe; but he is not primarily a constellation of such traits—he is a way of talking. When Rex Stout creates another character, Tecumseh Fox, who shares many of these traits but is seen only from the outside, the result is completely different. Whatever characters are made of, it is not a body of traits preceding or underlying the diegesis, but some quality inherent in the diegesis itself (compare the homespun rascal Huckleberry Finn in *Tom Sawyer* with the prodigious figure who bursts forth in the opening paragraphs of *Huckle-berry Finn*). Whether or not characters define themselves through their speech, it is only the storyteller's way of talking about them or displaying them that makes them more than the sum of their traits.

Describing characters as the sum of their traits also raises the problem of the relation between characters and people. Most people do not think of themselves as collections of traits but rather each as an incessant conscious-ness shaped by fluctuating dispositions. Instead of mental attitudes, I have a psychology which is both more and less constraining than habitual or characteristic traits: more, because my genetic and infantile background makes it more likely that I will act in certain ways; less, because my acting irritably ten times or a hundred does not simply make me an irritable person who will always necessarily act that way. Of course, psychology, like character itself, offers descriptive models for human behavior rather than a privileged account, but the real issue here is that characters cannot be explained in the same way human behavior as such is explained, because characters differ from people in being incompletely specified (how many characters are said to have armpits?) and intentionally intelligible, as human behavior is only among highly histrionic people or people perform-ing for an audience. We might be said always to be acting ourselves, but characters are always on display in a more radical sense: They are designed to be apprehended, and that is all they are designed for. The identity of narrative characters, unlike that of real people, is a uniquely discursive function. We can impute traits to characters in order to recover or justify problematic aspects of the narrative discourse, but it is those discursive aspects, not the corollary traits, that characters are made of.

Characters and People

Just as we can speak of plot as no more than an intelligible sequence of events, we can speak of characters who are no more than plot functions or illustrations of a particular emotional or intellectual humor. But when we ascribe depth or authority to characters, when we talk about what makes them compelling or memorable, even when we describe them as realistic, we are really talking about what makes them tellable, how they are displayed apart from the way the plot, the narrative world, or the discur-sive style is displayed. The problem of creating tellable characters is frequently the storyteller's leading mimetic concern. It therefore makes sense to ask, given their status as a discursive function, what makes characters tellable. The customary answer to this question, as my description of character as an amalgam implied, is that they are collections of traits or of different kinds of functions which have a putative authority beyond that of any particular trait or function. That is, different traits operate within a complex character like Dmitri Karamazov in much the same way that different characters operate in the world of Robert Altman's film *Nashville;* the functions seem more interesting than they actually are because we are prevented from considering them in isolation. Hence Charlie Chaplin is a social and physical type plus his fictional role in any given film; Huck Finn is voice, agent, and conscience; and Dante's Virgil is at once sinner, ideology, allegorical prefiguration of Beatrice and Christianity, exemplary poet, and beloved guide and father. What makes most characters tellable, however—and this rule applies to Virgil, Chaplin, Huck Finn, and Dmitri Karamazov—is subtraction rather than addition, the presentation of a character in terms of a type which is ultimately inadequate, or in terms of a role which is obscurely or incompletely defined.

Even the simplest characters begin to take on the illusion of life when their relation to their function or role is defined negatively. Dickens's minor characters, as Price suggests (36), imply an existence outside the frame of their novels simply by virtue of having nothing to do with the plot. This is true of even so important a minor character as Sarah Gamp, whose imaginary friend Mrs. Harris, a woman described more extensively than most "real" fictional characters, seems to testify by the very solidity of Dickens's gratuitous specification to Mrs. Gamp's own existence. Since no mere plot function could be as thick with detail as Mrs. Gamp, she appears, despite her limited range, as something more. In the 1934 version of *The Man Who Knew Too Much,* Hitchcock complicates his routine characters—the stiff-upper-lip husband and wife, the sinister head conspirator, and assorted secondary figures—through modulations of tone that allow most of the characters to step outside their conventional types. Even though the hero Bob Lawrence leaps only from one type to the next—from dry wit to amateur sleuth to protective father to self-satisfied Briton—the changes are so rapid and unexpected that the imposed types seem to supply partial views of some larger conception. And stories of all kinds are filled with characters who are defined by ironic analogy to what they are not, from Patroclus, who is not Achilles, to Terry Molloy, in *On the Waterfront,* who could have been a contender. Defining a character like Terry in terms of his frustrated potential is a particularly effective way to encourage the audience to impute a resonant and inclusive context to everything he does.

Leo Braudy has written that "the basic nature of character in film is omission. . . . Film character achieves complexity by its emphasis on incomplete knowledge."[14] Film can give us knowledge of a character's actions, habits, speech, appearance, and external circumstance, but never authoritative knowledge of his or her thoughts. Hence, as Braudy contends, "there is always something more" (184) than we see to a given character, something we supply for ourselves. The exception, the use of voice-over narration which gives us direct access to the narrator's mind, tends to prove this rule, for voice-over narration involves such ready access to the narrator's thoughts that it is notoriously difficult to use effectively except in films (*The Lady from Shanghai, Sunset Boulevard*) whose heroes are fundamentally ignorant or self-deceived. Braudy contrasts the incomplete knowledge film gives of its characters with the exhaustive observation of consciousness in Sterne or James. Certainly we have a kind of knowledge about Tristram Shandy or Maggie Verver that we never have about characters in movies; still, the similarities outweigh the differences. Novelists provide us with a record of their characters' thoughts which is voluminous but not exhaustive. We recover the characters precisely by generalizing or extrapolating the exemplary thoughts we are given to cover the passage of years, the subjects which arise only briefly (Strether's feelings for his dead son) or not at all (Dorothea Brooke's sexual desires), or the dimensions of experience which are not specified but which we take for granted (Emma Woodhouse's religion, the economic status of Mrs. Ramsay and Lily Briscoe). The exhaustiveness which Braudy attributes to the novelistic rendering of characters is a relative plenitude, but the example of James's heroes and heroines, of whom we are given a great deal of knowledge of a limited kind, should remind us that we never know everything about any fictional character. Apparent exhaustiveness is a feat of legerdemain. Even if a storyteller could actually reveal everything about a character, that character would be reduced to an untellable map of behavior whose interactions, completely determined, left no room for speculation. The audience's narrativity requires incomplete characters in whatever presentational mode.

Braudy suggests that film characters, whose incompleteness invites the imputation of continuity (for example, between onscreen and offscreen behavior), achieve depth through these putative but unspecified continuities, and this is true *mutatis mutandis* for characters in novels and plays as well. The fascination of Hamlet and Cleopatra is not that they specify their thoughts and feelings precisely but that they speak and act in a way that allows us to recover those feelings precisely ourselves by assuming that we are observing the most important moments in their lives, that their language and behavior are an accurate index of their natures, and that those lives and natures continue and extend in certain ways beyond the words we hear and the gestures we see. It is not that we try to reconstruct Hamlet's career at Wittenberg, but that we believe he once loved Ophelia, that secures his status as a character and not as anthology of stirring and mordant speeches. Shakespeare's Hamlet is not a real person (though no doubt the illusion is fostered by his being impersonated by someone real) but the product of a contract whereby the audience agrees to accept certain cues which allow them to impute to him a life offstage.

Film characters often acquire a resonance from the audience's awareness of the actor's personality or previous roles, an awareness exploited, for example, by Cary Grant's reference in *His Girl Friday* to his private identity ("The last person who told me that was Archie Leach, a week before he cut his throat"). An audience's memory of the earlier roles of Humphrey Bogart, Marlene Dietrich, or Marlon Brando adds increased complexity to their roles in *The Treasure of the Sierra Madre, Destry Rides Again,* and *Last Tango in Paris.* But audiences often define characters in noncinematic stories in terms of putative continuities as well. Characters within episodic or discontinuous works (Alice in Wonderland, Dante the pilgrim, Eugenie Grandet), or in novels that cover a long period of time, are often perceived as growing in response to different episodes or as living between the times and incidents which are presented. Characters who appear in more than one distinct work (Calandrino, the Princess Casamassima, Krazy Kat) assume a putative life, if not a complexity, of their own. It is a testimonial to the peculiar force of character that the public refused to accept the death of Sherlock Holmes, not an especially complex character, though one whose stories often display him more successfully than his adventures; that they wished not only further adventures (for *The Hound of the Baskervilles,* presented as a posthumous adventure, did not quiet the clamor) but the specific reassurance that he had not died; that later authors have often revived the character with success; and that for years many members of the Baker Street Irregulars conducted themselves as if they believed he were still alive. Even a character not literally reprised can assume the illusion of life—that is, can arouse expectations based on more than his reported circumstances and behavior—if he incarnates a recognizable type like Molière's elderly husbands, James Thurber's wives and dogs, and characters in the commedia dell'arte or the Punch and Judy show. Such characters seem by their qualities to invoke a previous life rather than comprising merely a series of details or attitudes.

More generally, characters can be made tellable through underspecification by trading on the audience's identifications. A character who is identified with a likely object of the audience's fear, moral revulsion, or desire (Dracula, Jason Compson, and Marilyn Monroe in *Some Like It Hot*) can assume the specific qualities appropriate to the emotions of each member of the audience. Every skilled director of horror films follows James's dictum: "Make [each member of the audience] *think* the evil, make him think it for himself, and you are released from weak specifications."[15] More often, identifications are urged in terms of the character's own consciousness, as in the case of James's heroes and heroines, whom the reader identifies with himself or herself rather than with his or her desires or fears. Even when we are never told what a character is thinking, a strong identification can be formed on the basis of situational empathy. The crowd on the Odessa steps in *Potemkin* is shown to us mainly as the faces of people shot down by Cossacks, but the shocking injustice of the massacre and the power of particular images (the fleeing citizens stepping on the wounded boy's hand, the baby carriage clattering unheeded down the steps) to arouse our emotional identification imply a world and a welter of lives behind Eisenstein's montage. Finally, the very remoteness or obscurity of characters like Kurtz, Hitchcock's Rebecca, or Lawrence of Arabia makes them touchstones for the audience's imagination.

Character in general is the result of the storyteller's sleight-of-hand, and most characters are analytically reducible to constellations of external details, mental attitudes, dramatic roles, and covert appeals to the audience to fill a discontinuity or form an identification. Indeed it is not going too far to say that all tellable characters are based ultimately on identification. But some characters are invoked by a peculiarly psychological—or, more accurately, narrative—use of identification. In Max Ophuls's *Letter from an Unknown Woman*, Joan Fontaine plays Lisa, a young woman who falls in love with pianist Stefan Brand (Louis Jourdain) when he moves upstairs from her mother's apartment in Vienna and remains in love despite her removal to Linz with her mother, the proposal of an eligible young cadet, her lack of opportunities to see Brand, his dubious character—he is a vapidly handsome womanizer—and his complete unawareness of her existence. After they finally meet and spend one night together, he forgets her again, despite the fact that she bears his son, protects him by refusing to name him as the father, and marries a wealthy man only to give her son a home. Some ten years later they meet again; she has left husband and son to resume her romance, but leaves Brand as well when she sees that he does not even recognize her. Shortly afterwards she and her son both die of cholera.

This summary will indicate the problematic nature of Lisa's character, a character some audiences find unrealistically masochistic and dominated by an incredible fantasy. Many audiences, however, have no difficulty accepting Lisa and her romantic story: Somewhat like the characters in comic strips, she becomes compelling without ever being believable. Lisa is displayed in large part through Ophuls's handling of mise-en-scène—idealized costumes, incessantly sentimental music, and especially the motivic use of floridly graceful pans and tracking shots up stairs, along streets, around a railroad station, and between characters (in the one long scene in which Lisa and Brand are both stationary in the frame, the scenery literally unrolls between them)—which defines Lisa in terms of the scene-agent ratio. Ophuls's control of Lisa's surroundings works to make us accept her desire for Brand and so display her character as such. Audiences who accept this desire and consider the film successful do so not because the desire is rationally intelligible—romantic love is by nature rationally obscure, and nothing about Brand's behavior justifies such extraordinary devotion—but because the conventions of the film and Ophuls's control of mise-en-scène establish their identification with Lisa, through whose eyes we see many of the film's images and who serves as the focal point for most of the others.

Ophuls's example suggests first, that most fictional characters to whom we impute a full-blown psychology solicit our interest principally through identification (Lisa falls in love with Brand because, since she lives in a world charged with romantic sentimentality, the audience wants and expects her to do so); second, that a character's psychology can be established externally, by control of the scene-agent or act-agent ratio; and third, that desire, the basis of psychological theories of character, is not reducible to a series of predicates or mental attitudes. The difference between "Lisa loves Brand" and "Lisa has a high opinion of Brand" or "Lisa thinks Brand handsome" or "Lisa is very sentimental" is that the first formulation, unlike the others, describes an unstable situation, Lisa's wish to possess something beyond her reach, rather than a reflection in repose. It implies further development without implying a teleology (Lisa may never get close to Brand; she may get him and lose him; she may get him and live happily ever after). It marks, in short, a narrative approach to character, the display of a character in terms of a story implied by an imbalance of desire.

Although Ophuls's frame-story imposes certain teleological restrictions on his material (Lisa has written to Brand a letter which begins: "By the time you read this letter, I may be dead"), in general he presents her desire as a narrative principle whose ending the audience cannot determine. *Citizen Kane*, which is structured as an inquest into the life of the late Charles Foster Kane, adopts the opposite procedure. How can Kane's last word, and by implication his whole life, be explained? The final identification of "Rosebud" as the name of Kane's sled implies that his whole life has been spent nostalgically longing for the nurturing love he lost as a child and attempting to buy or coerce that love from others. We have by this time seen Kane more and more explicitly trying to buy other people's respect and affection, and two characters, his friend Jed Leland and his second wife Susan Alexander, have commented at length on this behavior;

the revelation of "Rosebud" simply explains why Kane has been doing what we have seen him doing all along. In revealing the rationale behind Kane's actions, the film substitutes a predicate (Kane is unloved) for Kane's narrative project (to win the love of others). Audiences who find the revelation of "Rosebud" unsatisfactory, anticlimactic, or designedly ironic[16] are demonstrating a preference for conceiving character in terms of narrative projects rather than in terms of psychological predicates.

Kane's project makes him seem more interesting than his memories of his old sled because his project unfolds in circumstances largely contingent. It is in the nature of Kane's monomania to be attracted to Susan as, in Leland's words, "a cross-section of the American public," to insist that the voters will forgive his extramarital liaison with Susan, to push her into an operatic career, and to retreat with her into a private kingdom when that career fails. But nothing in Kane's psychology predicts that Susan will have the toothache that brings them together or that she will be an untalented singer. Kane's character is conceived in narrative terms not only in the sense that his desire for love projects a story but also in the sense that his life is shaped, like those of Julien Sorel and Thomas Sutpen, by the polytropic interaction between an obsessive project and a largely contingent world of circumstance; it is the interaction, and not only the desires which engendered the project, that makes these characters what they are. For this reason a character like Kane can seem different at sixty than he was at twenty by virtue of experiences which have changed him without changing his project.

Defining characters like Ophuls's Lisa or Welles's Kane in terms of an informing narrative project is the most important way storytellers have presented characters who change while remaining consistent. Just as the projection of followable chains of events whose teleology becomes explicit only in retrospect is the essential problem in the creation of narrative plot, the problem of making characters change consistently is essential to making them polytropically—that is, narratively—tellable, and is of course a contradiction in terms as well. In a tactical sense, developing a character without inconsistency involves steering a middle course between two errors. The character must not behave uncharacteristically—that is, the audience must accept the change as expressive, not imposed by the requirements of plot or theme. Since any change a character undergoes is imposed by the storyteller, successful character development requires a great deal of authorial tact. Critics have regarded with particular suspicion the final revelations concerning Estella's love for Pip (in the revised ending of *Great Expectations*), Noddy Boffin's slyly constant virtue (here, paradoxically, the earlier degeneration of Boffin is more authoritative than the announcement that he has never really changed), and Huck Finn's acquiescence in Tom Sawyer's plans to rescue Jim. On the other hand, the character must be felt as genuinely altered, not merely placed in a different situation or seen, like so many of Dickens's characters, in a new light. Price has cogently described the "other self" (xiv) that characters in Lawrence and elsewhere seem to discover or reveal in the course of their novels, an identity comprehending all their earlier behavior but somehow deeper and truer, as if the movement of the novel allowed them to become more completely or authentically themselves. Speaking of the reader's experience, we can say more generally that character development is prospectively gratuitous (for if a character implies a teleology, the sequel merely makes his or her implicit features explicit rather than projecting any change) but retrospectively logical (or the whole change would be dismissed as inconsistency). The process of character development is polytropic: Tellable characters, like tellable plots, imply some later development without committing themselves *a priori* to any given line of development, and their development has a retrospective, though not perhaps a necessitous, logic.

9
Narrative Fiction and Nonfiction

My discussion of plot, character, and the narrative world, tropes normally associated with fictional narrative, as proper to narrative generally raises a problem implicit throughout this book: Is narrative fiction truly representative of fiction in general? How far can we generalize from an analysis based almost exclusively on fictional narratives to the analysis of all narrative? My assumption throughout has been that narrative fiction is indeed representative of all narrative; now I wish to defend that assumption by examining more closely the relation between narrative fiction and nonfiction.

Fiction and nonfiction are most often distinguished in terms of their subject matter or their status as speech acts. In "The Fictions of Factual Representation," Hayden White has contended that "historians are concerned with events which can be designed to specific time-space locations, events which are (or were) in principle observable or perceivable, whereas imaginative writers—poets, novelists, playwrights—are concerned with these kinds of events and imagined, hypothetical, or fictive ones."[1] John Searle offers a different distinction in "The Logical Status of Fictional Discourse" between "fictional and serious utterances" by defining fiction in terms of "the illocutionary stance that the author takes toward it," a stance which frees the author from certain commitments of serious or nonfictional discourse: "If the author of a novel tells us that it is raining outside he isn't seriously committed to the view that it is at the time of writing actually raining outside."[2] Authors of fictional works, according to Searle, perform utterance acts indistinguishable from serious utterance acts but invoke "horizontal conventions that suspend the normal illocutionary commitments of the utterances" (68), so that their serious utterance acts are only pretended illocutionary acts. This chapter will examine Searle's argument in some detail; the following chapter will explore some implications of this examination for White's argument.

The Commitments of Nonfiction

Searle's general conclusions are based on his analysis of two brief passages. The first, by Eileen Shanahan, is from *The New York Times* of 15 December 1972:

> Washington, Dec. 14—A group of federal, state, and local government officials rejected today President Nixon's idea that the federal government provide the financial aid that would permit local governments to reduce property taxes.

The second, by Iris Murdoch, is the opening of the novel *The Red and the Green:*

> Ten more glorious days without horses! So thought Second Lieutenant Andrew Chase-White, recently commissioned in the distinguished regiment of King Edward's Horse, as he pottered contentedly in a garden on the outskirts of Dublin on a sunny Sunday afternoon in April nineteen-sixteen.[3]

According to Searle, the difference between these two utterances is based on their differing commitment to four rules governing the illocutionary act of asserting:

1. that the proposition asserted be true;
2. that the speaker be able to provide reasons or evidence for its truth;
3. that it not, in its immediate context, be self-evidently true;
4. that the speaker sincerely believe it to be true.

If Shanahan fails to comply with these rules, which "establish the internal canons of criticism of the utterance" (62)—that is, for example, if there is at the time of writing no such person as President Nixon, or Shanahan does not believe there is such a person—then her utterance is defective. Murdoch's utterance, on the other hand, does not commit her to the truth of the proposition it expresses, that on a sunny Sunday afternoon in April

1916 a recently commissioned cavalry lieutenant named Andrew Chase-White pottered in a garden in Dublin looking forward to ten more glorious days without horses: "Such a proposition may or may not be true, but Miss Murdoch has no commitment whatever as regards its truth" (62–63), nor is she held responsible for observing any of the other rules governing serious assertions.

Searle aptly observes that "the test for what an author is committed to is what counts as a mistake. If there never did exist a Nixon, then Miss Shanahan (and the rest of us) are mistaken. But if there never did exist an Andrew Chase-White, Miss Murdoch is not mistaken" (72). Because the notion of what counts as a mistake is so important in determining what an author is committed to—Searle goes on to discuss what does and does not count as a mistake in fictional works in order to define the kinds of commitments different kinds of fictional utterances make—it is worth exploring in detail. Suppose, for example, the idea that the federal government provide the financial aid that would permit local governments to reduce property taxes did not originate with President Nixon but with a member of his staff; suppose that staff member, under approval from a higher-ranking staff member, made the proposition public without Nixon's ever having heard of it; or suppose, on the other hand, that Nixon, hearing of the proposal, made it public himself without any particular interest in whether or not it were accepted; and suppose, in either case, that Shanahan knew the proposal had come from a member of the White House staff and was not, except in a very broad sense, "President Nixon's idea." Even though that phrase would be misleading to a great number of Shanahan's readers, it is safe to say that it would not count as a mistake. As Searle has noted in "Literal Meaning": "For a large class of unambiguous utterances . . . the notion of the literal meaning of the sentence only has application relative to a set of background assumptions."[4] In this case the sense in which the proposal in question is "President Nixon's idea" depends on institutional contexts Shanahan is not responsible for clarifying. (Her utterance *would* be defective if a White House spokesperson substantiated the assertion that neither Nixon nor any of his officially delegated authorities had ever sanctioned the proposal.) Since a phrase like "President Nixon's idea" may be misleading or insincere (in the middle of writing the phrase Shanahan may have turned to another reporter and said, "I'll bet this proposal never even crossed his desk," without rendering the illocutionary act her sentence conveys defective) without counting as a mistake, it evidently commits its author in some ways but not in others, and these ways are not always accurately defined by Searle's rules.

Consider a few more obvious mistakes with particular respect to their consequences. What would have happened if Shanahan or a *Times* com-

positor had accidentally typed "President Noxon"? Probably nothing—
the very obviousness of the error would have allowed the *Times* editors to
assume that readers would substitute the correct spelling. A later edition of
the *Times* might have printed a correction or rescission, but typographical
errors are so common in newspapers that most of them go uncorrected;
hence, in all likelihood, Shanahan and the *Times* would have gone on
record as committed to the truth of the proposition that the President of
the United States was named Noxon. The only circumstances under which
a rescission and apology would certainly follow would be the appearance of
a typographical error verging on slander—"President Noxious," for example—and then not because the error was any more misleading than
"Noxon," but because the association of ideas and the malicious intention
it implied would be more embarrassing to its subject.

Even when obvious mistakes are at issue, then, there is considerable
latitude as to the ways in which something can count as a mistake.
Journalistic errors may be treated in several different ways. Most typographical errors are allowed to stand without further comment; embarrassing errors are corrected or rescinded; occasionally reporters are disci-
plined or fired for deliberately falsifying data; and newspapers themselves
are liable to legal prosecution for misrepresenting certain states of affairs.
But the relative seriousness of these mistakes, the degree to which they
count as mistakes, is determined by custom and convention, by courtesy
and prudence, or by a court of law, and determined in accordance with
how embarrassing, slanderous, and detectable they are—not by a committee of philosophers of language in accordance with how far they deviate
from the rules governing assertive illocutions.

Furthermore, certain kinds of errors in journalistic discourse are commonly agreed not to count as mistakes. When a candidate for public office
coughs, stutters, or begins a sentence several times over in response to a
difficult question, his or her response is almost certain to be transcribed as
a series of declarative sentences or of grammatically correct clauses.
Speeches are reported in the *Congressional Record*, for example, as their
speakers would have liked them to be heard, not as anyone necessarily
heard them. In fact, speeches routinely appear in the *Congressional Record*
whether or not they were ever delivered on the floor of Congress.

What are we to conclude from this? Does it follow from a newspaper's
tolerance of certain types of factual error or from the *Congressional Record*'s
continual subversion of the rules governing assertions that journalistic
assertions are nonserious in Searle's sense? Obviously not; such utterances
clearly make certain commitments fictional utterances do not. But the
difference between serious and fictional discourse cannot adequately be
summarized by characterizing the first as committed, the second as un-

committed, to the truth of the propositions it advances. Journalism as such is committed, not to propositional truth, but to the accurate reporting (accurate within certain limits established by custom, courtesy, and the law) of particular kinds of information. Journalism, that is, cannot simply be identified with some unmarked case or null context called "nonfiction"; it is a particular kind of nonfiction with its own distinctive tropes that determine its characteristic illocutionary stance toward the propositions it asserts.

To say this does not invalidate Searle's rules for assertions, but suggests that they would require modification to describe more exactly the rules governing journalistic assertions and casts some doubt on the degree to which they accurately describe any actual utterances. Shanahan may in fact fail to comply with one or the other of Searle's rules without rendering her assertion defective according to the special requirements of journalistic reporting, which, like language generally, is a rule-governed form of behavior. If a high-ranking government official told Shanahan, "This isn't for attribution," or, "This is off the record," and she quoted and attributed the remarks in question, with or without qualification, she would be letting her regard for propositional truth get the better of her responsibilities as a reporter. This would be true even if the remarks she was not permitted to quote contradicted the sincere but mistaken assertions of a story she was preparing; she might delete part of the story or choose not to publish it at all, but she could not amend it until she had independent, producible evidence for her amended assertions. This hypothetical situation makes it clear that what journalism is actually committed to is facts, events, and statements which are, or can legally be made, a matter of public record. Within the limitations of this commitment reporters will comply with the rules governing assertive illocutions if they can, but whenever the two commitments are at odds, they will usually, and legitimately, give up the second for the first.

When Murdoch writes, "Ten more glorious days without horses! So thought Second Lieutenant Andrew Chase-White . . ." she is using the word "thought" in a construction ("he thought such-and-such," as against "I thought" or "he said he thought" or "it seemed that he thought") in which it can legitimately appear only in a work of fiction, for we can never, outside of fiction, have absolutely authoritative knowledge about what anyone else is thinking. The pretense that fiction can give us such knowledge, even about people who never really existed, obviously constitutes an important part of its appeal, but this is an appeal it shares, for better or worse, with certain kinds of nonfiction (e.g., most history and journalism), which also claim to give information about what other people are thinking but differ in the kind of information they give. Historians frequently claim to be reporting what other people have thought. The difference between Herodotus, who invents thoughts and speeches to which no one could have been privy, and historians more tentative or circumspect is mainly a tactical matter, for the majority of historians and journalists, perceiving their subjects as rational agents, are constantly hazarding guesses about their motives, intentions, and opinions. Because the rules governing the public availability of evidence are especially strict in journalism, reporters become adroit at imputing thoughts to public figures by describing a selection of their words and actions and allowing their readers to draw the desired inferences.

The more pointedly journalists and historians make and encourage inferences about other people's thoughts, the more evidence they offer. In biographical works, for example, such inferences will be documented by letters and diaries, conversations with friends or relatives of the subject (and ideally the subject himself or herself), and close inquiries as to matters of public record which might reasonably be construed as influencing or reflecting the subject's thinking. Still, since journalists and historians can never say with complete assurance what anyone else thinks or thought, and since the attempt to do so often violates the second (and sometimes, surely, the first) of Searle's rules governing assertions, the question arises why such writers would so frequently and openly court failure.

Two answers seem plausible. First, the imputation of purpose and intention is often necessary in order to impose a pattern on what might otherwise seem arbitrary or meaningless behavior. White has argued that "a mere list of confirmable singular existential statements does not add up to an account of reality if there is not some coherence, logical or aesthetic, connecting them one to another" (122); imputations of coherence, psychological or not, are both necessary for followability and unverifiable. Second, readers have a keen appetite for the thoughts of other people living and dead, for an intimacy, however spurious or attenuated, which can overcome their sense of isolation or satisfy their voyeuristic curiosity. Biographies are often written precisely in order to encourage and justify inferences, for example, about the private thoughts of public figures. In journalistic terms, the thoughts of many such figures are newsworthy in themselves; if *Newsweek* interviews Nancy Reagan, anything she says is news just because she has said it. More fundamentally, the thoughts of many public figures, if only they could be authoritatively documented, would be more newsworthy than their verifiable public actions, because it is only their putative thoughts which make the actions newsworthy. If Senator Edward Kennedy, asked if he intends to campaign for the Democratic presidential nomination in the coming election, replies that he will support his party's candidate, that answer will be faithfully reported, but only because the reporters have no direct access to Kennedy's private reaction to the question. Indeed, reporters will routinely follow a would-be candidate, filing reports about his or her speeches, activities, and public appearances, expressly in order to motivate or justify theories about his or her private thoughts, which can never be known directly.

Since journalists and historians often have a leading interest in, indeed often write in order to substantiate, motives, intentions, and mental states they can never authoritatively document, what makes a journalistic assertion (for example) newsworthy is often at odds with what makes it true. Moreover, the institution of journalism makes the issue of truth secondary to the issue of newsworthiness; or, to speak less cynically, considers truth as a means to newsworthiness as an end. Searle's rules for Shanahan's assertive illocution assess the success of her performance with some accuracy in regard to propositional truth, but seem oddly irrelevant to its ultimate end, what Searle calls its illocutionary point. Newspapers are typically published with the view of informing the public about certain kinds of events in order to secure their readership and so their financial patronage. Business and legal sense encourages newspapers to adhere to certain standards of truth, but the illocutionary point of truthful reporting is to sell more newspapers. Since newspapers always omit many true propositions (the sort of information, for example, that almanacs and encyclopedias provide)[5] and include many items like editorials, advertisements, and comic strips which are not reducible to assertive illocutions (but including, in Searle's terms, directives, expressives, and sometimes declarations), it seems clear that journalism is concerned with the true only as a special, though predominant, case of the newsworthy—and occasionally, as the *Congressional Record* shows, with the newsworthy at the expense of the true.

The same point may be made in another way. Imagine a reader seeing Shanahan's article in the *Times*. Surely his or her leading reaction to the sentence Searle quotes would be not (as Searle's rules imply) "Is this really true?" but rather "How will this affect me?" or "So what?" Searle's third rule acknowledges this point but not the consequence which follows. The assumption that allows newspapers to build their circulation is that public events do affect their readers, but a given news story seldom makes that connection explicit, even though it is what makes the news newsworthy. Almost all news stories necessarily establish their newsworthiness through implications about the mental states of their subjects and the likely consequences of the reported events on their readers; but the rules for assertive illocutions govern only their explicit propositional content, not their implications, even though it is precisely these implications which make them newsworthy. A news story about how warmly Walter Mondale and other party officials praised Geraldine Ferraro at the 1984 Democratic National Convention makes no commitments whatever regarding their true feelings for her, even though it is for the sake of its implications about those feelings that it is being read. Since journalism and history, like fiction, present themselves as satisfying our interest for a kind of knowledge which is ultimately unverifiable, and for which they offer only token verification, they cannot be distinguished from fiction on the basis of their commitment to the truth of their discursive representations. They are committed to the truth of their explicit propositions, but in a fundamental sense that commitment is beside the point.

Like other ordinary language philosophers, Searle tends to assume that one particular use of language is more ordinary—that is, closer to an unmarked case or zero degree—than any other: the answering of questions which presuppose the questioner's ignorance and interest. But this privileged status is institutional, as several recent commentators on Searle have remarked. Barbara Herrnstein Smith notes that *"the fact that something is true is never a sufficient reason for saying it":* In a language transaction, "as in any social transaction, each party must be individually motivated to participate in it."[6] Searle himself acknowledges that "one cannot just express a proposition while doing nothing else and have thereby performed a complete speech act";[7] we might go further and say that asserting does not in itself constitute a complete speech act, that all assertions are made, and all speech acts performed, for some purpose not governed or recognized by Searle's internal canons of criticism and cannot be adequately described apart from that purpose. Stanley Fish contends that "these canons are indeed internal, and that what counts as a mistake is a function of the universe of discourse within which one speaks, and does not at all touch on the question of what is ultimately—that is, outside of and independent of, any universe of discourse—real."[8]

It would seem then that there is no question of opposing a normal and normative "committed" nonfictional discourse to a fictional discourse which is "uncommitted" because there is no such thing as nonfiction. Or rather, there is, but it is institutional and multifarious, not natural and monolithic. In libraries which catalogue books according to the Dewey Decimal System, works of fiction are kept in separate shelves, often in a separate room, alphabetically under the author's name, but what is kept on the remaining shelves is not simply "nonfiction," but titles in philosophy, religion, the social sciences, and so on. This institutional division between fiction and nonfiction acknowledges that there is no such thing as untroped nonfiction, nonfiction pure and simple, works whose sole intention is to assert the truth of certain propositions without regard to the social and institutional requirements of nonfictional genres like journalism and history.

The Commitments of Fiction

Searle correctly notes that the opening sentences of *The Red and the Green* do not commit Murdoch to the truth of any propositions concerning the existence, qualities, or thoughts of Andrew Chase-White. This lack of commitment is characteristic of all fictional openings, even those which seem to assert truthful propositions ("Happy families are all alike"), for only the total context of a given fictional utterance can establish its illocutionary point. Another of Searle's examples, the opening of Vladimir Nabokov's *Ada* ("All happy families are more or less dissimilar; all unhappy ones more or less alike"), although a proposition of the same form as Tolstoy's, could not possibly be taken as a propositional truth by anyone familiar with the whole of *Ada*, but its lack of commitment, like Tolstoy's commitment, to propositional truth is made clear only in the total context of the utterance it introduces. Indeed this lack of commitment to propositional truth on the part of any given fictional sentence unmediated by its total context is an essential convention of fiction. Jonathan Culler, opposing writing to speech, has observed that writing promises, "by its solidity and apparent autonomy, meaning which is momentarily deferred";[9] whether or not this is true of Shanahan's sentence, it is certainly true of Murdoch's.

Readers of fiction accept the indefinite deferral not only of meaning in the sense of propositional commitment (which propositions embedded in this discourse are true? to what general propositions is the discourse as a whole committed?) but of tellability. News stories generally begin with a summary of their most important point, which is elaborated by the rest of the story; they are under a conventional obligation to demonstrate at the outset what makes them newsworthy. Even given the difference between newsworthiness and tellability, fictional utterances are under no such obligation. Most readers of fiction will not insist that a novel, for example, establish itself as tellable by the end of its opening sentence or paragraph, or even its opening chapter. (The opening chapter of *The Red and the Green*, a rehearsal of family relationships which become tellable primarily in retrospect, is at first reading rather arid.)

Since fictional utterances do not characteristically establish their tellability at the level of the single sentence, it would be misleading, as Mary Louise Pratt points out, to accept for fictional utterances Searle's rule that "the characteristic grammatical form of the illocutionary act is the complete sentence."[10] (White would dispute this rule with reference to history as well.) Fictional sentences removed from their contexts make no commitments whatever because the fictional conventions which endow them with meaning seldom operate within the level of individual sentences. The units of meaning and illocutionary force are not given in fictional discourse; instead, readers commonly approach fictional texts with conventional expectations—what Culler calls "literary competence" (114), based on, and presupposing, conventional rules of meaning characteristic of fiction: "the rule of significance," whereby the work at hand is read "as expressing a significant attitude to some problem concerning man and/or his relation to the universe"; the conventions of "metaphorical coherence" and "thematic unity" (115), whereby puzzling or arbitrary details are assumed to require integration into intelligible larger structures of meaning; and what might be called the convention of tropic generalization, whereby particular language may be read in figurative terms (as metaphor, synecdoche, and so on) "in order to attain the level of generality required" (177) and the work itself may be taken in its totality as a discursive figure for the experience it represents.

It is through such conventions that fictional works establish their commitments. In the most general terms, the commitments of fiction are always tropic or figural; a work of fiction is not committed at the level of the propositions it advances (or, Searle would say, pretends to advance), but rather at the level of what those propositions implicate through the conventions of particular fictional genres. I am using *implicate* (and its related terms *implicature*, or "act of implicating," and *implicatum*, or "what is implicated") to apply in H. P. Grice's technical sense to whatever a speaker or written text has "implied, suggested, or meant," as "distinct from what [he or she or it has] said,"[11] providing the audience must postulate such an implicature in order to reconcile the meaning of a given sentence (say) with the conversational rules or generic conventions governing the utterance of which that sentence is a part. If a friend tells me she has been burning the candle at both ends, I need to posit a metaphorical implicature ("my hours have been too long") to make sense of her remark; if I read in Donne's "Canonization" that "we are tapers too, and at our own cost die," I need to recall the immediate fictional situation (a man defending his love to a skeptical friend), the commonplace Renaissance pun on "die" ("achieve sexual consummation"), and the contemporary belief, frequently attested by Donne, that lovemaking shortens one's life, in order to make this proposition not only intelligible as a sentence but appropriate to its context. Grice's analysis focuses on conversational implicatures; mine will focus on conventional implicatures, those an audience must posit in order to reconcile the meaning of a given utterance with its generic conventions.

Although the constitutive role of generic conventions is firmly established in literary criticism, much less has been written about the conventions of nonfictional discourse—the conventions, for example, that make
news stories newsworthy. That observing such conventions is essential to
success in a given nonfictional genre, however, cannot be doubted. Beginning reporters, however great their respect for the truth, need to learn the
conventions of journalistic writing, the sort of conventions defined pre-
scriptively in style sheets and journalism textbooks. Moreover, these conventions vary greatly within the institution of journalism and even within
the context of a given newspaper. If a baseball pitcher marries a debutante
between games of a Saturday doubleheader at Yankee Stadium, the event
will be reported differently in the first section, the society section, and the
sports section of the Sunday *Times* because each section will have its own
conventional rules for determining what makes the event newsworthy.

Because newsworthiness or tellability is necessarily a function of a
specific generic context, terms like "totality" and "total context" are
ambiguous and somewhat misleading, and the institution of fiction is far
too broad to define the commitments of a given work with any precision.
Chekhov anticipates Culler's rules of significance and unity in his remark
that if a gun is shown hanging on the wall in act one it must be fired before
the final curtain, but this commitment would be interpreted differently in
different contexts. *The Red and the Green* might be approached in the
context of other works of fiction, other novels, other historical novels, or
other novels by Iris Murdoch; in each case the context would modify the
reader's response to particular details. Considering the book a novel would
imply commitments regarding circumstantial and psychological verisimilitude which might not be fulfilled by prose romances, allegories, or sagas;
considering it in the context of historical fiction would imply further
commitments about the public significance of private motives and actions;
considering it in the context of Murdoch's other work would imply still
more precise commitments about, for example, the metaphorical significance of Andrew Chase-White's name (especially given Murdoch's title)
and of the garden he is pottering in, and about the likelihood of thematic
analogies between characters, unexpectedly passionate relationships, and
acts of violence. A primary convention of the novel as genre is its promise
of a plot which economically realizes the potential of its characters, but
insofar as a reader approaches a given novel in a more specific context, that
promise will be framed in more specific terms. Many novels, moreover,
presuppose an acquaintance with not only the general conventions of prose
fiction but also specific works. The opening of *Ada*, which misquotes and
parodies the opening of *Anna Karenina*, depends for its adequate interpretation on some knowledge of that novel (which it explicitly identifies,

though again inaccurately), of the institutions of the Russian novel and the family novel, and of Nabokov's parodic habits in general. Murdoch's title echoes Stendhal's title *The Red and the Black* in a way which arguably makes Stendhal's novel part of Murdoch's total context. *Finnegans Wake,* going further, presupposes a vast array of general and particular knowledge on the part of its reader. For these reasons the total context of a given fictional sentence must be defined as *at least* the context which the author controls and presents as unitary—all the words of the poem or play or novel in which the sentence appears—but which may in fact be much wider.

Given the range and variety of contexts a particular fictional utterance may invoke, and especially given the ability of fictional works to define their own contexts and redefine their relation to them, it might seem impossible to pin down a fictional work to any commitments whatever. Is it possible for a novelist to make a mistake in the same way a journalist might make a mistake? Most fiction respects the physical limits of human experience, but it does not count as a mistake that Superman can fly, or that Billy Pilgrim can visit the extraterrestrial world of Trafalmadore. If Murdoch made Andrew Chase-White fly through space, would that count as a mistake? This question can be answered only with reference to the generic conventions Murdoch is invoking. If *The Red and the Green* were a comic strip like *Superman,* it might be entirely appropriate for Andrew Chase-White to fly, even though other comic strip characters like Blondie and Mary Worth could not. If *The Red and the Green* invoked the conventions of science fiction in the same way that *Slaughterhouse-Five* did, it might even be appropriate for Andrew Chase-White to fly only under certain conditions. Since, as Vonnegut's novels testify, it is always possible for fictional works to change their relation to a given genre in the middle of the discourse—so that a story which seems bound by the conventions of verisimilitude and physical realism can suddenly present a supernatural or unrealistic aspect—it would theoretically be possible for Murdoch to have Andrew Chase-White behave normally through the entire novel until he took off on the last page.

In each of these cases, whether or not Murdoch had made a mistake— whether or not her fictional discourse was felicitous—would depend entirely upon its acceptance by an audience. If an audience accepted Andrew Chase-White's ability to fly on the last page, then Murdoch's discourse would be successful; if not, it would be unsuccessful. Murdoch's success would vary with different audiences, but all of them would probably agree in taking Chase-White's powers of flight, however lately developed or revealed, as part of a significant larger concept rather than an isolated characteristic. If he flew only on the last page, then his flight would be construed as commenting on the entire work and redefining its generic allegiances, as Chance's walking on water in the last shot of *Being There* does. A given work may invoke any number of contradictory generic conventions and may freely adapt or combine the conventions it invokes (as John Barth's *Chimera* is an amalgam of classical myth, psychological novel, moralistic essay, and self-reflexive commentary), but its relation to those conventions, however complex, problematical, and unique, is ultimately stable; if it were not, the work would be impossible to read at all. Moreover, the more adventurous an author is in combining or transforming generic conventions, the more openly she courts the most calamitous failure possible in fiction, the loss of her audience. What counts as a mistake in fictional discourse, then, is entirely a function of the reader's expectations, based on the generic conventions a given work invokes. If an author fails to invoke the conventions which would give his material tellable implicata, fails to indicate his work's relation to the manifold conventions it invokes, or fails to fulfill the expectations aroused by the conventions to which he refers, then he has made a mistake.

If the commitments a given work of fiction makes depend on satisfying its readers' conventional expectations, then it is impossible to examine the commitments Murdoch's opening sentences incur without assigning them a generic context more specific than "fiction," which in itself commits an author to no more than does the context "nonfiction." Out of many possible contexts operating simultaneously I shall focus on one, the genre of the historical novel. Assuming that we approach *The Red and the Green* within the context of historical novels, to what are its opening sentences committed?

The defining convention of historical novels is that recognizable events and perhaps figures from public history will play an important role in the work. Murdoch's unusually precise references to time and place—April 1916 in Dublin—make no commitments to propositional truth, but they do arouse certain expectations based on this defining convention. Readers who know of the Easter Uprising of 1916 will expect the novel to refer in some way to that event. Even if the uprising is never mentioned, the story will be taken as making oblique reference to it; otherwise the references to Dublin and April 1916 would be as uneconomical and pointless as Shakespeare's introducing into *Julius Caesar* a soothsayer whose predictions were unreliable. Within the generic context of the historical novel, Murdoch's references to Dublin and April 1916 commit her, in Searle's terms, to some serious illocutionary act concerning the Easter Uprising.

This illocutionary act is normally an assertion; for historical novels, whatever else they do, undertake to explain the historical situations and events to which they refer. Historical novels invoke conventions which assume generally that the historical events they recount are intelligible, and more especially that public events are shaped by private and personal motives inaccessible, for instance, to the readers of newspapers. By making authoritative statements about what historical figures and invented characters *thought*, historical novels pose explanations of historical events which could not be properly documented according to the conventions of journalism or history.

In order to escape the charge of proposing a hypothetical explanation of public history in terms of private motives and then inventing private motives in order to support that hypothesis, historical novels incur the further commitment of making their fictional characters typical or representative and their invented situations plausible and figuratively apt. The leading characters in historical novels, although they do not represent actual individuals, are offered as representing general social, cultural, intellectual, or political types which do exist or have existed (an implication reflected in the use of the term "figure" for fictional characters, but only rarely for actual people, except in the metonymic phrase "public figure"). When Dickens in *Barnaby Rudge* presents as the leaders of the Gordon Riots of 1780 a public hangman, a murderer's half-mad son, and the illegitimate son of a gypsy and an English nobleman, he is committing himself through this convention to an implied assertion about the riots. Although Dickens's use of figurative tropes allows a certain latitude in interpreting his implicatum, it obviously excludes certain alternatives (e.g., "the rioters were concerned primarily to consolidate their already considerable power" or "the rioters were impelled by a profound sense of political commitment"); and it would count as a mistake if Dickens summarized his action in terms of such alternatives, or if a reader inferred them from his story. In presenting Andrew Chase-White as a newly commissioned young English cavalry officer, Murdoch commits herself by implication to the truth of certain yet unspoken general assertions about young men, young Englishmen, and young cavalry officers, and also to the relevance of this invented character to an explanation, on a level of generalization yet to be determined, of the Easter Uprising. As is customary in works of fiction, Murdoch is committed at the level of her implicata, not at the level of her explicit propositions. According to the conventions of the historical novel, she may not contradict or alter any accepted fact of public history without adducing specifically historical evidence (as Josephine Tey does, for example, in her novel *The Daughter of Time*). Within these conventions, her implicated explanations, even though based on invented particulars, are arguably true.

How can invented characters and incidents implicate truthful explanations? Murdoch's references to horses provide one example. Andrew

Chase-White, newly commissioned in the regiment of King Edward's Horse, is looking forward in the opening sentence of the book (a position which invites figurative imputation) to ten more glorious days without horses. This apparent discrepancy could be inconsequential; it could simply be a way of saying that Andrew had had enough of horses to be glad of a respite; it could even be a sign of Murdoch's carelessness. But all these eventualities would disappoint Murdoch's commitment to the implicatum that Andrew's relation to horses is equivocal and that this contradiction is thematically significant, the vehicle ultimately of some serious illocutionary force. Murdoch makes this commitment explicit a few pages later when she writes, "Andrew detested and feared horses," and continues with an explanation of why he should have felt compelled to master this fear: "The key to this phenomenon lay in Andrew's Irish cousins. . . . Andrew's now so distressingly close association with horses had come about through a simple desire to impress his cousins. There was in it, too, though Andrew recognized this less clearly, an element of masochism" (6). Andrew's relation to horses, then, is established very early in the novel as a prefiguration of his relation to his Irish cousins and, by a further figurative abstraction, of England's relation to Ireland. Since fictional works are committed at the level of their implicata rather than of their explicit propositions, Murdoch is not committed to the proposition, "Andrew detested and feared horses," even though that is what she explicitly says. But she is committed to some such proposition as, "The British attitude toward Ireland was compounded of cultural kinship, revulsion, a determination to achieve mastery, and a masochistic lack of decisiveness," even though she never says so.

Such an implicated proposition is of course not demonstrably true, but only because propositions of this sort—explanations on this level of abstraction—never are. Even in avowedly nonfictional works, historical explanations, though normally the implicata for whose sake a given work has been written, are never more than arguably true, that is, more or less convincing, because such explanations are by nature hypothetical. Readers of history assess its explanations as more or less satisfactory according to the explanatory power of the hypotheses offered, the adequacy of the evidence, the fairness and acuteness with which it is selected and weighed, and the openness with which alternative hypotheses are considered. In the case of historical novels, in which a good deal of the evidence for the implicated explanations is invented, this evidence must be made convincing in other ways: Characters must be made vivid and recognizable, their motives, actions, and relationships plausible in view of their historical circumstances. Readers who accept Andrew Chase-White as a plausible and compelling figure whose interests, desires, and fears are made accessible by appeals to their own experience, and historically apt by their figurative manifestation of public events and abstract relations, will be persuaded by Murdoch's presentation of the Anglo-Irish conflict his personality and situation embody. Within the generic context the historical novel provides, Murdoch's implicated explanation of the Easter Uprising can be as true as any other.

It does not follow from this that the primary meaning of *The Red and the Green*, and by extension of all fiction, is allegorical, and that the appropriate procedure in reading fiction is to infer general implicata from its fictional propositions and then analyze these implicata as if they had been inferred from serious discourse. Only a very limited amount of fiction undertakes to demonstrate the truth of general propositions even in figurative terms. Insofar as we consider *The Red and the Green* in the context of the historical novel, its primary commitments are to the hypothetical explanation of historical events. Although fictional works are committed only within particular generic contexts, however, no single generic context exhausts the meaning of a given work: *The Red and the Green* is a member of the set of historical novels, modern novels, Anglo-Irish novels, love stories, and so on; and each of these generic contexts arouses in the audience expectations which establish the author's commitments.

To a certain degree we can generalize from this analysis. Not all novels are historical novels; not all novels pose as explanations of specific historical events by creating characters and incidents which embody specifically historical forces. But all novels, whatever else they do, pose as explanations, on a further level of abstraction, of human behavior and human identity, whether shaped by historical forces or not.[12] Every novel is, among other things, a complex of hypotheses about human nature. Not all fiction, however, is committed to such hypothetical explanation; neither hard-core pornography nor "The Hunting of the Snark" makes any such commitment.

In that case, is there any commitment common to all fiction—anything to which fiction as such is committed? In order to answer this question, it is necessary to return to Searle's question of what counts as a mistake in fiction. Searle himself offers one example: "If Sherlock Holmes and Watson go from Baker Street to Paddington Station by a route which is geographically impossible, we will know that Conan Doyle blundered" (72). This suggests that fictional discourse is committed to the conventions of nonfictional discourse (geographical, historical, and physical verisimilitude, and so on) unless it establishes conventions at odds with these (the conventions, say, of science fiction or of fairy tales); but since any departure from a given convention may serve to establish an alternative convention, Searle's rule seems tendentious and unhelpful. More important, it is oddly irrelevant to what is surely the illocutionary point of most fiction. The voluminous researches of the Baker Street Irregulars on apparent inconsistencies and factual errors in the Holmes corpus (the location of Watson's old wound, the number and dates of his marriages, the Christian names of the Moriarty brothers) show that, at least for a large audience, these fictional stories have a scriptural authority which, excluding the very possibility of error, simply provides an invitation to recover any apparent errors as logical and true propositions. It would count as a far more serious, perhaps a fatal, blunder if Conan Doyle's stories had projected fictional characters and events so unremarkable, inconsistent, obscure, or unmoving that they aroused no reaction but bewilderment or boredom; for the primary commitment of fiction is not that it be circumstantially accurate but that it be tellable. Since tellability is also the primary commitment of a good many nonfictional utterances like anecdotes and journalism, it cannot be used to distinguish between fiction and nonfiction.

If fiction as such is committed only to an ideal of tellability it shares with many nonfictional utterances, then fiction and nonfiction cannot be differentiated with respect to their commitments, because the commitments of any discourse, fictional or nonfictional, are defined in terms of generic conventions within the general categories "fiction" and "nonfiction." Fiction, like nonfiction, is an institutional and multifarious category; there is no such thing as untroped fiction, or a trope purely and simply fictional, for the same reason that there is no such thing as untroped nonfiction. Nor is it possible to distinguish even between the range or repertory of commitments fiction and nonfiction make, because some of the generic conventions which define these commitments cut across these broader categories: Historical novels like *Barnaby Rudge* and *The Red and the Green* make the same commitments to historical explanation as the histories of Tacitus, Gibbon, and Braudel. Searle notes that accounts of how fiction conveys serious speech acts tend to be "ad hoc and particularistic" (75), but this limitation is inevitable because the notion of commitment is meaningful only within a particular generic context whether or not the utterance is fictional.

Hence fictional works convey serious speech acts in the same way nonfictional works do: through the implicata required by the particular generic conventions they invoke. Although fictional works are committed to the serious speech acts they convey, however, it is not a defining commitment of fiction to convey a serious speech act; no work of fiction is committed as such to anything more than the minimal criterion of tellability. Many formulaic works—comic books, thrillers, gothic romances, pornography—fulfill this minimal commitment adequately. But it does not follow that all fiction is by definition inconsequential. Searle makes a distinction, according to the intention of deceiving an audience, between "pretend[ing] to be Nixon in order to fool the Secret Service into letting me into the White House" and "pretend[ing] to be Nixon as part of a game of charades" (65). The intention to deceive evidently has consequences in the first case which are suspended in the second. Since Searle defines fiction as a "nondeceptive pseudoperformance"—that is, as inconsequential pretending—the terms of his argument make it impossible to explain how fictional works can have serious consequences. But the consequentiality of an utterance has nothing to do with its fictive status. If I stand on a street corner telling passersby, "I've just killed a man," my utterance, whether or not it is true, is far more likely to have serious consequences than if I tell them, "My favorite kind of ice cream is vanilla." In the same way, fictional works like *Crime and Punishment,* which commit themselves to altering and renewing the reader's perceptions in ways that persist beyond the boundaries of the work itself, are more consequential than works like *The Murder of Roger Ackroyd.* We might define works which made and fulfilled such commitments as "literature" (an institutional category which appropriately includes both fictional and nonfictional works), but in that case there would be no more correlation between literariness and fictiveness than between inconsequence and fictiveness.

This analysis may seem to imply that it is impossible to make a distinction between narrative fiction and nonfiction. But although it is impossible to make such a distinction in the terms Searle proposes, an examination of the way stories engage their audiences' narrativity suggests another way in which such a distinction might be maintained.

10
Toward Narrative Aesthetics

It would be highly satisfying if this chapter, and this book, could conclude by proposing a general theory of narrative aesthetics, an indication of what audiences value in stories as stories, apart from what other values— gnomic, propagandistic, pornographic—stories may offer in passing. Given the tentativeness of my suggestions about what stories display, however, it would be more accurate to say that in this chapter I shall pursue the argument of the previous chapter concerning the relation between narrative fiction and nonfiction until it becomes an argument about narrative aesthetics—that is, about what stories display.

In examining Searle's argument in Chapter 9, I concluded that fictional stories could not be differentiated from nonfictional stories on the basis of their lack of commitment to the truth of the propositions they advanced because the commitment of nonfiction to verifiable truth extended only to its explicit propositions, not to the implications that made it tellable, and because at least a large number of fictional stories were also committed to the arguable truth of their implicated propositions. In general, however, the commitments of fictional stories are different from those of nonfictional stories because the former display something different from the latter. The task of this chapter will be to distinguish between what fictional and nonfictional stories display; why this distinction will be an appropriate conclusion to this book will become evident in the course of the chapter.

The Documentary Event

If narrative fiction cannot be distinguished from nonfiction, as Searle claims, in terms of the commitments it makes, can it be distinguished, as

Hayden White claims, in terms of its material? The documentary film seems to confirm the intuitive distinction on which White's formulation is based. Frank Capra's *Why We Fight* series and *Casablanca* are both about World War II, but *Casablanca* is also concerned with the romantic relationship of Rick Blaine and Ilsa Lund, a relationship which never actually took place; hence the Capra series is documentary, *Casablanca* fictional. Pare Lorentz's films *The Plow That Broke the Plains* and *The River* and John Ford's *The Grapes of Wrath* all dramatize the tragic erosion of topsoil from the Great Plains, but the Lorentz films are concerned only with actual events, whereas the Ford film focuses on the plight of the Joads, an imagined family. Hence *The Grapes of Wrath* is fictional, even though the migration of the Okies to California is not.

Documentary film is a useful focus for the attempt to distinguish between fiction and nonfiction because the problematic relation between fiction and nonfiction is at the heart of its definition. In a widely quoted phrase, John Grierson once defined documentary as the creative treatment of actuality. The World Union of Documentary has defined the form at greater length: "By the documentary film is meant all methods of recording on celluloid any aspect of reality interpreted either by factual shooting or by sincere or justifiable reconstruction, so as to appeal either to reason or emotion, for the purpose of stimulating the desire for, and the widening of, human knowledge and understanding, and of truthfully posing problems and their solutions in the spheres of economics, culture and human relations."[1]

Neither of these two definitions acknowledges a problem Satyajit Ray has noted: "Even fables and myths and fairy tales have their roots in reality. . . . Therefore, in a sense, fables and myths are also creative interpretations of reality. In fact, all artists in all branches of non-abstract art are engaged in the same pursuit that Grierson has assigned exclusively to the makers of documentary films."[2] This problem—the fact that Grierson's definition of documentary is too broad to distinguish it from fictional cinematic modes—recurs in a subtler form in the World Union's definition, in the imprecision of terms like *aspect of reality, factual shooting, sincere or justifiable,* and *truthfully posing problems and their solutions.* The difficulty in defining documentary film in a way that will include all documentaries but exclude everything else suggests that documentary may well inhabit a gray area between fiction and nonfiction.

Certainly a primary lesson of documentary theory has been that it is impossible to distinguish between film fiction and nonfiction without acknowledging a large and untidy frontier between the two. Most audiences would agree that the *Why We Fight* films are nonfictional and *Casablanca* fictional. But on what basis is this distinction made? If the

presence of professional actors is the criterion, then the films of Sergei
Eisenstein and Roberto Rossellini are nonfictional, and the presence of the
veterans Harold Russell and Audie Murphy makes *The Best Years of Our
Lives* and *To Hell and Back* less fictional than they would be with John
Wayne in their roles. Unless we consider *To Hell and Back*, starring
Murphy and based on his autobiography, less fictional than his other films,
and think it would be more fictional with Wayne in the starring role, we
must conclude that the presence of professional actors is not itself a reliable
distinction between fictional and nonfictional films.

A distinction more frequently urged is based on the staging of events
especially for the camera. The positions in the often heated debate over
whether Leni Riefenstahl's *Triumph of the Will* is a work of fiction or of
nonfiction have characteristically been based on beliefs about whether and
to what degree the events of the 1934 Party Congress in Nuremberg were
staged expressly in order to be photographed. But this rule would categorize as fiction many films now accepted as documentary. Dai Vaughan has
pointed out that the British documentarist Humphrey Jennings "would
rehearse a man countless times in an action which was already part of his
everyday routine."[3] Robert Flaherty went still further in his pioneering
documentaries *Nanook of the North, Moana,* and *Man of Aran,* filling them
with cultural anachronisms, recreations of a way of life that even his
primitive heroes had already outgrown.[4] The issue here is not whether an
event is actually taking place—Hitler is surely landing in Nuremberg and
Nanook is spearing a seal, whether or not the films are fictional—but
rather whether the deliberate staging of an event makes it a fictional
representation. Vaughan has argued that since the mere presence of the
camera in certain intimate situations distorts the behavior of the principals
whether or not their actions are staged, "we must rely upon the integrity of
the artist for [the creation of authenticity] and upon the judgment of the
viewer for its proof" (58).

Because the distinction between staged and unstaged events is itself
problematic, it seems safer to adopt White's distinction between fictional
and nonfictional events. But the nature of cinematic representation poses
difficulties for this distinction as well. In one episode of Jennings's *Listen to
Britain,* Dame Myra Hess is playing a Mozart concerto; the music continues as the camera cuts freely to several overhead extreme-long-shots of
London. In *The Battle of San Pietro,* John Huston originally showed the
bodies of dead soldiers being put into sacks over the sounds of their voices,
recorded earlier. In both cases image and soundtrack combine observed
(and overheard) events to produce a new event not even, in White's
phrase, "in principle observable." A more common version of this problem arises in what Jay Leyda has called compilation films—films editing

existing footage to illustrate new meanings and perhaps to create new events. In 1898, Francis Doublier's company took advantage of the widespread interest in the Dreyfus case by editing together "a scene of a French army parade led by a captain, one of their street-scenes in Paris showing a large building, a shot of a Finnish tug going out to meet a barge, and a scene of the Delta of the Nile" with a commentary that "told the following story: Dreyfus before his arrest, the Palais de Justice where Dreyfus was court-martialled, Dreyfus being taken to the battleship, and Devil's Island where he was imprisoned, all supposedly taking place in 1894."[5]

Even filmmakers determined not to fictionalize their material can hardly help creating events by the editing of images in continuity. The most common sequence in narrative films, the shot-reverse shot, often creates an event which never took place because such sequences are almost always projected more rapidly than they took place, since new lighting and camera setups are often required for each shot in a conversation between two people. Although few documentaries film conversations in shot-reversal sequences, most of them use continuity editing based, for example, on the alternation of event shots and reaction shots. But even a documentary which avoids such an alternation will represent, when projected, only a fraction of the footage originally shot, and this footage will in nearly every case be edited into a new, more intelligible sequence. The issue in this connection is not the mere selection of material, for the principle of selection is as common to history as to fiction, but the fact that the audience will assume that shots presented in immediate sequence stand in a causal or logical relation with each other, and that this relation is in fact rarely a reflection of a relation inherent in the process of shooting. In other words, all but the most primitive films present chains of events which are constituted as events by connections and imputations which are not and cannot be observable.

Imagine a television photographer sent into combat to film a battle. Decisions about cutting (when a soldier shoots a rifle, does the camera hold on him or cut to whatever he is shooting at?), about camera placement, about the choice of lens (a wide-angle lens, exaggerating spatial perspective, would probably make the space between opposing forces appear greater; a Panavision lens would reproduce an image proportionately much wider, including more combatants and cutting off vertical lines, for example of trees which might be hiding ambushers), about the choice of filmstock and focus, about the placing of microphones and the mixing of the soundtrack, would to a great extent determine how the audience perceived the event—that is, what kind of an event it was, what the relation was between individual subjects and the image, between individual images and the entire segment. Although there is no zero-degree or unmarked set of conventions for filming a given event, a peculiarity of film for many audiences is that its images appear as unmarked, as the only way, or the best way, an event could have been represented. But in fact the notion of an "event" which is in principle observable overlooks the fact that even to consider a series of states of affairs an event already entails imputations of sequence, causality, and significance. States of affairs may be observed, but events, whether in fiction film or documentary, are always constructed or reconstructed by the audience.

These arguments are meant not to indicate that it is impossible to distinguish between fictional and nonfictional films, but to suggest that a large number of films are neither clearly fictional nor clearly nonfictional. Are *Ten Days That Shook the World* and Maya Deren's *Study in Choreography for Camera,* which are "concerned" entirely with "events which are (or were) in principle perceivable," fictional or not? Clearly the answer depends on the way the audience construes the word *concerned.* Are the short subjects Allen Funt arranged for "Candid Camera," in which unwitting subjects are filmed under provocation by staged dilemmas, fictional? Such events are staged, but staged without the knowledge of their principals, and then projected as observed. Are the instructional films *(Our Mr. Sun, Hemo the Magnificent, The Strange Case of the Cosmic Rays)* Frank Capra made for Bell Laboratories in the 1950s—films which use fictional characters like Dr. Research, animated figures like Hemo the Magnificent, and marionettes representing Poe and Dostoevsky speaking about cosmic rays—fictional? Such films stage nonhistorical events (for instance, the meeting of Poe and Sherlock Holmes) as a way of presenting scientific observations. Which events, the invented incidents or the scientific explanations, carry more weight in establishing their ontological status?

The problem is compounded by another peculiarity of motion picture viewing. Events in a movie generally seem to be taking place as the audience watches; many documentaries, and nearly all fiction films, have a much more equivocal relation to the historical past tense than do prose fiction and history, or indeed than still photographs seen in a book or mounted in an album. If the audience's assumption in watching a film is that these states of affairs are coming about in the present, then all films are fictional, since the only state of affairs taking place during the time of viewing is the projection in a darkened room of twenty-four photographic images per second. If, on the other hand, the audience's assumption is that these states of affairs actually did come to pass at some point in the past, then all films are in a fundamental sense nonfictional, since, with the exception of special effects shots like those in *2001: A Space Odyssey* and *The Birds,* everything the audience is seeing is a record of something that actually did happen. Hundreds of men really did use a wooden scaffolding to scale a high wall during the filming of *Intolerance*. James Cagney really did push a grapefruit into Mae Clarke's face during the filming of *Public Enemy*. Ingrid Bergman really did tell Humphrey Bogart that she couldn't live without him during the filming of *Casablanca*. It does not follow, of course, that Ilsa Lund really told Rick Blaine that she couldn't live without *him*, or (to put it another way) that Bergman really meant what she said to Bogart, any more than it follows that Cagney was actually bored and annoyed with Clarke, or that Griffith's extras were really trying (or were under the impression that they were trying) to besiege the city of Babylon. What makes these films fictional, Searle would say, is that although the actors are going through the motions of certain actions, they are not committed to the beliefs or consequences normally attendant upon those actions. The fact is that although the camera does not lie in a certain obvious sense, it does not simply tell the truth either, because it reproduces motion without establishing its status as action. Even within the context of its invented story, a film does not commit itself explicitly to the truth of its characters' expressed sentiments. When Ilsa Lund says she can never give up Rick again, the film makes no unequivocal commitment as to whether or not she means it; earlier, Rick's headwaiter had assured a customer that the roulette wheel in the back room was not fixed, and he turned out to be lying. Ilsa does establish the commitment of her emotion in other ways, for example by making her confession directly after calling Rick names and pulling a gun on him, but this commitment is based on the audience's knowledge of a set of representational conventions, not on any explicit propositions. Images themselves evidently cannot advance propositions; they can only illustrate propositions advanced in some other way.

This may seem a perverse conclusion in light of the documentary value traditionally ascribed to photography. A photograph of John Dillinger hanging in the post office would presumably assert the proposition, "The wanted man looks like this." Most of the sequences in Frederick Wiseman's documentary *Hospital* seem to assert the proposition, "The medical staff has difficulty in dealing with a great number of illnesses." A photograph or motion-picture sequence showing a revolver asserts, "A revolver was placed here," or, "Here is a revolver!"[6] Since altering the context of any of these images, however, would alter its propositional content—placing the photograph of Dillinger next to one of W. C. Fields, for example, would assert the proposition, "The man on the left is thinner," or, "Mr. Dillinger's face is not suited to comedy"—that content is clearly not inherent in the photograph itself. Photographic images can of course support propositions, but as the Allied documentarists who plundered *Triumph of the Will* for footage which would help establish the inhumanity of Hitler's regime have demonstrated, they have no necessary allegiance to any given proposition; the same shot of Hitler reviewing his troops can carry very different meanings in different contexts.[7]

This problem may be illuminated by adapting Searle's distinction between speech acts and the propositions they advance to suggest that although symbolic acts like filmmaking, like the speech acts of verbal discourse, can express or illustrate true propositions, symbolic acts themselves can be neither true nor false. Hence Capra's educational films can assert true propositions (e.g., the heart pumps blood through the arteries) by means of a symbolic act which is neither true nor false. Because films, like other discursive entities, are neither true nor false, the question about the fictionality of documentary films becomes another question: Do fictional films (e.g., *The Grapes of Wrath*) and documentary films (e.g., *The Plow That Broke the Plains*) assert propositions in ways so different as to amount to a distinction between fictional and nonfictional discourse? Hayden White would argue that only fictional films support their propositions by invented incidents, but this distinction is, as we have seen, unsatisfactory for two reasons. First, the reproductive nature of film means that every incident observable in a film was observable before it was filmed. If we observe Bergman telling Bogart that she cannot live without him, that is because she really did tell him that as the cameras rolled. The effect of *Casablanca* on the audience depends, of course, on the implication that we are watching Ilsa Lund tell Rick Blaine that she cannot live without *him*, but we do not simply observe this incident; instead, we reconstruct a series of such fictional incidents about the characters Bogart and Bergman are playing by means of inferences that we make about the motions that are actually presented, and action, unlike motion, is never simply observable. Second, the grammar of cinematic presentation (e.g., the mechanics of continuity editing) incessantly constructs incidents whose sequentiality and causality are putative, based on the conventions of representation rather than on simple observation, whether the film at hand is fictional or not. The criterion of invented incidents at best indicates modes or degrees of fictionality; it cannot distinguish between fictional films on the one hand and nonfictional films on the other.

Although a photographic image cannot explicitly assert a proposition, films constantly seem to be asserting and defending propositions because of the conventions of cinematic storytelling (which place unusual emphasis, for instance, on metonymy); because of the audience's narrativity, which assumes a purposefulness behind the sequence of images projected on the screen; and because films are frequently used to illustrate propositions established by a speaking voice, whether in fictional films (as when Bogart, as Rick Blaine, says, "I stick my neck out for nobody") or documentaries (as when, in *The Plow That Broke the Plains*, a farmer tips his hat and looks at the sky as a voice-over narrator says, "High wind and sun. . . . A country with little rain"). Since most films cannot adequately be described as explicit verbal commentaries with visual illustrations, however, the relation between image and proposition must be more complex. In H. P. Grice's terms, cinematic images advance propositions through conventional implicatures which the audience must recover in order to appreciate the point of each sequence or episode.

The assumption that cinematic images assert propositions through implicatures echoes the belief of John Grierson and Paul Rotha, the leading British theorists of documentary film, that documentaries do not (or, in their argument, cannot) simply depict motion or embody pictorial values. Grierson argued in 1932 that "the artist need not posit his ends—for that is the work of the critic—but the ends must be there, informing his description and giving finality (beyond space and time) to the slice of life he has chosen."[8] In 1935 Rotha advanced a similar argument about documentary film: "If its aim were simply to describe for historical value, accuracy would be its main endeavour. But it asks creation in dramatic form to bring alive the modern world. . . . The documentary film has an important purpose to fulfil in bringing to life familiar things and people, so that their place in the scheme of things which we call society may be honestly assessed" (26). Documentary films, according to Grierson and Rotha, display the implicated propositions that make them tellable. Although Grierson and Rotha assume in their terms "finality," "their place in the scheme of things," and "honestly" that the implicata of documentaries are simply true, the use of Riefenstahl's footage in myriad anti-Nazi documentaries suggests that the implicated propositions of documentary film, like those of history, are arguable rather than true. But this account of documentary film, as Satyajit Ray indicated, overlooks the fact that fictional films can also implicate arguable propositions, though they often offer different kinds of evidence. Rotha implicitly acknowledges the dependence of documentary on the methods of fiction when he observes that "a full and real expression of the modern scene" depends on "establishment and development of character. There must be growth of idea, not only in theme, but in the minds of characters" (113). This formulation collapses the distinction between the people who are presumably the material of documentary films and the putative characters and the sense of character common to fiction films. It is of course not true that fictional characters display nothing but their implicata; if this were so, then the power of the Joad family in *The Grapes of Wrath* would be exhausted by Ma Joad's closing speech: "They can't keep us down. . . . We're the people." Even though this proposition is essential to the coherence of the film, it is not the propositions it implicates that make Ford's film tellable (or watchable), but the way it implicates them, through Jane Darwell's performance, Gregg Toland's photography, and so on. The difference between implicated propositions and the way in which they are implicated—that is, between implicata and implicatures—indicates a way of distinguishing between documentary and fictional films: *Documentary films display their implicata; fictional films display their implicatures.* The agents and principals of film become "characters" (and so fictional) to the degree that the audience is made interested in their nonpropositional content, in the problems and eccentricities that would not be exhausted by an explicit statement of the propositions they implicate. In Thorold Dickinson's *Next of Kin,* which is presented as a fictionalized account of an actual wartime incident, Nova Pilbeam plays a shopkeeper who inadvertently discloses information about troop movements to enemy spies and is killed when she learns what she has done and confronts one of the spies. To the degree that the film emphasizes the poignancy of this invented character's death, it gravitates in the direction of fiction; to the degree (in this case predominant) that it treats her as a statistic or a moral exemplum (implicating the proposition, "loose lips sink ships"), it gravitates toward documentary. This is not to make a distinction between fiction films and documentaries on the basis of their emotional appeal. In Sidney Meyers's documentary *The Quiet One,* the poignancy of the central figure, an emotionally disturbed boy, is primary. But this emotion is material to the leading proposition the film implicates ("delinquent children often need and respond to psychiatric care") in a way that the emotion attendant on the Pilbeam character's death is not. The salient distinction between documentary and fictional film is a difference in emphasis between the propositions implicated and the nature of the act of implication.

This distinction is not as satisfyingly simple as the distinction between actual and invented events, or between unstaged and staged action, but it has the virtue of accounting for numerous problems in documentary film. It explains, for example, in what sense Bergman's expressions of love for Bogart are fictional: They are fictional to the degree that the audience's narrativity is engaged by the manner in which information about the characters is disclosed to them. (If a biography of Hitler, for example, were organized around the primary goal of arousing and fulfilling the audience's narrativity, it would become thereby fictionalized.) It explains how a documentary can use fictionalized situations and characters in order to implicate serious propositions: In Capra's Bell Labs films, the invented figure of Dr. Research is displayed secondarily as a fictional character with an interest of his own, but primarily for the sake of the scientific propositions he advances. It explains how documentaries can make use of staged action and preexisting footage without jeopardizing their status as documentaries: If Flaherty rehearses Nanook in his daily routine to film it more economically, he is doing something different from rehearsing Nanook in a new routine in order to implicate the proposition that this is how Nanook actually lives; if he rehearsed Nanook in a song-and-dance routine, the film would be even more frankly fictional, because the audience would presumably refuse to accept the implicatum that this routine was characteristic of Nanook's daily life and would be free to enjoy it as a triumph of Flaherty's resourcefulness and wit. Finally, it explains how the same sequence can be either fictional or documentary, depending on its context: When Gene Kelly dances in *Singin' in the Rain*, his behavior is referred at least in part to the emotions of the fictional character he is playing—"Even though it's raining, he's still happy"—but when the same sequence appears in *That's Entertainment*, his behavior is referred to a different proposition—"What a great dancer Gene Kelly is"—which exhausts a much greater portion of its interest. The second sequence, unlike the first, is designed primarily to display the proposition it implicates, and is therefore primarily nonfictional.

The distinction between displaying implicata and displaying implicatures, though based on the specific problems of documentary film, has obvious applications to other kinds of symbolic action as well; it may be used, for example, to distinguish between narrative histories, which display their implicated propositions, however arguable, and historical novels, which display their implicatures rather than their implicata. Hence *Gone with the Wind* engages the audience's narrativity in order to display the nature of Scarlett O'Hara's involvement in the Civil War and Reconstruction rather than using that involvement primarily as a means of historical analysis. Another implication of this analysis is that "fiction" and "documentary" are terms more proper to impulses or procedures than to completed works, which normally combine both impulses in different ways. Finally, the problematical status of documentary film suggests that theorists of fiction might do well to accept what documentary theorists have long believed: Whatever the opposite of fictional discourse may be, it is neither nonfictional discourse nor truth.

The Aesthetics of Hollywood Storytelling

Although both fictional and nonfictional discourse are committed at the level of their implicata, they are committed in very different ways. The success or failure of a work of history clearly depends on the status of the implicated propositions. No matter how close Barbara Tuchman makes us feel to Enguerrand de Coucy,[9] her study of the fourteenth century, presented as history, will be dismissed by historians who find her dates and figures inaccurate, her descriptions of Coucy's adventures improbable, and her discussion of the effects of the Black Death exaggerated, because such errors would undermine her implicated propositions about the nature of Coucy's life, his representative status, and the pivotal importance of the period as marking a transition between the Middle Ages and the modern world. As I argued in Chapter 9, fictional stories are also committed at the level of their implicated propositions, insofar as they commit themselves to the truth of any propositions. Most fictional stories, however, are not primarily concerned with this commitment. Even though historical novels like *The Red and the Green* may propose implicated explanations of historical events, and nonhistorical novels like *Joseph Andrews* may propose implicated (or indeed explicit) accounts of human nature, most fictional discourse does not display this commitment; the audience for most novels and films, that is, is less concerned with their implicated propositions than with the way in which these propositions are implicated. A brief consideration of the aesthetics of Hollywood films suggests that many different audiences, whatever else they may disagree about, agree in judging them on the basis of their implicatures.

American movie audiences prefer fictional narrative films to any other kinds of films. Despite the recent popularity of concert films like *The Last Waltz* and revue films like *Richard Pryor Live at the Sunset Strip*, the overwhelming majority of films shown in American theaters continue to be fictional narrative films. Of the ten top-grossing American films, most (e.g., *Indiana Jones and the Temple of Doom, Return of the Jedi, Jaws*) seem designed to support Searle's contention that fictional works do not assert anything, and it is obvious that audiences are not watching them for the sake of their implicated propositions. Action movies like these offer the pleasures of spectacle, adventure, and kinesthetic excitement. Instead of a catharsis which defines the action's unitary impact on the audience, such films present a series of dangers and triumphs which arouse a vicarious but nonetheless genuine sense of apprehension and relief, bewilderment and satisfaction. Watching them has thus been aptly compared to riding a roller coaster, an experience with even less propositional content, because in each case what the clientele seeks is precisely the nature of the experience rather than any conclusive result.

That this experience depends upon arousing and rewarding the audience's narrativity is also clear. Indiana Jones's adventures would seem far less dangerous, Luke Skywalker's far more puerile, if not for the rapid cutting that gives the audience segments of a single action—a slide down a cliff, the assault on the Empire's current stronghold—and forces them to integrate them, together with a musical track which indicates their importance or an effects track which indicates their violence, into a single chain of events. The audience for George Lucas's phenomenally successful *Star Wars* series is not primarily interested in the implicated proposition that trusting the instincts that bind one to the community will allow one to overcome one's dark side emotionally and politically; what they are after is the way such propositions will be implicated through a series of exciting adventures—ultimately, through a rapid series of images which they can integrate into a story. Their goal is simply to share, insofar as the limitations of film permit, the adventures and experiences of Luke Skywalker, Han Solo, and Princess Leia, and the films make these adventures available to them by displaying their implicatures about essentially banal propositions in an engaging way.

At higher levels of sophistication, however, it is less clear that critics are judging the relative success of a given film with reference to its implicatures. When critics review the films of Bergman, Antonioni, or Werner Herzog, aren't they assessing them primarily on the basis of their implicata, on the propositions they implicate about the world outside the frame? Even to speak of a film as "the expression of a director's vision,"[10] as Andrew Sarris does in "Toward a Theory of Film History," seems to emphasize the film's implicata over its implicatures. In promulgating what François Truffaut had called the *politique des auteurs*[11] and what he called the auteur theory to American audiences, Sarris insisted on "the distinguishable personality of the director as a criterion of value."[12] Since Hollywood directors normally worked under studio contracts which might well compel them to direct many different kinds of films whose subjects and screenplays remained outside their control, however, Sarris argued that a director's personal vision could seldom be defined in straightforwardly thematic terms—in terms of the recurring implicata of his films. Instead, Sarris defined "interior meaning" ("the ultimate glory of cinema as an art") in terms of "the tension between a director's personality and his material" ("Notes," 538). In other words, it was not what a director had to say (his implicata) that made him a significant artist; it was his success in imparting a sense of his vision to his films through the quality of his implicatures without losing his position in the studio.

This extreme version of auteur worship—the greater the constraints on the director, the more heroic his efforts to transcend them, and the more highly to be valued—has been widely criticized, most notably by Pauline Kael, who described Sarris's ideal auteur as "the man who signs a long-term contract, directs any script that's handed to him, and expresses himself by shoving bits of style up the crevasses of its plots. . . . Subject matter is irrelevant . . . and will be quickly disposed of by *auteur* critics who know that the smart director isn't responsible for that anyway; they'll get on to the important subject—his *mise-en-scene*"—that is, the visual devices he uses to smuggle his authorial signature into the frame of a story he has no other means of controlling. By contrast, Kael suggests, auteur critics would have no use for a filmmaker whose implicata were displayed for their own sake: "Poor misguided Dostoyevsky, too full of what he has to say to bother with 'technical competence,' tackling important themes in each work (surely the worst crime in the *auteur* book) and with his almost incredible unity of personality and material leaving you nothing left to extrapolate from."[13]

The debate between Sarris and Kael seems to reflect a disagreement about whether the success of fictional films should be discussed in terms of their implicatures (Sarris) or their implicata (Kael). In practice, however, the positions of the two critics are virtually indistinguishable. Sarris implicitly retreats in "Toward a Theory of Film History" from his earlier emphasis on the presence of a director's personality as a criterion of success. Auteur criticism, he contends, does not rejoice in detachable "bits of style" but rather emphasizes the connections implicit in the perception and definition of a filmmaker's style: "The auteur critic is obsessed with the wholeness of art and the artist. He looks at a film as a whole, a director as a whole. The parts, however entertaining individually, must cohere meaningfully." It is true, Sarris concludes, that he considers "the art of the cinema" to be "the art of an attitude, the style of a gesture. It is not so much *what* as *how*. . . . Auteur criticism is a reaction against sociological criticism that enthroned the *what* against the *how*. However, it would be equally fallacious to enthrone the *how* against the *what*. The whole point of a meaningful style is that it unifies the *what* and the *how* into a personal statement" (30, 36). Sarris's accounts of particular directors, however, continue to emphasize the how of their implicatures over the what of their implicata.

So, surprisingly, do Kael's. Her first collection of reviews, *I Lost It at the Movies*, reprints her attack on Sarris alongside an essay called "Zeitgeist and Poltergeist: Are Movies Going to Pieces?" which compares the recent work of Resnais and Antonioni unfavorably to exactly the Hollywood genre films Sarris was praising in the *Village Voice:* "There is more energy, more originality, more excitement, more *art* in American kitsch like *Gunga Din, Easy Living,* in the Rogers and Astaire pictures like *Swingtime* and *Top Hat,* in *Strangers on a Train, His Girl Friday, The Crimson Pirate, Citizen Kane, The Lady Eve, To Have and Have Not, The African Queen, Singin' in the Rain, Sweet Smell of Success,* or more recently, *The Hustler, Lolita, The Manchurian Candidate, Hud, Charade,* than in the presumed High Culture of *Hiroshima Mon Amour, Marienbad, La Notte,*

The Eclipse, and the Torre Nilsson pictures."[14] Since Kael never accuses "kitsch" films like *Top Hat* or *To Have and Have Not* of presenting original implicata about the relations between men and women, the originality of which she speaks here is clearly a question of technique. But she is not simply favoring kitsch films as the best of a bad lot, for she concludes that "if debased art is kitsch, perhaps kitsch may be redeemed by honest vulgarity, may become art. Our best work transforms kitsch, makes art out of it. . . . Our first and greatest film artist, D. W. Griffith, was a master of kitsch" (25).

The debate between Sarris and Kael, who continue twenty years later as the pre-eminent film critics in America, pits a critic whose principles are confused but consistent against a critic whose much more reasonable principles are flatly contradicted by her assessments of particular films. No matter how hard Kael tries to judge films in terms of their implicata, she is repeatedly overruled by her sensitivity to their implicatures. Nor is it difficult to find the source of her contradiction. When, in "Circles and Squares," she attacks Sarris's celebration of the tension between film-makers and their material as "the opposite of what we have always taken for granted in the arts, that the artist expresses himself in the unity of form and content" (302), she is adopting Renaissance standards of art which are often inapplicable to many works of art, not just films. When Hitchcock told Truffaut that people would complain about *Psycho*, "It was a terrible film to make. The subject was horrible, the people were small, there were no characters in it,"[15] he was echoing Henry James's reaction to *Sentimental Education* and *Nana*. The fact is that the unity of form and content, which Kael pronounces a universal criterion for success in the arts, is an ideal rooted in the aesthetics of the Renaissance, a period when, despite the efflorescence of work in architecture, painting, sculpture, drama, and music, the art of narrative fiction remained largely in eclipse.

The critical reputations of such great American filmmakers as Griffith, Chaplin, Keaton, Lubitsch, Hawks, Hitchcock, and Welles—to take a few figures whom Sarris and Kael agree in praising—are certainly based less on their implicata than on their implicatures. Griffith, as Kael acknowledges, was a commonplace thinker whose views of politics, history, and religion were almost ludicrously naive, but whose ability to translate psychological states and to compress social observations into expressive images has never been surpassed. Indeed, this ability constitutes Griffith's exemplary legacy to each of these later filmmakers. Chaplin and Keaton use their own bodies to focus rather commonplace emotions, and provoke laughter by the freshness with which they enact the contrast between personal aspiration and social or physical reality. Lubitsch is the master of the image or gesture which implies an entire relationship, or even the

history of a relationship, between characters. Hawks and Welles (whose
Citizen Kane Kael calls "a shallow masterpiece")[16] are noted for the
intensity with which they stage the clichés of conflict within the frame,
Hitchcock for the finesse and wit with which he provides visual metaphors
for his audience's apprehensions. All these directors have been honored
for what has been called "the Lubitsch touch," which is precisely the
ability to suggest more, and more interesting, implicata than are directly
shown—that is, to engage the audience's narrativity through the economy,
elegance, or precision of a film's implicatures. And this is not surprising,
for although it is a film's implicata which comprise the information necessary for an audience's comprehension of a story, it is the way in which
those implicata are established—the implicatures as such—which establishes a film's visual style, its narrative world, and which determines the
ways in which recovering this information will give the audience pleasure.

What Stories Do

Nonfictional stories, we may conclude, display their implicata, fictional
stories their implicatures. In Chapter 2, however, I argued that what
makes stories tellable, what they display, is the way in which they engage
and satisfy the audience's narrativity, the way the audience is made to
supply the explicitly omitted connections and resonances that allow them
to savor stories as stories. If all stories display their implicatures, does it
follow that nonfictional stories are not really stories, or that all stories are
fictional? It would be tempting to say at this point that to the degree that a
given utterance or discourse is narrative, it is so by virtue of displaying its
audience's narrativity through its implicatures, and so is to that degree
fictional. (Hayden White takes a similar position in "The Fictions of
Factual Representation.") Narrative itself would then be a fictional trope;
to narrate would be to fictionalize, as the title of the 1979 University of
Chicago symposium on narrative, "The Illusion of Sequence," suggests.

A concluding summary of what fictional and nonfictional narrative
display will indicate, however, that it is unnecessary to construe all narrative, insofar as it is narrative, as fictional. Nonfictional narrative, I have
said, displays its implicated propositions; although its explicit propositions
must be demonstrably true, or must be acceptable conventionally as
matters of public record, its implicata (e.g., "the temporary defeat of
revenue sharing will have a long-term impact on citizens' lives") are
seldom clearly true or false. Newspaper stories and histories—which are
read for the sake of implicata which remain merely arguable, a set of

theories or premises or guesses about the relation of historical events to the public, and indeed about which states of affairs are to count as historical events (a set of assumptions sharply challenged, for example, by recent feminist theorists)—may not display their implicatures, but they depend on implicatures for their authority; if historians were limited to asserting the explicit propositions they could prove, human history would become unthinkable. Indeed, as Paul Ricoeur and others have argued, it would become unnecessary, because history begins not in an attempt to document what can be demonstrated as true, but in an attempt to redeem the sense of being in time by advancing hypotheses about the connections among different human states of affairs; and to distinguish between absolutely true and false hypotheses—as, for example, the Acts of the Apostles undertakes to do—would preclude any further hypothetical investigations and so bring an end to history.

Would historians welcome this development? Probably not; they at least are more deeply committed to the act of implicating than to the propositions they implicate. A more interesting question is whether their audience would welcome an authoritative revelation which put an end to further historical speculation, a newspaper or history which would never be outdated. However we answer this question, considering it in these terms indicates that the habit of narrativity and the appetite for stories which are necessarily contingent are strong; audiences may prefer fictional stories to any ultimate teleological revelation.

Whatever the form of that revelation, it would certainly not be narrative; for stories, as I have maintained, are not primarily a means of communicating information but a transaction designed to arouse and satisfy the audience's narrativity, a sense of themselves as existing in a world of contingent meanings which encourages guesses about its order with intimations whose authority is never final. The narrative world—a world always betokening an apocalypse that never arrives—is surely not simply the world, but is it therefore simply a fictional world? If narrative is a trope, it seems, like the tropes of metaphor, synecdoche, and irony, not adequately described as a fictional trope; or, to put it more accurately, it is a fictional trope which mocks the possibility of any alternative, nonfictional trope. Stories are designed not primarily to provide information but to give their audience a certain kind of experience—the experience of making sense of a world designed precisely to respond to their attempts—and this experience is in itself simply an experience, no more or less fictional than the roller coaster ride it is sometimes said to resemble.

To compare stories to roller coasters may seem puerile. But in fact there is something adolescent about the very appetite for stories, particularly new stories. Very young children, as every parent knows, distrust new stories and are particularly intolerant of variation: "It's supposed to be 'So she knocked *twice* on the door.'" Their narrativity is subordinate to their desire for the kind of reassurance ritual provides, and their interest in open-ended stories can be exasperatingly limited ("But what did Cinderella and the prince do *after* they got married?"). Many readers in their old age develop similar attachments to a few favorite novels or poems which they return to repeatedly for the pleasure of an affirming order. The desire to spend time in a world which tantalizes us with the prospect of making sense just a little while later is one that, for most audiences, corresponds to a relatively limited period in their own lives; given the vicissitudes of life, not everyone is prepared to indulge the suspension of certainties the narrative world provides.

Just as stories which aim to arouse and reward our narrativity do not appeal equally to audiences of all ages, not everyone will agree on what counts as such a story, or even whether a given story is fictional. In Chapters 1 and 2, I considered some minimal narratives which might or might not be stories depending on the conditions of judging. In general, the least sophisticated audiences will be more inclined to assimilate stories as true, and therefore will attend most keenly to their explicit representations of states of affairs (as audiences for the Lumière brothers' first films ducked when they watched a train coming toward them on the screen); more sophisticated audiences will pay more attention to the implicata of a given story (so that only people of a certain age are interested in newspaper stories because they recognize their potential importance); and still more sophisticated audiences will concentrate on a story's implicatures (as teachers labor to direct their students' attention away from what *Huckleberry Finn* makes them think about slavery to how it makes them think that way). In discussing the fictional status of documentary film earlier in this chapter, I maintained that although there is no zero-degree way of photographing a given event, audiences assume that there is. But this is true only for some audiences; an audience of documentary filmmakers, for example, would never make this assumption. More generally, the assumption that cinematic stories unfold in the present is one that operates differently in different audiences; though the illusion that Indiana Jones is trapped in a cave *right now* is obviously responsible for the audience's excitement and apprehension, few audiences really believe that he is. Even the imputation that successive shots in a film stand in a logical or causal relation to each other operates very differently from one audience to the next: Very young audiences might enjoy documentaries like Disney nature films purely for their images of wild animals; more sophisticated audiences might take pleasure in their pictorial beauty; even an audience who perceived a narrative pattern in one of these films—a student writing a paper for a filmmaking class, for instance—might well be focusing instead on the film's expert use of telephoto lenses.

The point of these distinctions is to indicate that whether or not to count a given discourse as a story corresponds to a certain moment (which may last for years or centuries, but not forever) in the life of an individual or a cultural audience, that perceiving a given discourse as a story is not the only way or even perhaps the best way to perceive it, and that just as audiences develop the sophistication to grow into an appreciation of narrative, they may well acquire sufficient sophistication to grow out of it. I argued in Chapter 2 that the "story" Charlie Brown tells Lucy,

(1)   Once upon a time they lived happily ever after,

is not a story at all; it is simply an attempt to get out of telling a story. By contrast, many readers will find

(2)   Once upon a time they lived happily ever after

an adequate, complete, and highly amusing story. The storyteller provides just enough guidance to establish a certain pattern of expectations, then deftly reorders those expectations by posing a conclusion which, like the concluding couplet in Fulke Greville's sonnet, redefines the status of the discourse with respect to other discourses and so confirms the polytropic nature of the audience's experience. But such an audience, which is capable of recovering anything as a story, is already moving away from the experience of story to the experience of analysis.

This rather Borgesian example, which suggests that narrativity is in the eye of the beholder, is offered as a cautionary parable. Throughout this book I have made distinctions between stories and other things on the basis of cultural and institutional presuppositions I hope my own audience will share; if they do not, my analysis will suffer, but it will not therefore be superseded by some metacultural analysis, for there is no way of defining the genre of narrative, or any literary genre, except within shared cultural presuppositions. More generally, although there is no zero degree of narrative presentation or narrative ontology—no way of presenting a discourse which will guarantee its status, irrespective of its situational context, as narrative—such indeterminacy is no cause for alarm. For studying the conditions under which stories and their worlds, plots, and characters are displayed—studying the conditions under which stories become stories—should not finally be an imperialistic endeavor which aims to define every intelligible discourse as narrative. The interest in stories, whether in analyzing them, cataloguing them, reading or watching or listening to them, must lead finally to an interest in something else.

Notes

Chapter 1

1. All references to Aristotle, unless otherwise noted, are to *The Basic Works of Aristotle*, edited by Richard McKeon (New York: Random House, 1941). The translation of the *Poetics* is by Ingram Bywater.

2. Robert Scholes and Robert Kellogg, *The Nature of Narrative* (New York: Oxford University Press, 1966), p. 4.

3. Recent research on the psychology of visual perception suggests that even photographs and sculptures are apprehended sequentially, and that the effect of a simultaneous impact of spatial elements is largely illusory. See David Noton and Lawrence Stark, "Eye Movements and Visual Perception," *Scientific American* 224 (June 1971): 34–43.

4. Seymour Chatman, *Story and Discourse* (Ithaca, NY: Cornell University Press, 1978), p. 19.

5. See, for example, Robert L. Caserio, *Plot, Story, and the Novel* (Princeton: Princeton University Press, 1979), on the analogues among narrative sequence, mental sequence, and the intelligible sequences of the physical world: "A story is . . . a relating of an intelligence of relations in such a way that further relational thought is incited" (p. 6)—a formulation which offers no way of distinguishing between narrative and non-narrative relations.

6. Percy Lubbock, *The Craft of Fiction* (1921; reprint, New York: Viking, 1957), p. 251.

7. Henry James, *The Art of the Novel*, edited by R. P. Blackmur (New York: Scribner, 1934), pp. 106, 108.

8. *The Notebooks of Henry James*, edited by R. P. Blackmur and Kenneth B. Murdock (New York: Oxford University Press, 1947), p. 263.

9. David Bordwell and Kristin Thompson, *Film Art* (Reading, MA: Addison-Wesley, 1979), pp. 49–51.

10. For a detailed analysis of such "classic" narrative structures, see Tzvetan Todorov, *Grammaire du Décaméron* (The Hague: Mouton, 1969).

11. See Charles F. Schulz, *Good Grief, More Peanuts!* (New York: Holt, Rinehart, Winston, 1956), n.p.

12. Gerald Prince, *Narratology: The Form and Functioning of Narrative* (Berlin: Mouton, 1982), p. 4.

13. Schulz, *You're Out of Your Mind, Charlie Brown!* (New York: Holt, Rinehart, Winston, 1959), n.p.

14. Shlomith Rimmon-Kenan argues in *Narrative Fiction* (London: Methuen, 1983) that although "there would be something very odd" about such a story, "if we accept this as the possible paraphrase of *some* text (perhaps a narrative pastiche by Robert Coover or Donald Barthelme), then the temporal conjunction requires us to imagine some world where these events can coexist" (p. 19). But a paraphrase or pastiche of narrative, as the ensuing discussion will demonstrate, is not necessarily narrative itself.

15. E. M. Forster, *Aspects of the Novel* (New York: Harcourt, 1927), p. 86.

16. Cf. John Gerlach, *Toward the End* (University, AL: University of Alabama Press, 1985): "Middles are not crucial to our sense of story," because "if we move from one extreme to another, if nothing indicates additional oscillation, then the thing perceived is presumably whole" (p. 11). Even this "oscillation," however, depends on a conceptual reversal, a realignment of the audience's expectations, absent from "the king died, and then the queen died of grief."

17. "Infant Innocence," in *A. E. H.*, edited by Laurence Housman (London: Jonathan Cape, 1937), p. 236.

18. Nelson Goodman, "Twisted Tales; or, Story, Study, and Symphony," *Critical Inquiry* 7:1 (Autumn 1980): 115.

19. Frank Kermode, *The Sense of an Ending* (New York: Oxford University Press, 1967), p. 4.

20. Kermode, *The Genesis of Secrecy* (Cambridge: Harvard University Press, 1979), p. 113.

21. Kermode, "Secrets and Narrative Sequence," *Critical Inquiry* 7:1 (Autumn 1980): 86.

22. Jonathan Culler, *The Pursuit of Signs* (Ithaca, NY: Cornell University Press, 1981), pp. 186–87.

23. Culler, p. 171; see Mieke Bal, *Narratologie: Essai sur la signification narrative dans quatre romans modernes* (Paris: Klincksieck, 1977), p. 6. Bal's book has recently been translated by Christine van Boheemen as *Narratology* (Toronto: University of Toronto Press, 1985).

24. Tzvetan Todorov, *The Poetics of Prose*, translated by Richard Howard (Ithaca, NY: Cornell University Press, 1977), p. 55.

25. In offering its own definitions of these terms, this book is following in a long tradition, for narrative theorists have used them to mean very different things. Forster's definition, which I have already considered, stresses causality as a requisite of plot. Bordwell and Thompson define plot as the order in which story events are presented in a narrative (p. 52). Caserio makes plot identical with story (p. 4). Peter Brooks, in *Reading for the Plot* (New York: Knopf, 1984), defines plot as "the design and intention of narrative, what shapes a story and gives it a certain direction or intention of meaning" (p. xi)—a definition which, though apparently remote from the others, is actually the most Aristotelian of all.

Chapter 2

1. Cf. Hayden White, who argues in "The Value of Narrativity in the Representation of Reality," *Critical Inquiry* 7:1 (Autumn 1980), that there is no such thing as a chronicle without some imputation of selection and causality (pp. 13–17).

2. Northrop Frye, *Anatomy of Criticism* (Princeton: Princeton University Press, 1957), pp. 246–47.

3. Cf. Käte Hamburger, *The Logic of Literature*, 2nd edition, translated by Marilynn J. Rose (Bloomington: Indiana University Press, 1973), another important generic study which does not consider narrative as a distinctive genre or mode.

4. Paul Hernadi, *Beyond Genre* (Ithaca, NY: Cornell University Press, 1972), pp. 165–66.

5. E. M. Forster, *Aspects of the Novel* (New York: Harcourt, 1927), p. 83.

6. See Hernadi, *Beyond Genre*, and Alastair Fowler, *Kinds of Literature* (Cambridge: Harvard University Press, 1982), for summaries and bibliographies of a wide range of theories conceived in representational rather than philosophical terms.

7. George Lukács, *The Theory of the Novel*, translated by Anna Bostock (Cambridge: MIT Press, 1971), p. 46.

8. Nelson Goodman, "Twisted Tales; or, Story, Study, and Symphony," *Critical Inquiry* 7:1 (Autumn 1980): 115–19.

9. Franz Stanzel, in *A Theory of Narrative*, translated by Charlotte Goedsche (Cambridge: Cambridge University Press, 1984), defines summary as "story-minus-mediacy or story-without-narrator" (p. 24), though without defining story itself.

10. Mary Louise Pratt, *Toward a Speech Act Theory of Literary Discourse* (Bloomington: Indiana University Press, 1977), p. 44.

11. Ross Chambers, *Story and Situation* (Minneapolis: University of Minnesota Press, 1984), p. 24.

12. William Luhr and Peter Lehman, *Authorship and Narrative in the Cinema* (New York: Capricorn, 1977), p. 291.

13. Seymour Chatman, *Story and Discourse* (Ithaca, NY: Cornell University Press, 1978), p. 37.

14. Barbara Herrnstein Smith, "Narrative Versions, Narrative Theories," *Critical Inquiry* 7:1 (Autumn 1980): 215, 219.

15. Seymour Chatman, "Reply to Barbara Herrnstein Smith," *Critical Inquiry* 7:4 (Summer 1981): 804.

16. Walter Benjamin, "The Storyteller," in *Illuminations*, edited by Hannah Arendt, translated by Harry Zohn (New York: Schocken, 1969), p. 89.

17. Robert Scholes, "Narration and Narrativity in Film and Fiction," in *Semiotics and Interpretation* (New Haven: Yale University Press, 1982), p. 60.

18. Wolfgang Iser, "The Reading Process: A Phenomenological Approach," *New Literary History* 3:2 (Winter 1972): 285. Cf. Iser's later discussion of "blanks" in *The Act of Reading* (Baltimore: Johns Hopkins University Press, 1978), pp. 180–231.

19. Cf. Giovanni Boccaccio, *The Decameron*, translated by G. H. McWilliam (Harmondsworth, England: Penguin, 1972), p. 68.

20. *The Novels and Tales of Henry James* (26 volumes; New York: Scribner, 1907–17), vol. 9, 160.

21. Martin Price, "The Irrelevant Detail and the Emergence of Form," in *Aspects of Narrative*, edited by J. Hillis Miller (New York: Columbia University Press, 1971), p. 89.

22. Cf. Chatman, *Story and Discourse*, on "reading" versus "reading out" (pp. 41–42), and Frank Kermode, *The Genesis of Secrecy* (Cambridge: Harvard University Press, 1979), on narrative as "interpretation" (pp. 81–82).

23. John Crowe Ransom, *The New Criticism* (Norfolk, CT: New Directions, 1941), pp. 213–14.

Chapter 3

1. E. M. Forster, *Aspects of the Novel* (New York: Harcourt, 1927), p. 27.

2. Barbara Herrnstein Smith, *Poetic Closure* (Chicago: University of Chicago Press, 1968), p. 34.

3. Alexander Welsh, "Foreword," *Nineteenth-Century Fiction* 33 (June 1978): 1.

4. Kenneth Burke, *A Grammar of Motives* (Englewood Cliffs, NJ: Prentice-Hall, 1945), p. 475.

5. *Poetics*, in *The Basic Works of Aristotle*, edited by Richard McKeon (New York: Random House, 1941), 6.1450a.

6. S. H. Butcher, *Aristotle's Theory of Poetry and Fine Art*, 4th edition (1911; reprint, New York: Dover, 1951), pp. 284–85. For a thorough examination of the relation between ends and endings which reaches quite different conclusions, see David H. Richter, *Fable's End* (Chicago: University of Chicago Press, 1974).

7. Ronald S. Crane, "Critical and Historical Principles of Literary History," in *The Idea of the Humanities* (Chicago: University of Chicago Press, 1967), vol. 2, 57.

8. George Lukács, *The Meaning of Contemporary Realism*, translated by John and Necke Mander (London: Merlin, 1962), p. 55.

9. Boris Ejxenbaum, "O. Henry and the Theory of the Short Story," in *Readings in Russian Poetics*, edited by Ladislav Matejka and Krystyna Pomorska (Cambridge: MIT Press, 1971), pp. 231–32.

10. Norman Friedman, "What Makes a Short Story Short?" in *Form and Meaning in Fiction* (Athens: University of Georgia Press, 1974), pp. 174–75.

11. Kenneth Burke, *A Grammar of Motives*, pp. 39–40; Francis Fergusson, *The Idea of a Theater* (Princeton: Princeton University Press, 1949), p. 18.

12. O. Henry, *Strictly Business* (1910; reprint, Garden City, NY: Doubleday, 1920), p. 172.

13. Ian Reid, *The Short Story*, volume 37 in The Critical Idiom Series (London: Methuen, 1977), p. 56. Cf. Thomas Docherty's distinction in *Reading (Absent) Character* (Oxford: Clarendon, 1983) between realistic fiction, which transmits "epistemological information from the author to the reader . . . *via* character," and contemporary fiction, in which "description is a phenomenological process which allows the reader to inform character" (p. 42).

14. Cf. Charles E. May, "The Nature of Knowledge in Short Fiction," *Studies in Short Fiction* 21 (Fall 1984): 327–38, on the "defamiliarizing" wisdom of the short story; and Susan Lohafer, *Coming to Terms with the Short Story* (Baton Rouge: Louisiana State University Press, 1983): "Every story shows us someone either coming home or leaving home" (p. 95). My argument has been that the story of homecoming is a subset of the story of departure or home-leaving.

15. Paul Ricoeur, "Narrative Time," *Critical Inquiry* 7:1 (Autumn 1980): 178.

16. Barbara Herrnstein Smith, "Narrative Versions, Narrative Theories," *Critical Inquiry* 7:1 (Autumn 1980): 227.

17. " 'Tess' and *Tess*: An Experiment in Genre," *Modern Fiction Studies* 28 (Spring 1982): 38.

18. Page references are to the Nonesuch edition of Dickens (Bloomsbury, 1935–37).

19. See G. W. Kennedy, "Dickens's Endings," *Studies in the Novel* 6 (Fall 1974): 283–84.

20. This pattern was first remarked by J. Hillis Miller in *Charles Dickens: The World of His Novels* (Cambridge: Harvard University Press, 1958), pp. 36–84.

21. Bernard Bergonzi, "Nicholas Nickleby," in *Dickens and the Twentieth Century*, edited by John Gross and Gabriel Pearson (Toronto: University of Toronto Press, 1962), p. 71. The recent success of the Royal Shakespeare Company's eight-hour production of *Nicholas Nickleby*, which breaks the novel into a rapid series of comic and pathetic scenes, tends to confirm Bergonzi's terms, if not his sentiments.

22. To be more exact, David is the first such character in Dickens's longer fiction. The problems of closure in his nonserialized short fiction are tactically very different.

23. See, for example, Lionel Trilling's Introduction to the Oxford Illustrated edition of the novel, reprinted in *The Opposing Self* (New York: Viking, 1955), pp. 50–65.

24. John Kucich, "Action in the Dickens Ending: *Bleak House* and *Great Expectations*," *Nineteenth-Century Fiction* 33 (June 1978): 102.

Chapter 4

1. Barbara Hardy, *The Appropriate Form* (London: Athlone, 1964), p. 49.

2. Frank Kermode, *The Sense of an Ending* (New York: Oxford University Press, 1967), p. 7.

3. Sigmund Freud, "Fragment of an Analysis of a Case of Hysteria," in *The Complete Psychological Works*, standard edition, edited by James Strachey (London: Hogarth, 1953–74), vol. 7, 12–13.

4. Freud, *The Complete Psychological Works*, vol. 23, 219–20.

5. Philip Rieff, Introduction to *Dora: An Analysis of a Case of Hysteria* (New York: Collier, 1963), p. 10.

6. D. A. Miller, *Narrative and Its Discontents* (Princeton: Princeton University Press, 1981), pp. ix, xi.

7. In *How to Write Short Stories*, reprinted in *The Best Short Stories of Ring Lardner* (New York: Scribner, 1957), p. 37.

8. Alain Robbe-Grillet, "Time and Description in Fiction Today," in *For a New Novel*, translated by Richard Howard (New York: Grove Press, 1965), pp. 152–53.

9. Alain Robbe-Grillet, Introduction to *Last Year at Marienbad*, translated by Richard Howard (New York: Grove Press, 1962), p. 14.

10. Roland Barthes, *Image—Music—Text*, translated by Stephen Heath (New York: Hill and Wang, 1977), pp. 124, 120–21.

11. Jonathan Culler, *Structuralist Poetics* (Ithaca, NY: Cornell University Press, 1975), p. 189.

12. Lionel Trilling, "Manners, Morals, and the Novel," in *The Liberal Imagination* (1950; reprint, Garden City, NY: Anchor, 1953), pp. 215, 205.

13. Consider Vonnegut's affinities with the forms and conventions of science fiction, a genre which typically displays the exposition of an invented situation rather than the development of a plot.

14. Donald Barthelme, *Sixty Stories* (New York: Putnam, 1981), pp. 214–15, 226.

15. *The New Fiction: Interviews with Innovative American Writers*, edited by Joe David Bellamy (Urbana: University of Illinois Press, 1974), pp. 51–52.

16. Woody Allen, "My Philosophy," in *Getting Even* (New York: Random House, 1971), p. 33.

Chapter 5

1. Patricia A. Parker, *Inescapable Romance* (Princeton: Princeton University Press, 1979), p. 4.

2. Walter L. Reed, "The Problem with a Poetics of the Novel," in *Toward a Poetics of Fiction*, edited by Mark Spilka (Bloomington: Indiana University Press, 1977), p. 64.

3. Mark Spilka, Introduction to *Toward a Poetics of Fiction*, p. ix.

4. Northrop Frye, *Fools of Time* (Toronto: University of Toronto Press, 1967), pp. 3–4.

5. Patricia Tobin, *Time and the Novel* (Princeton: Princeton University Press, 1978), p. 5.

6. Robert Champigny, *What Will Have Happened* (Bloomington: Indiana University Press, 1977), pp. 6, 5.

7. Stanley Fish, *Is There a Text in This Class?* (Cambridge: Harvard University Press, 1980), pp. 3–4.

8. Cf. Robert Gessner, who observes in *The Moving Image* (1968; reprint, New York: Dutton, 1970) that "the first five minutes on a screen are a precious gift placed tenderly in the hands of the writer-director. . . . The viewer is anxious not to have wasted his money and time; he is apperceptively willing to give the writer-director the most eager greeting and the benefit of any doubt" (p. 85).

9. E. D. Hirsch, Jr., *Validity in Interpretation* (New Haven: Yale University Press, 1967), p. 76.

10. This paragraph is indebted in a general way to W. B. Gallie, *Philosophy and the Historical Understanding* (New York: Schocken, 1964), pp. 34–39.

11. David L. Minter, *The Interpreted Design as a Structural Principle in American Prose* (New Haven: Yale University Press, 1969), especially pp. 17–35, 161–219.

12. Martin Price, *Forms of Life* (New Haven: Yale University Press, 1983), p. 20.

13. Leo Braudy, "Popular Culture and Personal Time," *Yale Review* 71 (July 1982): 495, 489.

14. Frank Kermode, *The Sense of an Ending* (New York: Oxford University Press, 1967), pp. 71–72, 74.

15. Paul Ricoeur, "Narrative Time," *Critical Inquiry* 7:1 (Autumn 1980): 178. See Ricoeur's much fuller discussion in *Time and Narrative*, Volume I, translated by Kathleen McLaughlin and David Pellauer (Chicago: University of Chicago Press, 1984), especially pp. 52–87, 175–225.

16. Quoted by Ernest Samuels in his Notes to *The Education of Henry Adams* (Boston: Houghton Mifflin, 1975), p. 540.

17. Michael McCanles, "Mythos and Dianoia: A Dialectical Methodology of Literary Form," in *Literary Monographs IV*, edited by Eric Rothstein (Madison: University of Wisconsin Press, 1971), p. 4.

18. Lionel Trilling, "Manners, Morals, and the Novel," in *The Liberal Imagination* (1950; reprint, Garden City, NY: Anchor, 1953), p. 202.

19. Many fictional portraits of the modern consciousness involve little or no dramatic action, but these are either ironic (like "The Beast in the Jungle," whose point is the lack of engagement between Marcher's imagination and the requirements of his world) or marked by a tendency away from narrative altogether (like Woolf's novels, which often seem organized around the exposition of intersubjectivity rather than its narrative development).

20. See, for example, Marius Bewley, *The Eccentric Design* (New York: Columbia University Press, 1959); A. N. Kaul, *The American Vision* (New Haven: Yale University Press, 1964); and Nicolaus Mills, *American and British Fiction in the Nineteenth Century* (Bloomington: Indiana University Press, 1973).

21. Richard Chase, *The American Novel and Its Tradition* (Garden City, NY: Anchor, 1957), pp. 1, 11.

22. Kenneth Burke, *Permanence and Change*, second revised edition (1954; reprint, Indianapolis: Bobbs-Merrill, 1965), pp. 71–74.

23. Quoted by Erich Auerbach in *Mimesis*, translated by Willard R. Trask (Princeton: Princeton University Press, 1957), p. 5.

24. Line references are to the Loeb edition of Virgil's works, translated by H. R. Fair-clough (revised edition, 2 volumes, Cambridge: Harvard University Press, 1965).

25. The translation is Allen Mandelbaum's (New York: Bantam, 1971), p. 263.

26. Line references are to John D. Sinclair's bilingual edition of the *Comedia* (3 volumes, New York: Oxford University Press, 1939).

27. Francis Fergusson, *Dante's Drama of the Mind* (Princeton: Princeton University Press, 1953).

Chapter 6

1. Shlomith Rimmon-Kenan, *Narrative Fiction* (London: Methuen, 1983), p. 125.

2. Leo Braudy, *The World in a Frame* (Garden City, NY: Doubleday, 1976), p. 37.

3. All quotations are from the Authorized Version.

4. Tony Tanner has suggested that these two kinds of wonder are more intimately connected. See *The Reign of Wonder* (Cambridge: Cambridge University Press, 1965), p. 309.

5. Cf. the analysis of A.-J. Greimas in *Structural Semantics*, translated by Daniele McDowell, Ronald Schleifer, and Alan Velie (Lincoln: University of Nebraska Press, 1983), p. 79.

6. For the concept of "motivation," see Boris Tomaskevskii, "Thematics," in *Russian Formalism: Four Essays*, edited by Lee T. Lemon and Marion J. Reis (Lincoln: University of Nebraska Press, 1965), pp. 78–87.

7. For representative closed theories, see Sergei Eisenstein, *Film Form*, edited and translated by Jay Leyda (New York: Harcourt, 1949), and Rudolf Arnheim, *Film as Art* (Berkeley: University of California Press, 1957); for open theories, see André Bazin, *What Is Cinema?*, selected and translated by Hugh Gray (2 volumes, Berkeley: University of California Press, 1967–71), and Siegfried Kracauer, *Theory of Film* (New York: Oxford University Press, 1960).

8. Barbara Hardy, *The Appropriate Form* (London: Athlone, 1964), p. 51.

9. Roland Barthes, *S/Z*, translated by Richard Miller (New York: Hill and Wang, 1970), p. 19.

10. Tzvetan Todorov, "Narrative-Men," in *The Poetics of Prose*, translated by Richard Howard (Ithaca, NY: Cornell University Press, 1977), p. 68.

11. The fact that *Psycho*, despite its emphatic use of terminal devices, has so far spawned two sequels (neither directed by Hitchcock) indicates some of the ways its world demonstrates greater staying power than its teleology.

12. François Truffaut, *Hitchcock* (New York: Simon and Schuster, 1967), p. 211.

13. *The Works of Geoffrey Chaucer*, edited by F. N. Robinson (Boston: Houghton Mifflin, 1957), C, 277.

14. Hayden White, "The Value of Narrativity in the Representation of Reality," *Critical Inquiry* 7:1 (Autumn 1980): 14. White's account implies another category of pure narratives: those whose thematic or verbal or pictorial resources are designed solely to arouse a certain response in the audience—the early comedies of Mel Brooks and Woody Allen, for example, or the cinematic offspring of *The Texas Chainsaw Massacre*—for here the continuity depends purely on what Poe called the unity of effect. Or it could be argued that pure narratives invoke the conventions of storytelling without their teleology; such stories would include not only the Physician's Tale but *The Hunting of the Snark*. These are skeletal narratives, whose

purity is a matter of what they leave out; Borges's garden of forking paths seems by contrast an imperialistic narrative, the story to end all stories.

15. Jorge Luis Borges, *Labyrinths*, augmented edition, translated by Donald A. Yates and James E. Irby (New York: New Directions, 1964), p. 26.

16. Alain Robbe-Grillet, "Time and Description in Fiction Today," in *For a New Novel*, translated by Richard Howard (New York: Grove, 1965), p. 152.

Chapter 7

1. *Poetics*, in *The Basic Works of Aristotle*, edited by Richard McKeon (New York: Random House, 1941), 6.1450a.

2. Erich Auerbach, *Mimesis*, translated by Willard R. Trask (Princeton: Princeton University Press, 1957), pp. 481–92.

3. Cyril Hare, "The Classic Form," in *Crime in Good Company*, edited by Michael Gilbert (London: Constable, 1959), p. 68.

4. Henry James, *The Art of the Novel*, edited by R. P. Blackmur (New York: Scribner, 1934), pp. 42, 47.

5. Henry Fielding, *Joseph Andrews and Shamela*, edited by Martin C. Battestin (Boston: Houghton Mifflin, 1961), p. 13.

6. Kenneth Burke, *A Grammar of Motives* (Englewood Cliffs, NJ: Prentice-Hall, 1945), pp. 430–40.

7. Herbert Ruhm, Introduction to *The Hard-Boiled Detective* (New York: Vintage, 1977), pp. xiii–xiv.

8. Harley Granville-Barker, *More Prefaces to Shakespeare* (Princeton: Princeton University Press, 1974), p. 150. For a more extended discussion of the relation between action and acting from a different point of view, see Michael Goldman, *Acting and Action in Shakespearean Tragedy* (Princeton: Princeton University Press, 1985).

9. T. S. Eliot, "Seneca in Elizabethan Translation," in *Selected Essays*, new edition (New York: Harcourt, 1950), p. 65.

10. *The Plays of Christopher Marlowe*, edited by Leo Kirschbaum (New York: Meridian, 1962).

11. Line references are to the Signet editions (New York: NAL).

12. The text of Greville's sonnet is taken from *Five Courtier Poets*, edited by Robert M. Bender (New York: Washington Square Press, 1969), p. 543.

13. Mario Praz, "Petrarch in England," in *The Flaming Heart* (1958; reprint, Gloucester, MA: Peter Smith, 1966), p. 267.

14. Paul Fussell, *Poetic Meter and Poetic Form*, revised edition (New York: Random House, 1979), p. 122.

15. Stephen Booth, *An Essay on Shakespeare's Sonnets* (New Haven: Yale University Press, 1969), p. 177.

16. C. S. Lewis, *English Literature in the Sixteenth Century, Excluding Drama* (Oxford: Clarendon, 1954), p. 327. We might consider George Meredith's *Modern Love* a sonnet sequence which displays (among other things) its teleology without displaying its events.

17. *The Novels of Dashiell Hammett* (New York: Knopf, 1965), p. 726.

18. Ronald S. Crane, "The Concept of Plot and the Plot of *Tom Jones*," in *Critics and Criticism*, edited by R. S. Crane (Chicago: University of Chicago Press, 1952), pp. 620–21.

Chapter 8

1. René Girard, *Deceit, Desire, and the Novel,* translated by Yvonne Freccero (Baltimore: Johns Hopkins University Press, 1965); Leo Bersani, *A Future for Astyanax* (Boston: Little, Brown, 1976).

2. For a useful corrective to this tendency, see Thomas Docherty, *Reading (Absent) Character* (Oxford: Clarendon, 1983).

3. Martin Price, *Forms of Life* (New Haven: Yale University Press, 1983), p. 37.

4. William H. Gass, "Philosophy and the Forms of Fiction," in *Fiction and the Figures of Life* (1971; reprint, New York: Vintage, 1972), p. 16.

5. *Poetics*, in *The Basic Works of Aristotle*, edited by Richard McKeon (New York: Random House, 1941), 6.1450a.

6. S. H. Butcher, *Aristotle's Theory of Poetry and Fine Art*, 4th edition (1911; reprint, New York: Dover, 1951), p. 340.

7. Erich Auerbach, *Mimesis*, translated by Willard R. Trask (Princeton: Princeton University Press, 1957), pp. 17–18.

8. *The Complete Greek Tragedies*, edited by Richmond Lattimore and David Grene (1942; reprint, New York: Modern Library, n.d.), vol. 1, 29–30. Quotations from all the tragedies are from this edition.

9. John Jones, *On Aristotle and Greek Tragedy* (New York: Oxford University Press, 1962), pp. 145, 153–54.

10. Paul Delany, *British Autobiography in the Seventeenth Century* (London: Routledge and Kegan Paul, 1969).

11. Gass, "In Terms of the Toenail," in *Fiction and the Figures of Life*, p. 55.

12. Kenneth Burke, *A Grammar of Motives* (Englewood Cliffs, NJ: Prentice-Hall, 1945), pp. 7–9.

13. Seymour Chatman, *Story and Discourse* (Ithaca, NY: Cornell University Press, 1978), pp. 119–131.

14. Leo Braudy, *The World in a Frame* (Garden City, NY: Doubleday, 1976), p. 184.

15. Henry James, *The Art of the Novel*, edited by R. P. Blackmur (New York: Scribner, 1934), p. 176.

16. See, for example, Pauline Kael, "Raising Kane," in *The Citizen Kane Book* (Boston: Atlantic/Little, Brown, 1971), pp. 59–61; and David Bordwell, *"Citizen Kane,"* in *Movies and Methods*, edited by Bill Nichols (Berkeley: University of California Press, 1976), pp. 273–90.

Chapter 9

1. Hayden White, *Tropics of Discourse* (Baltimore: Johns Hopkins University Press, 1978), p. 121.

2. John R. Searle, *Expression and Meaning* (Cambridge: Cambridge University Press, 1979), pp. 60, 65. All otherwise unspecified references to Searle are to this essay.

3. Iris Murdoch, *The Red and the Green* (New York: Viking, 1965), p. 3.

4. Searle, *Expression and Meaning*, p. 125.

5. An exception might be made for national newspapers like *USA Today*, which treat as potential news virtually any recherché information as long as it is true.

6. Barbara Herrnstein Smith, "Narrative Versions, Narrative Theories," *Critical Inquiry* 7:1 (Autumn 1980): 233.

7. Searle, *Speech Acts* (Cambridge: Cambridge University Press, 1969), p. 29.

8. Stanley Fish, "How to Do Things with Austin and Searle," in *Is There a Text in This Class?* (Cambridge: Harvard University Press, 1980), p. 238.

9. Jonathan Culler, *Structuralist Poetics* (Ithaca, NY: Cornell University Press, 1975), p. 134.

10. Mary Louise Pratt, *Toward a Speech Act Theory of Literary Discourse* (Bloomington: Indiana University Press, 1977), p. 85; cf. Searle, *Speech Acts*, p. 25.

11. H. P. Grice, "Logic and Conversation," in *The Logic of Grammar*, edited by Donald Davidson and Gilbert Harman (Encino, CA: Dickenson, 1975), p. 65.

12. The concept of human nature, however philosophically suspect, is essential to the novel as an institution, since novels customarily engage our interest in human thoughts and actions by assuming our natural community with the invented thinkers and actors.

Chapter 10

1. Quoted by Paul Rotha in his Foreword to the 3rd edition of *Documentary Film* (London: Faber, 1952), pp. 30–31.

2. Satyajit Ray, "The Question of Reality" (1969), reprinted in *The Documentary Tradition*, edited by Lewis Jacobs, 2nd edition (New York: Norton, 1979), p. 381.

3. Dai Vaughn, "The Man with the Movie Camera" (1960), reprinted in Jacobs, p. 58.

4. Flaherty's fondness for cultural anachronisms is itself well documented: see, for example, Erik Barnouw, *Documentary: A History of the Non-Fiction Film* (New York: Oxford University Press, 1974), pp. 44–48.

5. Jay Leyda, *Kino: A History of the Russian and Soviet Film*, 3rd edition (Princeton: Princeton University Press, 1973), p. 23.

6. This last example is based on Christian Metz, "The Cinema: Language or Language System?" in *Film Language*, translated by Michael Taylor (New York: Oxford University Press, 1974), p. 67.

7. Leyda, *Films Beget Films* (New York: Hill and Wang, 1964), pp. 49–55. Forsyth Hardy notes in "The British Documentary Film" that Alexander Korda's British propaganda film *The Lion Has Wings* was shown in wartime Berlin as a comedy. See Michael Balcon et al., *Twenty Years of British Film, 1925–1945* (1947; reprint, New York: Arno, 1974), p. 55.

8. John Grierson, "First Principles of Documentary," in *Grierson on Documentary*, edited by Forsyth Hardy, abridged edition (London: Faber, 1979), p. 41.

9. Barbara L. Tuchman, *A Distant Mirror* (New York: Knopf, 1978).

10. Andrew Sarris, *The American Cinema* (New York: Dutton, 1968), p. 37.

11. François Truffaut, "A Certain Tendency in French Cinema" (1954), reprinted in *Movies and Methods*, edited by Bill Nichols (Berkeley: University of California Press, 1976), pp. 224–37.

12. Sarris, "Notes on the Auteur Theory in 1962," reprinted in *Film Theory and Criticism*, edited by Gerald Mast and Marshall Cohen, 3rd edition (New York: Oxford University Press, 1985), p. 537.

13. Pauline Kael, "Circles and Squares," in *I Lost It at the Movies* (Boston: Atlantic/Little, Brown, 1965), pp. 302, 295.

14. Kael, "Zeitgeist and Poltergeist: Are Movies Going to Pieces?" in *I Lost It at the Movies*, p. 24.

15. Truffaut, *Hitchcock* (New York: Simon and Schuster, 1967), p. 211.

16. Kael, "Raising Kane," in *The Citizen Kane Book* (Boston: Atlantic/Little, Brown, 1971), p. 4.

Index

Books are listed under the author's name; films are listed by title, with a separate reference to the director only if his or her name appears in the text.